Praise for

Why the Dutch Are Different

A book as quietly appealing as its subject and full of fascinating details. Coates is entirely convincing in his affectionate portrait.
—Bronwen Maddox, *Prospect*

I thoroughly recommend this book. Why the Dutch are Different *provides the answers to all the questions I had but didn't dare ask about the Netherlands. I eagerly sat up late into the night reading, laughing often and enjoying the ride into my adopted homeland.*

—*DutchNews.nl*

Fascinating. Thoroughly researched and well thought out, Why the Dutch are Different *takes us on a journey that goes beyond red-lit windows and Anne Frank to the true depths of the country. Ben Coates's day-to-day life sits effortlessly alongside deeper dives into history and folklore. A friendly read that strikes the right balance between teaching and entertaining.*
—*The Bookbag*

Coates gets under the skin of a nation renowned for its liberalism.

—*The Bookseller*

For Kim, of course

Why the Dutch Are Different

A Journey into the Hidden Heart of the Netherlands

Ben Coates

NICHOLAS BREALEY
PUBLISHING
London • Boston

First published by
Nicholas Brealey Publishing in 2015

3–5 Spafield Street
Clerkenwell, London
EC1R 4QB, UK
Tel: +44 (0)20 7239 0360
Fax: +44 (0)20 7239 0370

20 Park Plaza
Boston
MA 02116, USA
Tel: (888) BREALEY
Fax: (617) 523 3708

www.nicholasbrealey.com
ben-coates.com

ISBN: 978-1-85788-633-7
eISBN: 978-1-85788-962-8

British Library Cataloguing in Publication Data
A catalogue record for this book is available from the
British Library.

Printed in the UK by Clays Ltd, St Ives plc.

Contents

The Netherlands

Preface

The Queen had resigned, and it was the new King's first day at work. Amsterdam was ablaze with colour, the city's narrow brick streets flooded with an estimated one million people celebrating the inauguration of the first King of the Netherlands in more than a hundred years. The concentric canals were gridlocked with small boats, many of them in danger of sinking under the weight of the scores of people drinking and dancing on board.

It was April 2013 and the Dutch capital had been hit by a serious outbreak of what the locals called *oranjekoorts*, or 'orange fever', a non-fatal disease whose chief symptom was the urge to cover oneself from head to toe in bright orange clothing. The choice of colour was a tribute to the Royal House of Orange, itself named after the small French town of Orange over which its members had once ruled. Orange banners floated from the windows of the slender canal houses, orange bunting spanned the crooked alleyways and orange balloons hung from the tilting iron lampposts. The cobbled floor was littered with discarded orange wigs, hats and miniature flags. Babies wore orange face paint and a barking dog sported an orange hat, coat and miniature feather boa. Wearing an orange T-shirt emblazoned '*IK HOU VAN HOLLAND*' ('I love Holland'), an orange top hat and orange sunglasses, I felt I hadn't really made enough of an effort.

In Dam Square, site of the dam on the river Amstel that gave the city its name, some 25,000 people had gathered to watch the retiring Queen Beatrix hand the family business to her son, the new King Willem-Alexander. At one end of the square, the six-storey Royal Palace was draped with Dutch tricolour flags, the golden railings of its first-floor balcony laced with orange flowers. In front of the palace was a vast crowd of well-wishers, many of them dressed in orange fur-trimmed capes and inflatable crowns. Necks craning and cameras held high, they strained for a view of the minor royals and celebrities walking to the palace from the ancient Nieuwe Kerk (New Church) where the King had just been formally approved by the Dutch parliament. The UK's Prince Charles sweated his way across the cobbles under a mass of gold braid and medals; Ghana's Kofi Annan grinned and waved to the cheering crowd.

Queen Beatrix had announced her intention to step down a few months previously, after thirty-three years on the throne. It was, she said, time for the crown to pass to 'a new genera-tion'. Now, appearing on the palace balcony above the square, the nation's kindly grandmother looked close to tears. 'Some moments ago I abdicated from the throne,' she told the tan-goed masses in Dutch, a light breeze ruffling her dark purple dress. 'I am happy and grateful to introduce you to your new King, Willem-Alexander.' The national anthem began to play, and the former Queen stood back from the balcony. The new King stepped forward, ruddy as a farmer in his dark suit and pale tie, flanked by his wife Maxima, an Argentinian beauty who had shaken off her past as a junta leader's daughter to win millions of Dutch hearts. Next to the royal couple stood their three cherubic daughters, visibly nervous but as pretty as Disney princesses in their matching yellow dresses. They waved to the tangerine crowd, and applause rippled through the city like thunder.

My own journey to Dam Square had begun some three years previously, more than five thousand miles away in the Caribbean. Until 2010, I had worked in London as a kind of low-rent political hitman, crafting snide talking points and tub-thumping speeches for ambitious politicians, skilfully misrepresenting opponents and raking over expense claims to force the resignation of otherwise competent cabinet min-isters. It was the kind of job that guaranteed invitations to cocktail parties and impressed girls in bars, and I didn't like it at all. When a national election and coalition agreement put my jubilant former colleagues in power, I found myself faced with a choice. I could either angle for work carrying a minister's bags around expensively catered international summits, or I could submit to the lucrative PowerPoint grind of a corporate lobbying job. After mulling over my options for an afternoon, I did what any sensible person would: I booked a one-way flight to Cuba.

By September that year, I was on a battered forty-foot sailing boat off the coast of Belize, in possession of little more than an oaky tan and the kind of beard that guaranteed a strip search at airports. The vessel's dreadlocked crew were more interested in listening to reggae than in actually sailing anywhere, and time had collapsed into a blissfully monotonous cycle of drinking rum punch, swimming with turtles and broiling gently in the sun. The House of Commons seemed a long way away.

The few other passengers on board included a pair of sunburned English girls celebrating their graduation and making plans to save the world, and four sunburned Dutch cousins with backpacks, boisterous and over-friendly in the way that tall people released from a small country usually were. Bored of the rum and the turtles, I struck up a conversation with the only girl in the Dutch group, a skinny blonde with salty hair, a starfish-patterned bikini and eyes the colour of the sea. We discussed nothing memorable, but when she disembarked that evening I somehow convinced her to leave behind her email address, scrawled on the back of a Cubana Airlines ticket stub.

Several months passed in a haze of beer, beaches and bus rides, and I had all but forgotten about the girl on the boat until a series of agitated messages from my bank indicated it was time to find a new job. Unfortunately, the plane carrying me back to Heathrow met with a sudden snowstorm and was diverted to Amsterdam. With all flights cancelled, an unkind security guard kicked me out of Schiphol airport and I trudged through thick snow to a series of hotels, each overcrowded with other stranded passengers. Shivering in a T-shirt and cotton trousers better suited to Caribbean climes, I was seriously contemplating sleeping in a subway station when I remembered that I did, in fact, know someone who lived in the Netherlands. Kneeling by a frozen canal, I dug a sun-bleached ticket stub from the bottom of my backpack and sent a message to the skinny girl asking if she'd like to meet for dinner. She invited me round to her place in Rotterdam that evening, and I never left.

Introduction

Almost Dutch

Rotterdam is not a beautiful city. A sprawling industrial conurbation of some 600,000 people, the Netherland's second largest metropolis has none of the canals, cobbles or picturesque bridges of its more famous rival, Amsterdam, and as such is rarely troubled by tourists. However, much to my surprise, it soon began to feel like home. Literally hours after walking out of the airport in the snow, I found myself living in a tall, crooked townhouse, on a tree-lined street between a canal, a tram stop and a bar selling tiny glasses of Heineken. My Caribbean suntan swiftly faded, and my long beard joined my tattered beach clothes in a rubbish bin on the rain-soaked balcony. By the time the snow melted, my belongings had already arrived in the post from England, and I was eating bright green *erwtensoep* (pea soup) with gusto. The skinny girl – a feisty, fiercely intelligent Rotterdammer with a pretty smile – showed no signs of kicking me out, and I began the slow process of integrating into Dutch society.

One of the first things to figure out was what to call my new home. Even the Dutch themselves couldn't quite decide, referring to their country as either *Holland* or *Nederland* (the Netherlands) interchangeably. Consulting a heavy book in the library, though, I learned that strictly speaking the country was actually called 'The Kingdom of the Netherlands'. Just as the United Kingdom included Wales, Scotland and assorted overseas territories, the Kingdom of the Netherlands included both the main territory in Europe – the Netherlands – and three colonial relics in the Caribbean: the islands of Aruba, Curaçao and St Maarten. (Three other specks in the Caribbean – Bonaire, St Eustatius and Saba – also had the status of 'special municipalities'.) The European part of the Kingdom could therefore be termed simply 'the Netherlands', but to label it 'Holland' was wrong, as that name referred only to the country's two most populous provinces: North Holland

and South Holland. Calling the whole country 'Holland' was therefore rather like calling the whole of the United Kingdom 'England' – a common mistake, but a mistake nevertheless. So the country was 'the Netherlands', and the people who lived there were Dutch, and spoke Dutch, a language that sounded to an outsider like a drunk man gargling soup.

Next were the bikes. In Britain, bicycles are sporting accessories used only by children, the fit or the foolhardy. In the Netherlands, though, a third of the country ride one as their main mode of transport. Within a few weeks I had bought two: a sturdy shopping bike with handlebars like a Frenchman's moustache, and then a lean white racing bike that weighed perhaps a fifth as much as the first one. A few weeks later came what the Dutch called a *snorfiets*, or miniature motor-scooter, an absurd little machine the same colour as a fire engine and almost as noisy. Helmets are optional, and the miles of flat, traffic-free cycle lanes are perfect for wobbling home after a few too many Heinekens.

Thirdly, unfortunately, I had to get a job. The generosity of the Dutch welfare system made it tempting to stay in bed, but sadly I soon found gainful employment – an incredibly lucrative but boring position with a major Anglo-Dutch company, sending emails from a cubicle in The Hague and trying to understand the curious habits of my Dutch colleagues.

Finally came the language. Nearly all Dutch people speak perfect English, thanks to an excellent education and a population small enough to mean it isn't worth dubbing American films and television programmes into the local language. However, outside of Amsterdam it is relatively rare to hear English spoken in the street, and I quickly became frustrated at being unable to follow conversations, read menus or tell the difference between alcohol-free beer and real beer in the supermarket. Dutch friends provided a crash course in key phrases every Englishman abroad should know: '*Mag ik een biertje*' (can I have a beer); '*Je bent mooi*' (you are beautiful); '*Ik heb het niet gedaan, ik wil een advocaat*' (I didn't do it, I want a lawyer). When this vocabulary proved insufficient I took a few lessons with a private tutor, a kind, curly-haired woman who'd broken her hip in a cycling accident and was consigned to a Hitchcockian convalescence watching the birds through her rear window. We never studied as such, but gossiped in a mixture of Dutch and English, and I quickly reached a level where I could understand almost everything people said and stammer my way through a reply. Reading was harder, though, and I battled my way through picture books belonging to a Dutch friend's eighteen-month-old daughter. *Miffy* (*Nijntje*) was fun, but *The Very Hungry Caterpillar* was beyond me. Out in public I still regularly made mistakes, such as the time when instead of asking someone whether she was cold, I accidentally called her something else beginning with 'c'.

Surprisingly quickly, the Netherlands began to feel like home. I learned how to cycle while holding an open umbrella, how to slip slimy pickled herrings down my throat in one vinegary gulp, and how to pronounce words like '*genoeg*' and '*hottentottentententententoonstelling*'. However, there was still much about the country that was deeply confusing.

For a tiny nation, smaller than Togo or Kyrgyzstan, the Netherlands has had a huge influence on the world. The Dutch ruled over an empire stretching from the Caribbean to East Asia, founded the city of New York, discovered Australia, played the world's best football and produced some of the finest art and architecture in Europe. Everywhere one goes in the world, one can always find Dutch people. A country half the size of Scotland, with a population of just seventeen million or so, claims to have invented the DVD, the dialysis machine, the tape recorder, the CD, the energy-saving light-bulb, the pendulum clock, the speed camera, golf, the microscope, the telescope and the doughnut.

The Netherlands has been, and still is, a kind of hidden superpower. Yet to many outsiders – including me – it remained a land defined entirely by clichés: clogs and canals, tulips and windmills, bikes and dikes, pot and prostitutes. Bookshelves in the leafy English village where I grew up groaned under the weight of volumes about Italian cuisine or the difficulties of assimilating in rural France, but when it came to the gastronomically and climatically challenged Netherlands, most people were completely uninformed. Those well versed in the history of the Berlin Wall or the French Resistance often knew nothing about swathes of Dutch history: the vast land bridge that once connected the Netherlands to England; the famine that devastated the country in the 1940s; the Catholic traditions of the carnival-loving south; the long battle for independence from Spain; the bloody wars against the English navy; the engineering marvel of the Delta Project; the poisonous politics of the Dutch far right. The millions of tourists who visit each year rarely leave Amsterdam, and many expats manage to live in the country for years without speaking a single word of Dutch. Like Canada or Sweden, the Netherlands is a place about which everyone knows a little, but no one knows very much.

As my own ties to the country deepened, I was determined to learn more. In 2013 I set out on a series of journeys through my adopted country. Some were many miles long, while others were confined to a single city or even building, but each aimed to understand a different aspect of the Netherlands' culture and history – the battle against the rising tides, the 'Golden Age' of empire, the Second World War, the effects of immigration, the liberal approach to drugs and prostitution – and how these shaped the Dutch themselves. This book is the story of those journeys. In the course of undertaking them I not only saw the new King inaugurated in Amsterdam, but dressed as a tiger for Easter, got drunk in a world-famous art gallery, had a picnic in a concentration camp, found Noah's Ark near the North Sea and watched small children put on blackface before Christmas. I even broke the habit of a lifetime and went to a football match. I learned why the Dutch are always cleaning their windows, why prostitutes pay income tax, and why the Netherlands are not quite as liberal as they seem.

Some things, however, remained a mystery. Chief among these was where the Netherlands was heading. During my first few months in the country, I often thought the Dutch had built something close to a perfect society. They live in one of the richest countries in Europe but work the fewest hours, with profitable multinational companies and excellent public services to boot. Compared to their British counterparts, the average Dutch person works an hour a day less but is about twenty per cent wealthier. Violent crime is almost unheard of and even major cities are bucolic, with little of the stress, pettiness and grime that plague places like London. With memories of my daily commute to Westminster fading fast, I cycled slowly to the office, worked a few hours a day and had my bank account replenished with an unspendable torrent of euros every month – with special extra pay cheques provided to cover the cost of Christmas and summer holidays. Despite drinking dozens of cups of coffee a day, the Dutch are relaxed about almost everything. Working on weekends is unheard of, while suits and ties are reserved for weddings and funerals only. (For a job interview, a clean T-shirt will suffice.) The Netherlands often seemed a charmingly time-warped place, with children playing safely in the streets at night, road-sweepers using wooden witches' brooms, and teenagers rollerblading in the park while listening to Michael Jackson. Wandering the canals of Delft or watching the royals wave from their balcony in Amsterdam, it was easy to agree with the German poet Heinrich Heine, who allegedly said that if a war ever broke out he would head straight for the Netherlands, because 'everything happens fifty years later there'.

Over time, though, it became clear that my initial impressions of peace and prosperity were not entirely accurate. Although there was much in the Netherlands to admire, there were also some things to be concerned about. For centuries the country had benefited from its exposure to the outside world. Its geographical position and long seaboard helped it get rich from trade, while its overseas empire funded the development of cities like Amsterdam and artists like Rembrandt.

The Dutch people's outward-looking, internationalist attitude had given them a place on the world stage that it was hard to imagine being rivalled by, say, Finland, or Montenegro.

However, in recent years, exposure to outside forces had also created challenges. A journalist from the *New York Times* had described how 'the Dutch... tend to be a little world-weary these days. The past 35 years of Dutch history is the story of innocence lost,' he wrote. 'The noxious malaise that has long been eating at the vitals of most of industrialised Europe seems finally to have reached the Netherlands, taking much of the bounce out of this quiet, bustling nation... [as] the stout-hearted Dutch got their first taste of domestic terrorism, racial extremism, corporate scandal and massive unemployment.' That was in 1976. Since then, the sense of uncertainty had only intensified. The economic crisis had hit the Netherlands hard, climate change had threatened the country's watery borders, and immigration had caused tensions in many communities. Perhaps most strikingly of all, many former liberals now thought the whole Dutch social experiment had gone too far. The country's famously permissive approach to tricky social issues had been questioned, and sacred cows like legal drug use and prostitution sacrificed. In the teenage years of the twenty-first century, one of Europe's smallest countries seemed to be a microcosm for the challenges facing the continent at large.

Would the Netherlands be able to maintain its traditional freedoms, or were the good times over? No one seemed entirely sure, but as Amsterdam erupted in orange, the country was determined to defy the doomsayers. In their laidback, pragmatic, untheatrical way, the Dutch were responding to change just as they always had: with drinking and dancing and a quiet determination to maintain their unique outlook on life. For now, the country remained an island in time: arguably the most tolerant, peaceful and prosperous corner of a generally turbulent world. 'We'll keep making the wrong decisions,' a friend told me, 'and we'll keep enjoying the consequences.'

One

Water, Water, Everywhere

*Windmills, Climate Change and the Battle
against the Tides*

One night, Johan dreamed it was going to rain. In his dream, it
rained for forty days and forty nights. The sea rose, the rivers
flooded, and still the rain kept falling. People raced for higher
ground, searching for tall trees and mountaintops where they
could survive the deluge, but it was no use. The waters kept
rising and the whole world was drowned. When Johan awoke,
he decided to build an ark.

Some two decades later, the completed ark floated in a
dock off the River Maas in Dordrecht, an ancient cathedral
city some fifteen miles southeast of Rotterdam. Approaching
on foot from the train station one grey February morning, I
had expected something smaller and, strangely, did not notice
the ark until it was right above me: a vast wooden box of overlapping, honey-coloured pine that towered over the weedy
wasteland around it. As high as a five-storey building, the
ark looked exactly like those I'd seen in illustrated bibles as a
child, with a bowed profile and a squat cabin on the top. The
high sides were studded with portholes and hatches, from
which plastic animals peered out at the empty car park: a
black-and-white cow at one window, a gloomy-looking horse
at another. More oversized toys gazed down from the open
top deck, including a life-sized plastic giraffe at the stern and
an elephant at the bow. On the murky water below, a single
live swan bobbed serenely like a bath toy; waiting, perhaps, to
be offered a place on board.

Of all the places in the world where a modern-day disciple
might choose to build an ark, the Netherlands was perhaps
the most logical. With more than a quarter of the country
lying below mean sea level, canals, rivers and lakes were

almost as common as trees. Even a short walk or drive would involve crossing countless bridges, and even the most modest homes could be fronted by open water. More than three thousand miles of waterway were used to transport everything from cars to cows, and many towns retained the names of the water features on which they were originally based, such as Amsterdam's dam on the River Amstel. 'The Netherlands isn't below sea level,' a Dutchman on a ferry once told me. 'The sea is above Netherlands level.'

Mark Twain was supposed to have said that any investor seeking profit should buy land, as it wasn't being made any more. In most countries that would be sound advice, but in the Netherlands the opposite is true. Huge swathes of the country consist of land reclaimed from the sea, including the entire province of Flevoland. While England and Belgium are rough patchworks of fields and forests, the Netherlands is a man-made chessboard of straight lines and sharp corners. 'God created the world,' as one popular saying goes, 'but the Dutch created the Netherlands.' Unsurprisingly, the endless battle to stay dry has had a profound effect on the country's history and culture. After living there for a while, I came to realise that almost every distinctive feature or cliché about the Netherlands was, in some way, a result of the country's unique relationship with water: from the windmills that were used to pump fields dry, to the flatness of the land that was left behind, to the bicycles that travelled easily across the smooth terrain. Bricks paved roads built on dangerously soft ground; tulips thrived in the silty reclaimed soil; cows grew fat on rich, moist grass; glasses of milk and beer were safe to drink when clean water was in short supply; people grew tall from drinking all the milk; and thick wooden clogs kept farmers' feet dry when trudging through boggy fields. Almost everything that an outsider might think of as typically Dutch could be attributed to the country's ongoing battle against the tides.

The omnipresence of water had also, I came to see, had a profound effect on the Dutch themselves. Earthy and honest,

with nothing to hide, the Dutch people I met were as depend-
able and unexotic as the landscape in which they lived.
Having worked together to build a country the way others
might build a house, they also had a deeply ingrained belief in
the need for hard work and order, equality and cooperation.
To begin to understand the Dutch, therefore, I had to understand their relationship with water. And a journey along one
of the Netherlands' largest rivers, from Noah's Ark through
my adopted home city of Rotterdam and on to the North Sea,
seemed like a good place to start.

Into the Ark

I walked along a narrow jetty, pushed open a wooden swing
door and entered the ark. Inside, a young Dutch woman in
a Noah's Ark fleece jacket sat behind a pine reception desk
in a pine reception area. I bought a ticket – €12.50 for eter-
nal salvation, paid with a credit card – and the receptionist
pointed out animal footprints painted on the rough wooden
floor, leading away from the counter and into the belly of
the ship. '*Volg de voetstappen,*' she explained. 'Follow the
footprints.' I did as I was told and soon reached a series of
nativity-style displays nestled in the curves of the hull, each
housing doe-eyed plastic animals waiting for the waters to
subside. Next to them, recovering in bed from his frenzied
carpentering, was Noah, his grey beard cascading over a
grubby smock, dead plastic eyes staring at a splintery ceiling. On the wall was an enlarged page from a Dutch bible:
'The flood continued forty days upon the earth... and all
flesh died that moved upon the earth... Only Noah was left,
and those that were with him in the ark.' The whole place
smelled like IKEA.

The ark had opened in 2012, some twenty years after
the Dutch creationist and amateur prophet Johan Huibers
had his apocalyptic dream. A well-off building contractor
sporting a Mario Brothers moustache, Huibers had become
convinced that the Netherlands would be submerged in an

Old Testament–style flood. In 2005 he built a half-size replica of Noah's Ark, followed by the full-size replica in which I now stood. Three years in the making, it reportedly cost well over a million euros to build. Huibers told reporters he hoped to offset the costs by taking thousands of passengers on a tour of London during the 2012 Olympic Games, but those plans were scuppered when British authorities refused the vessel permission to visit, understandably concerned that a huge floating wood pile filled with people and candles might present something of a fire hazard.

According to its creator, the scale of the vessel followed the instructions laid out in the Book of Genesis. However, some concessions to modernity had been made – unable to identify the 'gopher wood' stipulated in the Bible, Huibers had resorted to building a Scandinavian pine skin over the metal hulls of several old barges that had been welded together. In a more serious break with tradition, rather than two specimens of each living creature, the ark included only a handful of small farmyard animals, outnumbered by plastic zoo animals. Perhaps for this reason, visitors were not exactly flooding in. Newspapers had reported a recent spike in interest in the ark when an apocalyptic cult claimed the end of the world was nigh, but when I arrived the queue to board the ark was not long. In fact, it was non-existent, and the car park outside was nearly empty.

Passing the plastic Noah, I walked deeper into the ship, ascending a series of wooden ramps and walkways through the maze of animal pens and cabins that filled the belly of the ship. Most of the pens were empty, but some contained live rabbits that were scratching their way through a dusty carpet of straw. A black plastic monkey swung from the rafters overhead, and a pair of plastic rhinos thrust their horns menacingly in the direction of the ostriches and dodos. Elsewhere, a six-packed plastic Adam with a shaggy brown wig and amorphous genitals was ignoring a terribly sexy Eve, her generous breasts obscured by long blonde hair and a carefully placed plastic flamingo. Posters on the wall offered a creationist view of world history, implying that the Grand Canyon had been created by the same deluge that sent Noah to sea.

Ascending the sloping walkways, I soon reached the top deck, where an empty café offered *rookworst* (sausage) sandwiches but no alcohol. Outside was a panoramic view of the river Maas curving towards the steeples of Dordrecht city centre. Milky grey and as flat as a table top, the river isn't much to look at, but is in fact one of the continent's most important arteries, one main channel of what geographers catchily refer to as the Rhine–Meuse–Scheldt delta. Roughly 600 miles long, the Maas (or Meuse in French) flows north through France, Belgium and the Netherlands before bending eastwards and joining a dense web of other rivers on their way to the sea, including the Lek and the Waal and what Lord Byron called 'the wide and winding Rhine'. Before leaving home, I had tried to follow the course of the rivers on maps online, but quickly gave up – it was like trying to track the path of a single thread through a knitted jumper. Suffice to say that should they wish, a boat owner in Dordrecht could in theory sail upriver not only to Dutch cities such as Maastricht, but on to Strasburg, Mainz, Cologne and even Basel. Going in the opposite direction, the river carries traffic from Dordrecht to Rotterdam before reaching the sea at several points along the Dutch coast, most notably at Hoek van Holland, from where ferries continued the journey across the Channel to Essex. Although not widely known outside northern Europe, the Maas is mentioned in the first verse of the German national anthem ('We stand together as brothers/ from the Maas to the Memel'). The river even gave its name to a dinosaur: the Mosasaur, an alligator-like creature whose existence helped disprove the previously accepted theory that it was impossible for any animal to become extinct. The Maas is the lifeblood of the southern Netherlands, and I intended to make my way along it.

Dizzy from the smell of pine, I decided I had seen enough of the ark. I retraced my steps, resisted the temptation to buy stuffed toy animals from the woman at the reception desk, and disembarked. I had nearly an hour to spare before the ferry would depart for Rotterdam, and was happy to have the chance to explore Dordrecht, a city I had never visited before.

Dordrecht: A Smiling City

Just as Parisians must tire of fireworks over the Eiffel Tower, and Egyptians yawn at the sight of pyramids at sunset, a couple of years in the Netherlands had made me rather blasé about pretty little towns with historic churches and canals. Dordrecht, however, was undeniably charming: a warren of spindly old buildings tilting over rust-coloured brick streets dusted with fallen leaves. 'Dordrecht, a place so beautiful, tomb of my cherished illusions,' a lovesick Proust once called it. For Alexandre Dumas, it was 'a smiling city'. On a wintry weekday morning, the streets were quiet but the city felt quietly prosperous, unsullied by the tour groups and stag parties that blighted towns further north. Cyclists rattled over bumpy cobbled streets, weaving between shoppers carrying plastic bags filled with bread and potatoes. As in many Dutch towns, water was omnipresent. Around almost every corner came another small harbour, tucked between tall warehouses and houses lined up like books on a shelf. The city seemed like a jigsaw puzzle with many pieces missing, the gaps filled with spillover from the river.

Near one small harbour, I found the Nieuwe Kerk, an ancient colossus with curved brick walls and a wooden tower painted the colour of butter. Only in the Netherlands, I thought, could a building that was nearly a thousand years old still be known as the 'New Church'. Now deconsecrated, it had been converted into a home furnishing store where pilgrims could worship overpriced cookware and candles. A man passing by on a bicycle stopped to offer me a piece of bitter, coal-coloured Dutch liquorice, or *drop*. I declined, but took out my notebook and wrote: 'The people in Dordrecht are nice.'

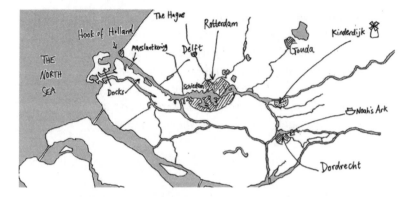

According to the books I'd consulted before arriving, Dordrecht was once a wealthy and powerful place. The city was encircled by rivers – the Maas, the Dordtsche Kil, the Hollands Diep, the Nieuwe Merwede – and its location made it a natural trading centre. A dense network of inland waterways enabled German merchants to travel all the way to Amsterdam, Antwerp or Bruges without breaching the stormy North Sea. Travelling downstream was relatively easy, but in the other direction teams of slaves were sometimes used to pull boats against the current. However, the city's prosperity was not to last. Ironically, the growth of waterborne trade proved to be its undoing: as trade volumes grew, larger boats were used, and Dordrecht's relatively narrow harbours and shallow channels became increasingly cramped. The city was eclipsed by larger ports elsewhere and slipped into relative obscurity, a mere spectator to much of the trade that continued to pass on the Maas. Once a major trading city, it was now a relatively sleepy backwater.

I wandered towards the river and found a row of small cafés squatting along the brick waterfront, each with the high glass screen the Dutch like to sit behind whenever they are compelled to go outside. A young waitress hustled past carrying a tray of traditional Dutch bar fare: greasy *bitterballen* hot snacks with mustard, and small glasses of beer wearing thick foamy hats. '*Lekker!*' the waiting customers cried in unison. 'Tasty!' I sat on a bench to take in the view of the river, and

13

was joined almost immediately by a girl of about sixteen with dyed pink hair, porcelain skin and a pierced nose. Opening a plastic shopping bag, she removed a cardboard shoebox and gazed lovingly at the hideous pink sports shoes nestled inside. '*Mooi, he?*' I asked, gesturing at the river and attempting to strike up a conversation. 'Beautiful, isn't it?'

'Yes,' she said, staring at the shoes. 'They are.'

The Mighty Maas

My allotted time in Dordrecht almost up, I walked along the river bank to a floating metal pontoon, where the Waterbus ferry service to Rotterdam was already waiting. I'd seen the same boat pass through Rotterdam at the height of summer, overloaded with middle-aged Dutch couples with bicycles and picnic baskets. Today, on an overcast Tuesday morning, I had the boat almost to myself, shared only with three lost-looking Polish men in tracksuits. Pausing on the gangplank, I bought a ticket from a young crewman who was dressed in a smart sailor's outfit, but apparently shared the common Dutch belief that there was no such thing as too much hair gel. When I asked for a ticket to Rotterdam, he requested I confirm my destination twice before obliging. 'Yes,' I said in Dutch and then in English, 'all the way to Rotterdam.' Fifteen minutes from Dordrecht by train but more than an hour away by boat, Rotterdam was an unusual destination at this time of year: a long haul on a vessel that was too slow for commuters and too cold for tourists.

A bell rang and the boat charged backwards at an alarming speed, sweeping through 180 degrees as it withdrew from the harbour's embrace. Following bitter experience with Dutch railways, I had expected the ferry's 'high speed' designation to be an ambition rather than a description, but for a boxy barge it moved surprisingly quickly and I scrambled to hold down my notebook and jacket as we roared away from Dordrecht. To the right lay the ridiculous ark, with a giraffe standing sentry on the bow. To the left was the first of a seemingly endless series of forks in the river. With a lurch, the boat surged down the righthand fork towards Rotterdam.

We swiftly overtook a boat piled high with dozens of shipping containers, stacked like bricks in a wall, and then another carrying a jumble of concrete blocks. The languages printed on the sides of the vessels we passed suggested their origins or destinations: German, French, British, Chinese and Norwegian. Along the riverbanks, high grassy dikes were washed by the ferry's milky wake. Atop one dike I saw a grey *reiger*, or heron, standing folded like a flick knife. Then came a fisherman wearing a long black cape, pointing across the river with a long carbon finger. Behind the dikes, small houses were clustered together like pieces on a monopoly board. Similar to many Dutch coastal and riverside homes, they had no view of the water, obscured almost entirely by the walls built to keep them dry.

A succession of small towns with names that could choke a child were quickly left behind: Alblasserdam, Papendrecht, Ridderkerk and Krimpen aan den Ijssel. Cycle route signs on the riverbank pointed to others well known to history: Gouda, of the cheeses; Oudewater, where suspected witches once were weighed to see if they were light enough to ride on a broomstick; Loevestein, where Hugo Grotius, the seventeenth-century father of international law, made his escape from a castle hidden in a wooden chest. Gradually, the landscape became less idyllic. The compact cottages of suburban Dordrecht gave way to the trappings of light industry: small factories and warehouses, cranes, piles of sand and sections of pipe waiting to be loaded onto barges. A string of three low-slung barges passed by in the opposite direction, each piled high with gravel and looking dangerously unstable as they bucked like a skipping rope in the ferry's wake.

We stopped at a small pontoon near a car park and picked up a few passengers: a dorky-looking father in a red baseball cap and three excited children, all waving goodbye to *oma* (grandma). As the ferry surfed away from the shore, the children leaned out over the railings while their father fussed, holding onto their belts and imploring them to hang on tight. '*Wees voorzichtig!*' he cried, 'Be careful!' He probably had good reason to worry: a couple of days previously, local newspapers had told the story of a nineteen-year-old woman who had nearly drowned not far from here. Thankfully, she was saved by a ninety-year-old fisherman who downed his rod and jumped into the river to save her. 'It was my duty,' Jaap Koppers told the local news. 'But it was just as well she was not too fat.'

I revelled in the wind and fresh air, but as we left the factories behind, what was most noticeable about the scenery was the lack of anything to notice. Apart from a few farms and spiky church towers puncturing the horizon, the landscape was almost completely featureless. The high dikes blocked the view from the river, and behind them lay not much to see anyway. I reread a page from a 1920s travel book that I had copied into my notebook: 'The stranger who cycles this way is unfortunate, but if he does it again he is a fool; the more especially as there is absolutely no interest on the way.' Another historical traveller had been even more succinct, proposing a mathematical formula to summarise the landscape in these parts: '[grass + water]'. For me, the scenery conjured up memories of a favourite book from my childhood, long before I ever set foot in the Netherlands: *The Cow Who Fell in the Canal*. Some twenty-five years after my parents read me the book, I could still remember almost every word.

Reclamation Nation

Thousands of years earlier, this whole corner of Europe had looked very different. During and after the last ice age, the western Netherlands was linked directly to the hunchback of East Anglia by a huge land bridge known as 'Doggerland'. This vast landmass – stretching nearly from Dover to Denmark – was often covered in thick snow, but in spring and summer the lagoons, mudflats and marshes made a rich hunting ground for the early Europeans who lived there. The rivers flowing across Doggerland, including the Rhine, the Maas and the Thames, were well stocked with trout and salmon, and the seas on either side teemed with eels, seals, shellfish and dolphins. Woolly mammoths roamed between Essex and the Netherlands along the routes now plied by giant passenger ferries.

Around 20,000 years ago, however, sea levels began to rise, and the tundra linking Britain to the continent gradually flooded. By around 10,000 years ago, the centre of Doggerland was dominated by a large freshwater lake, constantly refilled by the Thames from the west and the Rhine from the east. As sea levels rose further, the lake broke through to connect with the open water of the North Sea and the English Channel, sending hunter-gatherers fleeing to newly created small islands, early refugees from climate change.

Then, 8000 or 9000 years ago, a series of enormous landslides off the coast of Norway triggered a mega-tsunami that swept across what remained of Doggerland, erasing it from the map forever. Europe lost an area equivalent to an entire country, and Britain became an island. Within a few centuries, only a few traces of the land bridge remained, including the Dogger Bank sandbank off the coast of Britain and the Frisian Islands of the Netherlands, sandy, grassy humps strung along the coast north of Amsterdam like stepping stones. The landscapes of the east of England and the southeastern Netherlands would remain strikingly similar. Thousands of years after the tsunami, Dutch fishermen would still find antlers, stone tools and mammoth bones tangled in their nets.

Long after Britain broke away, the Netherlands had continued to be reshaped not by tsunamis and tectonic shifts, but by humans. At the dawn of the seventeenth century, much of the Netherlands was under water, with a coastline that varied from year to year depending on whether the sea or the sand dunes had the upper hand. Many of the parts that were above water were barely so, consisting of thick peat bogs and marshland. 'The Great Bog of Europe' was how an Englishman who toured the Netherlands in 1652 described it: 'the buttock of the world, full of veines and bloud, but no bones.'

Efforts to dry out this great bog began in earnest over 2000 years ago, when the northern Frisian tribe started constructing high mounds of mud and clay, known as *terps*, on top of which they could build their homes. As time went on, the *terps* were extended and joined together to form the first dikes: muddy sea walls reinforced with straw, household waste, wood and even cow hides. In 57 BCE, when the Romans invaded what would later become the Netherlands, the *terp*-dwelling Frisians were one of the few tribes in Europe successfully to resist Roman conquest. The edge of the empire was demarcated by a string of riverside army camps, with bridges and canals enabling troops to move quickly when a rebellion broke out.

Even Roman engineering could not keep the sea entirely at bay, and the east of the country continued to flood regularly. According to the Dutch historian Jacob Vossestein, one Roman soldier complained: 'On the hills, or rather on their handmade elevations, lives an unhappy population. At high tide they are like crew members, while at low tide they seem to be shipwrecked, picking up fish that want to escape with the retreating water.' Eventually, it all became too much for even the mighty Romans, and they quietly withdrew from the low waterlogged lands early in the fifth century. Their network of dams and canals remained – the foundation of what would become the world's greatest reclamation nation.

Around 600 years later, the physical geography of the Netherlands underwent another seismic shift, when peat – the rich, decayed plant matter carpeting much of the north of the country – was found to be an excellent fuel. The discovery sparked something of a peat rush. Huge areas of boggy land were dug up, cut into bricks and burned for cooking or heating. Peat fuelled everything from the kilns in Delft producing the famous blue-and-white pottery to the distilleries near Rotterdam brewing fiery Dutch *jenever*, the juniper-based spirit allegedly invented by a Dutch chemist for its medicinal properties, later popularised under its English name: gin. As the scars the peat-diggers left behind filled with water, the countryside became pockmarked with hundreds of shallow lakes.

The rush for peat had some serious side effects. The bogs consisted largely of water, and as the peat was removed the already low land sank even lower, becoming even more susceptible to flooding. Dikes around major settlements helped keep the water out, but crisis struck when woodworms began boring into flood defences. If the country was to survive, new techniques would be needed to keep it dry.

Windmills

The ferry surged onwards and the river forked again, the Lek joining the main channel of the Maas at a Y-shaped junction. I wanted to make a stopover and so changed to another vessel: a wide, flat ferry with an open deck to carry cars across a stretch of river where the road disappeared under water. A grey-bearded man in a pleasing sailor's hat came around collecting fares: 80 cents for a one-way crossing and a thumb-sized pink ticket stub. The boat growled away from the harbour, and immediately almost collided with another vessel: the *Anaconda*, cruising relentlessly upstream with a heavy cargo of jumbled bricks. I braced myself for a hasty swim to shore, but the ferry went hard into reverse and the barge slid by with a couple of feet to spare. A minute or two later we arrived at a slippery concrete ramp on the opposite side. A gang of six men sat waiting for the return crossing on restored vintage motorcycles, living out middle-aged James Dean fantasies in tasselled leather jackets, cigarettes dangling from their shivering lips.

At first glance, the village of Kinderdijk was an incongruous setting for one of the Netherlands' ten UNESCO World Heritage Sites, consisting of not much more than a concrete riverbank backed by a low grass-covered dike. Nevertheless, when I got behind the dike I found a rather pretty little village, with neat rows of gingerbread cottages down narrow lanes and a fine church tower peeking over grey-tiled rooftops. Walking away from the river, I soon came across all the usual indicators of an approaching tourist attraction: a cheesy art gallery, a café, an ice-cream shop with spinning racks of postcards cluttering the narrow pavement. Around a bend in the road, the attraction itself came into view. A few hundred metres from the river, on a green plateau speckled with cows and horses, lay four long canals, running in parallel for perhaps a mile like the curved prongs of a fork. All along the banks, at intervals of perhaps a hundred metres, sat bell-shaped brick windmills – a total of nineteen by my count, all spinning gently in the breeze. It was, an information sign at the roadside explained, the largest concentration of old-fashioned windmills in Europe. Despite the dreary weather, it looked like a tourist's fantasy of the Netherlands: a fistful of Dutch clichés crammed into a single postcard-worthy scene.

The area around Kinderdijk was, I later learned, named after a miraculous rescue that supposedly took place during a severe flood in 1421. A man walking on the dike spotted a cradle floating, Moses-style, in the raging flood waters, with a cat balanced precariously on top of it. He rescued the cat and then found, to his astonishment, a baby snuggled safe and dry inside the basket. Locals declared the incident to be a miracle, and rechristened the dike the *kinderdijk*, or 'child's dike'.

The area had been inhabited from around the tenth or eleventh century, when farmers began digging drainage ditches in an effort to convert boggy fields into usable farmland. At first excess water drained easily into the nearby rivers, but as river levels rose it became increasingly difficult to keep water flowing in the right direction. Around 1740, an ingenious solution was found: a series of windmills that would pump water up from the fields into an area of closed canals, and from there up and over the dikes into the river. With each windmill only able to pump water a few feet, the canals served as an intermediate storage tank between the farmland and the river, like a mezzanine floor enabling people to change elevators in a very tall building. It was this intermediate staging post – a dense concentration of canals and windmills lying lower than the river but higher than the surrounding fields – that made such an eye-catching spectacle today.

The Dutch began building primitive water-pumping mills around the end of the thirteenth century, based on designs they copied from Persia. Later, more complex designs from the Mediterranean were adapted to create distinctive brick towers with four spinning sails. As the technology proved its worth, Dutch windmills proliferated rapidly. They were expensive to build, but a growing population meant that good farming land was in short supply. By paying for new wind-mills to be built, investors could unlock huge tracts of land for housing or agricultural use, earning a handsome return on their investment.

According to one nineteenth-century travellers' guide, windmills were even sometimes used to pay dowries for brides. By the mid-1600s there were hundreds of the things, including more than two hundred in the northern town of Alkmaar alone. The high concentration of mills quickly became an early Dutch tourist attraction. In 1697, Russian tsar Peter the Great visited Zaandam, just north of Amsterdam, to study the revolutionary wind-powered sawmills there. Disguised as a common workman, the leader of one of the world's greatest empires stayed in a simple wooden cottage and worked as a carpenter in the shipyard.

The Netherlands soon became famous for its expertise in pumping water, with Dutch engineers helping drain large areas of land in other countries, including parts of Suffolk and Norfolk. The Dutch word for a tract of reclaimed land, *polder*, was (like the later 'apartheid') one of the relatively few Dutch words to be adopted into the English language. One particularly striking example of windmill-building prow-ess was the draining of the huge Beemster polder north of Amsterdam in the early 1600s. More than forty windmills drained a huge area of land that was then filled with densely packed villages laid out in a neat grid formation. At a time when much of Europe remained mired in poverty and conflict, it was an astonishing achievement. The wealthy merchants who had financed the windmills' construction earned handsome returns on their investments, while the grid-like layout of the new towns was sometimes said to have served as the inspiration for a city that the Dutch later founded overseas: New York.

Following the success of the Beemster scheme, investors looked for money-making opportunities elsewhere. These included draining large areas of land in Amsterdam, where concentric circular canals were dug and ringed with tall townhouses, creating another tourist attraction and a perennial hazard for cyclists wobbling home after too many Heinekens. Narrow streets radiated outwards from the central Dam Square like the spokes of a bicycle wheel, crossing the canals via dozens of picturesque bridges. A sequence of locks enabled the entire network of canals to be flushed regularly with water from the Amstel, keeping the canals relatively clean. Because the reclaimed land was so soft, new buildings often had to be built on top of long wooden pilings. Amsterdam's Central Station, for example, was built atop nearly 9000 poles, propping it up above soggy soil that was previously open water. Having paid for such elaborate foundations, developers had a strong incentive to increase their profits by adding extra floors to the buildings, much to the annoyance of later generations forced to struggle up ladder-like staircases with heavy bags of shopping. Such projects even helped shape the country's political system, with the need to coordinate the construction and maintenance of flood defences creating the famous 'polder model' of government, which depended on intense negotiation between numerous political parties. In the Netherlands coalition governments were the norm, as were mutually agreed policies that (critics said) left no one completely happy.

At Kinderdijk, a group of iPhone-wielding Chinese tourists vied for a prime viewing spot with a pair of watercolour painters working at their easels. I paused to watch them paint, and recalled reading somewhere how Rembrandt, born in a windmill near the Dutch city of Leiden, supposedly acquired his sensitivity to light and shade as an infant lying beneath spinning sails that gently strobed the sun. As I walked among the windmills I could see that many of them were still inhabited. Bicycles rested on fences, dogs slept in gardens and cheerful old women gazed out from behind chintzy curtains. Outside several mills, despite the grey skies, residents were indulging in the favourite Dutch pastime of gossiping with neighbours over thimble-sized cups of coffee.

In the windmills' heyday, millers themselves had also lived inside with their families, in round rooms with round furniture. They added fabric sections to the spinning sails to increase their surface area on less windy days, and even used the stationary sails to communicate with one another. By setting the resting sails in a certain position, a miller could broadcast news of a wedding, birth or death in the family, with sections of sail removed to indicate the gender and age of the departed. As well as draining land, windmills were employed to grind grain, tobacco, mustard seeds and building stone, and to saw wood for the country's rapidly growing shipbuilding industry. By the time Karl Marx visited the Netherlands in the 1830s, he could report some 12,000 windmills dotting the landscape. As another admiring visitor reported in 1836, the Dutch appeared to have found 'the means for creating a paradise, a new superior world, to effect in one year more than hitherto could be done in thousands of years'.

However, even thousands of windmills could not sate the Dutch appetite for land. During the seventeenth century alone the population of the Netherlands doubled, and more mouths to feed and people to house meant that even more land was needed. As the Industrial Revolution picked up speed, a new solution presented itself in the form of steam-powered pumps. Initially resisted by farmers, who thought the engine noise would scare cows, these quickly enabled massive new polders to be drained, including nearly 200,000 acres in the nineteenth century alone. In the 1860s, steam pumps helped drain a huge lake south of Amsterdam, including a certain part known, on account of its many shipwrecks, as the 'ship-hole'. The name survived at the airport built on the new polder – Schiphol – where planes could land and take off from an area that used to be several metres under water.

A few decades later came perhaps the most ambitious project yet: the closing of the mouth of the Zuider Zee, a huge tidal bay jutting deep into the coastline north of Amsterdam. Copying techniques used to build the Panama Canal, an engineer called Cornelis Lely directed workers on hundreds of boats to build an enormous clay wall across the mouth of the bay. Work was still underway when the Zuider Zee hosted the Olympic sailing competition in 1928, but within a few years the wall – known as the *Afsluitdijk* or 'closing-off dike' – was complete and the sea became a lake, enclosed behind almost twenty miles of perfectly straight causeway. Work to drain the lake began almost immediately, and within a few years thousands of people were living on land that had once been on the seabed. An inscription on the dike provided a summary of what had become the guiding philosophy of the Dutch people: 'A living nation builds its own future.'

A Land of Giants

Reclaimed land not filled with houses was often handed over to what would become another enduring symbol of the Netherlands: the dairy cow. As milk production soared, the Dutch began to devour enormous quantities of milk, yoghurt and particularly cheese – eventually consuming about 30% more milk products each year than their British, American or German counterparts. Wax-covered Dutch cheeses, many of them named after towns like Edam and Gouda where they were sold, became staples.

One consequence of this growing love of lactose was that the Dutch themselves grew incredibly tall. In the mid-1800s, the average Dutchman was about five feet four inches tall

– three inches shorter than the average American. One out of every four men applying to join the Dutch military was rejected for being too short. After 150-odd years of scoffing milk and cheese, however, the Dutch had soared past the Americans and everyone else. By the late twentieth century, the average Dutchman was a shade over six feet tall, and the average Dutch woman about five feet seven. The Dutch had gone from being among the shortest people in Europe to being the tallest people in the world.

By the time of my tour, building codes were regularly being adjusted to raise the standard heights for door frames and ceilings, hotels were offering twenty-centimetre bed extensions, and the national airline KLM had agreed a deal with the Tall People's Club to give extra-legroom seats to lanky Dutchmen. According to news reports, it wasn't unusual for Dutch ambulances to keep their doors open on the way to hospital, so patients' legs could stick out the back.

Scientists predictably argued over the causes: improved nutrition, democratisation of wealth, better hygiene and genetic factors were all thought to play a role. Research published in 2015 suggested that because taller Dutch men were statistically less likely to be single, and more likely to have children, natural selection was also at work. But it was generally agreed that the growth of the polders, and the resulting love of all things dairy, had played a major role in turning one of the world's flattest places into a land of giants.

Cold, Flat and Crowded

At Kinderdijk, it started to rain. I was shaken from my reverie by a cacophony of clicks, as three dozen Chinese tourists opened three dozen black umbrellas. Leaving the windmills behind, I walked towards the Maas, pausing at a small gift shop to buy a postcard for my mother. Nearby, a sign pointed out the modern replacement for the windmills: a pair of giant metal screws, each the size of a minibus, which could churn excess water up over the dikes and into the river. As I took a photo, a large yellow tour bus pulled up and deposited a flabby couple in the car park, unmistakably American in pristine running shoes and neatly pressed polo shirts, their baggy sleeves flapping in the wind like wings. The man raised a wrinkled hand and pointed at the windmills in the distance. 'Honey, do you want to walk over and take a closer look?' 'I think we've pretty much seen it,' his wife replied, already turning to get back on the bus.

Having pretty much seen it myself, I followed the road back to the river and boarded another Waterbus heading further along the Maas towards Rotterdam. A small yacht chugged by, carrying five tattooed men dancing to the arrhythmic house music so beloved of Dutch people, followed by a chunky barge stacked with containers labelled YANG MING, with a crewman washing a greasy sheet in the foamy white water behind. The ferry passed through a small shipyard, where a boat lay stricken on the riverbank like a beached whale, three men in blue overalls tending to a gaping hole in its side. The river meant leisure for me, but for others only work. Mostly, though, the landscape remained empty, with little to see other than high dikes and flat polder.

The featureless landscape pointed to an obvious consequence of manufacturing a country from below sea level: that it is totally, utterly flat. Soon after arriving in the Netherlands, I'd read in an atlas that the highest point in the country was at an impressive 887 metres above sea level, not too much lower than the highest point in Wales. That lofty point, however, turned out to be the aptly named Mount Scenery, a volcano in Dutch territory in the Caribbean. In the Netherlands proper, the terrain peaks at a rather less impressive 322 metres – and even that is in Limburg, the narrow finger of land protruding from the southeastern corner of the country into Germany. The northwestern areas where most of the population live are truly, extraordinarily flat, lacking any elevation beyond the occasional sand dune. Many places struggle to register any altitude at all: a sign in the Rotterdam satellite of Nieuwerkerk aan den IJssel notes proudly that it is the lowest point in Europe, wallowing almost seven metres below sea level.

As someone who had grown up in the kind of corrugated English village where collecting a pint of milk required a brisk walk up a 45-degree slope, I found this lack of altitude genuinely disconcerting. In place of the softly swelling landscapes and gently curving lanes of my homeland, the Netherlands had only starkly androgynous terrain and featureless, arrow-straight roads. There were no hill starts on driving tests and no front brakes on bicycles. When it snowed, local parks were filled with Dutch parents wheezing and grumbling as they dragged children around on sledges that had nowhere to slide.

Before moving to the Netherlands I had been a keen runner and cyclist, but both activities seemed futile without either the challenge of an incline to ascend or the reward of a view from the top. The main road near my house was named Bergweg – 'Mountain Road' – but inclined so insignificantly that I couldn't roll down it on my bike. When I did enter a short running race in Rotterdam, I received in the post written instructions on 'How to Run Uphill', lest I be unprepared for the slightly sloping bridge over which the race would pass. For the Dutch, life was lived in two dimensions.

The flatness of the landscape also had a strange effect on perceptions, helping make an already small country seem even smaller. In much the same way that hills and winding roads serve to magnify distances in hilly countries, adding hours to road journeys and isolating towns on the far side of mountains, the opposite was true in the uniformly level Netherlands. Journey times were shortened and fields of vision lengthened. On train journeys, for example, Rotterdam's jagged skyline would become visible on the horizon perhaps fifteen miles before arrival. The constant presence of rivers and canals also warped dimensions in curious ways, causing frequent lengthy diversions. It was rarely possible to walk directly to a destination without taking several detours to cross stretches of water. 'The bridge was up' was a trusted excuse for Dutch office workers running late.

In 2011, a Dutch journalist became briefly famous after suggesting, only partly in jest, a bold solution to the country's altitude problem. 'I have dreamed of having a mountain in Holland since I was fifteen,' Thijs Zonneveld told reporters. 'Being flat is really useful for growing beets... but it's a disaster when it comes to sports.' His proposal to build an artificial mountain won the backing of Dutch cycling, skiing and climbing federations, and Zonneveld was invited on national chat shows to discuss the idea. One major stumbling block was the cost of the project, estimated at a modest €1 billion, including cost savings achieved by making the mountain hollow. Construction of the 2000-metre peak was initially due to be completed by 2018, but at the time of my tour it had yet to begin, and the country remained as flat as a Dutch pancake.

Another national challenge was how to squeeze a relatively large number of people onto a rather small area of land. Despite relentless efforts to increase its landmass, at the time of my journey the Netherlands still had by far the highest population density in northern Europe, with an average of almost 500 people in every square kilometre. By international standards, Dutch population density was simply astonishing. The Netherlands was, according to my calculations, more than three times more crowded than China, while if the United States was as crowded as the Netherlands, it would contain more than four billion people. In the *Randstad* – the diamond-shaped constellation of Rotterdam, Amsterdam, Utrecht and Den Haag that formed the heart of the Netherlands – the situation was even more extreme. There, roughly 1500 people lived on every square kilometre of urban land. Not coincidentally, one of the few places to come close in terms of density was similarly waterlogged Bangladesh.

Over time, things were only getting worse – between 1960 and 2020 the population of the Netherlands was forecast to increase by 50 per cent, compared with 20 per cent growth in the UK and 15 per cent shrinkage in Belgium. Hardly anyone I knew lived in a proper house, rather than a cramped apartment or a *woonboot* (houseboat) bobbing on a canal.

Even the wealthy lived in homes that were – by international standards – small, with tiny gardens and dozens of neighbouring properties visible from the windows. Space was at such a premium that graves in the Netherlands were usually only rented for a decade or two, after which their inhabitants would be dug up and reburied in a communal *knekelput*, or mass grave.

Until relatively recently, large areas of the Netherlands remained almost empty. As late as 1900, the total population of the country was only five million or so, and major cities were separated by swathes of open countryside. Over the following century, however, the national population tripled. The *Groene Hart* ('green heart') of virtually undeveloped land between the major cities grew steadily smaller, with urban areas expanding to fill the gaps like ink blots on paper. The urban area of the *Randstad* – first identified by the co-founder of the airline KLM as he looked down on it from a plane – grew steadily until it formed one of the largest urban conurbations in Europe.

For a time the Netherlands was viewed as a model for sustainable growth, with Pete Hall's 1966 book *The World Cities* heralding the Dutch for preventing the *Randstad* from becoming 'another formless urban sprawl'. To me, though, it seemed that some of Hall's worst fears had been realised. Although the historic centres of Dutch cities were often achingly pretty, outside them much of the country was a New Jerseyesque sprawl of motorways, drive-through restaurants, backlit billboards and monolithic superstores. Many Dutch commute by car, creating fearsome traffic jams even on routes served well by public transport.

One consequence of all this has been that despite the rural imagery adorning the postcards sold to tourists – all dairy cows, green fields and windmills – most Dutch people live a lifestyle that is almost entirely urban. In Britain, one is rarely more than a couple of miles from a patch of open countryside or pristine woodland. In most of the Netherlands, though, one is rarely out of sight of a road or town. The Dutch talk about the *Groen Hart* in reverential terms, as if it were one of Europe's last great wildernesses, but in truth much of it is practically suburban, filled with roads, railways, petrol stations and even sizable towns. The few Dutch national parks are pleasant enough but would pass unremarked in Germany, France or the UK, crammed as they are with tarmacked paths, trimmed trees, car parks and cafés. 'Holland' may have been named for its abundance of *holtlant* (wooded land), but centuries later it was hard to find much of it.

Manhattan on the Maas

Fifteen minutes or so after leaving Kinderdijk, the Waterbus entered the suburbs of Rotterdam. Verdant river banks gave way to concrete walls and piers, and little Monopoly cottages were supplanted by glass-fronted apartment blocks and office complexes. The river swept leftwards in a great arc, cradling the city. On the left, I caught a glimpse of the bowl-shaped Feyenoord football stadium, De Kuip ('The Tub'), followed by one of the city's two major mosques, its spindly minarets echoed by the brick church spires behind them. Nearer the water, a circular gas storage facility looked strangely like another mosque, its domed roof decorated with golden stars.

Passing under a long, rust-coloured suspension bridge, I recognised a small harbour fronting the Witte Huis (White House), a Disneyesque office tower built in the 1890s. At ten storeys high, it was once the tallest building in Europe. Further back from the river, a cluster of glassy office buildings and apartment blocks shone in the weak winter sunshine. Perhaps forty storeys tall, their size would be unremarkable in many countries, but was something of a rarity in the Netherlands, and explained why Rotterdam's marketing board had tried to brand the city as 'Manhattan on the Maas'. Although the country was famous for its tall townhouses, the soggy terrain put a natural limit on the height of buildings. Old church towers and tall houses often exhibited an alarming sideways tilt.

The nineteenth-century townhouse where I lived listed like a sinking ship, with the front end of the living room lying about ten inches closer to street level than the back, requiring wedge-shaped slices to be sawn from the bottom of new flat-pack furniture. As a result, the country's tallest building – one of the towers I could see on Rotterdam's skyline – was barely half the height of the Eiffel Tower, and wouldn't even make the top hundred in New York City.

Entering Rotterdam, the Maas widened and straightened. The city's most famous landmark filled the horizon: the Erasmusbrug, a car, tram and cycle bridge linking the northern and southern halves of the city. According to my guidebook, the bridge was known locally as the Swan, although I couldn't quite see why; it looked to me more like a great white harp toppled sideways across the river, with dozens of slender cables radiating from its inverted V-shaped peak down to the opposite bank. As a rare focal point in a city that had been hollowed out by wartime bombing, the bridge had come to epitomise Rotterdam's post-war reconstruction and the architectural renaissance led by another of its famous sons, the architect Rem Koolhaas. Some two decades after its construction, its status as a local icon was assured: Rotterdam's own Eiffel Tower or Brandenburg Gate, available in plastic miniature from the tourist information office.

I had now lived in the city for a while, but it felt strange to arrive by boat for the first time, approaching from behind and below like a predator creeping up on its prey. I was also surprised by how busy the river itself was. In contrast to the miles of quiet water on which I'd just travelled, in Rotterdam the Maas was alive with activity. Small black-and-yellow water taxis buzzed across it like bees, ferrying passengers to hotels and office blocks on the south bank. Up on the Erasmusbrug, jangling trams vied for space with bicycles, cars and lorries. Just past it, a large cargo ship pulled up to the riverbank, its horn honking like an angry goose. A tour boat passed by, zoom lenses pointing from its sides as if pirates' cannons.

Rotterdam originally took its name from a dam built on the river Rotte, and had once been a key gateway for the Dutch Golden Age of trade and exploration. However, the city's nautical heritage received a serious blow during the Second World War, when Nazi bombing raids erased much of the historic centre. In their haste to rebuild, the authorities ordered dozens of canals and harbours to be filled with rubble from the ruined city, in a strange reversal of the usual reclamation process. Today only the main channel of the Maas and a few side harbours remain, most of them murky dead-ends lined with cheap restaurants and bars. Even the Rotte itself has all but disappeared from the city, blocked from the centre by a road and a subway station.

The Waterbus came to a halt just past the Erasmusbrug, on the north bank. Despite the frenetic activity all around, it was a pleasant spot to disembark, with a few trees lining the river and a small grassy park overlooking the water. Young couples sat along the high walls, their legs hanging over the water as they shared wine from paper cups and pointed at passing boats. The bridge itself cast a long shadow downstream towards my ultimate destination, the sea. I disembarked onto a steel jetty, and was hailed by a man of about fifty in stained blue overalls, drifting in a small white speedboat – another friendly Dutchman keen to chat with a stranger. Steering with his knees while trying not to spill the open wine bottle between his thighs, he cut the engine and started telling me something the singer Tom Waits had said in a recent radio interview. I struggled to understand his Dutch, but it was about the important things in life and not working too hard – clearly a philosophy with which he had a great deal of sympathy. I said little in reply, and he seemed to like it that way. An old brown dog on the passenger seat started awake, and the man reached out to fondle its ears before refiring the engine. '*Veel plezier!*' he shouted, 'Have fun!' as his boat muttered slowly away.

After the old-world charm of Dordrecht and the scenic boat ride, arriving in Rotterdam felt like entering another world. Traffic rumbled over the bridge and the streets were filled with cyclists, motor scooters and people talking loudly. Walking away from the jetty, I was very nearly run down by a suicidal pizza delivery boy on a speeding moped, beeping his horn insistently as he hurtled down a cycle lane. Nearby, three men in tracksuits were having a noisy argument outside a dingy café. A police car crawled past in an effort to intimidate them into good behaviour, with no effect. Two blonde women in matching pink vests jogged by, silencing the three men far more effectively than a carload of glowering policeman had. Trying and failing not to stare myself, I waited a couple of minutes before boarding a tram, a clanking grey box with small Dutch flags adoring its front corners, like a diplomat's limousine. It trundled away from the Maas, towards the central train station.

Jerking up and over a low dike, the tram passed the squat grey Kunsthal art gallery, from where thieves had recently removed priceless Picassos and Monets via an unsecured door. Gazing through a grimy window, I got a clear view of the legendary *Kabouter Buttplug* ('Gnome Buttplug') statue. I had originally assumed the name was an unfortunate colloquialism, but no – it seemed to be an accurate title for a massive piece of public art celebrating the union between a cheerful elf and a rocket-shaped toy. In front of the statue, another tram lay stranded across a junction in the tracks, painted white and festooned with L-plates, an anxious trainee tram driver sweating over the controls.

Riding the Rails

After perhaps ten minutes, the tram arrived at Rotterdam's central train station. A lavish extension was nearing completion and workmen were busy cleaning the shiny triangular façade of a new station entrance. A few skateboarders surfed lazily across the concrete, and a group of Italian tourists were taking photographs of the enormous new multistorey bicycle park. Inside the station, a woman in a pink cap and low-cut

T-shirt was handing out free newspapers to passing commuters. Behind her, three uniformed policemen stared at her tight blue trousers like hungry dogs at a barbecue.

I was hoping to take a train further along the Maas towards the coast, and with luck found one that was leaving almost immediately, a short string of yellow-and-blue carriages that looked like a child's toy. The name of the service – 'Sprinter' – turned out to be ironic, and it dawdled out of the city at little more than jogging speed. Across the aisle from me, a clean-shaven young man in jeans and T-shirt consulted the compass on his iPhone and began to pray, kneeling between the seats and mumbling under his breath as he bowed towards Mecca. An old lady with purplish hair frowned and muttered and moved to another seat further down the carriage.

The railway ran roughly parallel to the Maas, and as we left the gleaming office blocks behind, the train windows offered glimpses of the flat, chalky river and the enormous docks beyond. As the city receded, the industrial landscape became increasingly fantastical. We passed a dock filled with equipment for building bridges or dams: monstrous towers adorned with pulleys, chains and extendable arms. Painted in bright primary colours, they looked like collapsed rollercoasters ready to come to life. This was a side of Rotterdam that visitors rarely saw, but it was arguably the city's true heart – the source of not only its wealth and status, but its character. The docks were by far the largest in Europe, sprawling along some twenty-five miles of river-bank as well as a large area of reclaimed land jutting out into the sea. As a major source of local employment, and of pride, the docks had provided Rotterdam with a tough, working-class character that meant it was the polar opposite of refined, stylish, tourist-friendly Amsterdam. Young hipsters occasionally tried to give the city a makeover along the lines of Berlin or Brooklyn's grimy chic, but to little avail. It was, as an expat once grumbled to me, perhaps the only major city in northern Europe in which it was impossible to buy a decent croissant.

Tracking the river, the train trundled over or around dozens of small harbours. Some of them were quite pretty, lined with old wooden sailing barges and churches, but most were more industrial, housing solid barges, tugboats and brightly coloured police cruisers. After ten minutes or so, the train drew into the gin-brewing town of Schiedam, once a distinct settlement but long since absorbed into Rotterdam's outer suburbs. A bell rang and the train jerked to a halt at the small station. The conductor announced something over the tannoy, but I understood only one word: *helaas*, 'unfortunately' – the first word of Dutch that anyone travelling on the delay-plagued railways would learn.

The doors hissed open and I got out to see what the problem was, feeling like an African adventurer hindered by lions on the line. There were no lions, but a large white motor cruiser waiting to traverse a canal that passed under the railway line. More bells rang, red lights flashed and three bridges – one road, one rail, one bicycle – raised so that the boat could pass, sliding slowly behind railway tracks lofted temporarily skywards. I found it hard to imagine a train in Britain stopping to let a boat through, rather than the other way round.

The bells stopped ringing and I returned to the train. It lumbered on through a succession of unpronounceable small towns, several of which looked barely big enough to merit a station – Vlaardingen Centrum, Vlaardingen West, Maasluis, Maasluis West. Each seemed pleasant enough, but more people would leave the train at each stop than would join, and there was little to see other than modest apartment blocks, old ladies with shopping trolleys and bored children on bikes. Sometimes small towns are buoyed by their proximity to big cities, but here the opposite appeared to be true. With all the necessary jobs and attractions available in nearby Rotterdam, these towns had been drained of life and colour. As the train stopped at yet another empty platform, a tall man sitting behind me announced, to no one in particular, 'I think I am going to the end of the earth!'

Right on cue, the train reached the end of the line. Hoek van Holland is a compact town that has been saved from obscurity by its sandy beach and its large ferry terminal, popular with caravanners and truck drivers making their way to and from eastern England. It is, literally, the 'Corner of Holland', where the great rivers meet the jagged North Sea. According to a book I'd seen in Rotterdam's central library, no fewer than a million people pass through here on their way to Essex every year. A road sign outside the station pointed incongruously to destinations near and far: turn left for England, right for 's-Gravenzande.

The Great Disaster

Reversing course, I walked back towards Rotterdam, in search of the penultimate stop on my journey. At an otherwise featureless stretch of riverbank, a group of hikers pointing cameras indicated that I had found what I was looking for: the Maeslantkering storm-surge barrier, a massive set of flood gates that prevented the sea rushing upriver to Rotterdam. The gates would probably have been of little interest were it not for their sheer size. Each of the two white metal structures – one on the near riverbank and one on the far – was about the size and shape of an Eiffel Tower toppled on its side. As a sign explained, whenever a storm surge was predicted, the huge girders would automatically pivot across the river like a pair of swing doors closing, sealing it against the tide. Today, the gates lay dormant on the riverbanks, an object of curiosity for passers-by. To the Dutch, however, they were a key component of what some claimed to be 'the eighth wonder of the world', the huge network of dams and floodgates that cobwebbed the southern Netherlands, known as the Delta Works.

The impetus for building the Delta Works had come almost sixty years previously, on the night of 31 January 1953, the date of the greatest natural disaster in the history of the Netherlands. An unprecedented combination of high spring tides, strong winds and a major storm had pushed sea levels along the Dutch coast to several metres higher than normal. The poorly maintained flood defences were quickly over-whelmed. As the country slept, water poured over the dikes. In Rotterdam, the first sign of trouble reportedly came when hordes of rats ran from subways and cellars, fleeing the rising tide. In a belated effort to warn people of the impending disaster, church bells were rung and rusted air-raid sirens were set howling into the fierce wind, but it was too late. In the village of Stavenisse, for example, a group of locals rushed towards a crumbling dike with tools in hand, only to be swept back when it collapsed, carrying them through the village on a twelve-foot wave. Houses near the dike were destroyed instantly, with beams and sections of wall turning into floating battering rams, punching holes through the houses behind them. One man and his wife awoke to find their upstairs bedroom knee-deep in water. As the water rose further, the wife climbed out of the window to call for help, only to see her husband swept out of the front door to his death. Similar stories played out across the country.

By the time the waters receded, nearly 2000 people had drowned and another 70,000 had been forced to flee their homes. Dikes along roughly a third of the Dutch coastline were destroyed, and some 200,000 hectares of land submerged, including dozens of towns and villages previously thought safe from flooding. In scenes eerily reminiscent of the still recent war, thousands of refugees fled across wintry landscapes, through fields littered with the upturned corpses of thousands of cows. Survivors exchanged terrible stories, such as that of the man who had helped his wife give birth as the flood waters rose around her bed, then gone to find a doctor and returned to find both wife and child swept away. Another said he had clung to telegraph wires for two days to stay alive.

As the scale of the *watersnoodramp* (flooding emergency disaster) became apparent, the Dutch were determined to prevent a similar disaster from happening again. An official book published to raise funds for survivors set the tone, adopting

military terminology familiar to a country that had been liberated from the Nazis less than a decade before. 'The great
counter-attack begins,' the official account said. 'Not an inch
of land now taken by the sea in these floods will be given up.'
A caption accompanying a photo of a new-born baby noted
that he was 'a citizen of a land of unmeasured confidence'.
Within a year all the broken dikes had been resealed, but that
was not enough. A national commission proposed a bold solution to the existential threat facing the country: the construction of a vast network of dams and gates that would close
the tidal mouths of the great rivers, preventing future floods
while leaving major waterways open to shipping.

By 1958 the first component of the Delta Works had been
completed, a pair of giant steel floodgates suspended over a
river near Rotterdam like guillotines waiting to fall. Despite
opposition from environmentalists and fishermen, over the
next three decades many other barriers followed, including
the Maeslantkering where I now stood. The geography of the
Netherlands was transformed, with huge tidal bays turned
into tranquil lakes and miles of new highway running along
the tops of enormous dams. Altogether, the length of the
Dutch coastline was reduced by nearly half.

Fighting Mother Nature

After living in the Netherlands for a while, I realised that
experiences such as the 1953 flood, and the subsequent dam
building, had had a profound effect on the way in which
the Dutch viewed the world. Initially, I had been under the
vague impression that it was one of those eco-friendly countries where environmental protection was a top priority – a
nation of cyclists, vegetarians and hard-core recyclers. In reality, however, after centuries of battling against the water, the
Dutch tended to view Mother Nature not as a life-giving provider, but as a menace to be tamed. They even had a word
for it: *maakbaarheid*, the capacity to remake and control the
world around you. I often noticed that things someone who

was British or French or German might think of as beautiful – a wild meadow, a tangled hedge, a stormy beach – my Dutch friends viewed as an affront to common sense and discipline. Humans, they thought, had a duty to bring nature under control wherever they found it. Trees were meant to be neatly trimmed, wildlife fenced in, and beaches enjoyed from behind high glass screens providing protection against the pesky wind. There were few wildlife programmes on television, and most Dutch took their holidays not in mountains or forests but in cities like New York.

According to one EU survey, although the Dutch generally were aware of and concerned about environmental issues, there were two major exceptions, issues about which they demonstrated less concern than the citizens of other countries: the need to keep their homeland 'green and pleasant', and the importance of 'protecting nature'. In a minor example, when new neighbours moved in next door I was astonished to see them take a chainsaw to anything resembling greenery. In less than an hour, a pretty garden of wild flowers, tall trees and bushes had been reduced to a drab concrete patio adorned only with two chairs and a table, surrounded by tree stumps and trampled flowers. 'Beautiful, eh?' the neighbour called to me over the fence, thrilled with his ability to get unruly nature under control.

Dutch people's tendency to view the environment not as something to protect, but as something to protect *from*, was also reflected in the country's environmental record. The Netherlands' enormous ports, acres of gas and chemical plants and seemingly endless sprawl of greenhouses meant that, per capita, its carbon emissions were almost double those of France. As the home of Europe's largest airport and biggest oil refinery, the Netherlands was failing to meet Kyoto emissions reduction targets, and had particulate air pollution roughly 50 per cent higher than the developed-country average. For a supposedly liberal, eco-conscious people, the Dutch were very fond of their cars, and surveys showed that almost half of them thought that the seriousness of climate change was exaggerated. Despite all the cycling and recycling, the Netherlands actually wasn't very green at all.

Another consequence of the need for constant vigilance against flooding was Dutch people's deep attachment to order. In a country where poor maintenance of a dike or wall could – and often did – result in catastrophic flooding, people had a natural tendency to prioritise keeping things ship-shape. As an English traveller observed in the nineteenth century: 'One of the principal characteristics of a Dutch street is its scrupulous, or it would be more correct to say, elaborate, cleanliness. A grand scrubbification of the exteriors as well as the interiors of the houses takes place every Saturday.' Any man wanting a quiet moment to smoke his pipe, the traveller said, would have to climb a church tower to escape 'the army of restless brooms and scrubbing brushes'. Visiting the Netherlands in 1874, the novelist Henry James noted that even the tree trunks looked as if they were 'carefully sponged every morning'.

Centuries later, the same attitudes still prevailed. Even at riotous public events like King's Day, as the last partygoers schlepped home at 4am the streets would already be busy with cleaning trucks inhaling orange bunting and beer cans, so that by daybreak everything would be spotless again. In the area where I lived, cleanliness was a mark of respectability. Doorsteps were scrubbed and hedges neatly trimmed. My neighbours also all seemed to be obsessed with cleaning their windows, not only so they could see out, but so passers-by could have an unobstructed view of the immaculate living rooms inside. Almost everyone I knew paid for the services of a professional window cleaner, and even on rare sunny days it was wise to carry an umbrella to shield oneself from the armies mopping top-floor windows with long-handled brooms and dripping hoses. I often got the impression that many Dutch people would find it perfectly acceptable for their children to be gay, divorced, unemployed or transsexual, but to have dirty windows or an untidy living room would bring great shame on the family. It was perhaps not a coincidence that the Dutch word for 'beautiful' and the Dutch word for 'clean' were one and the same – *schoon*.

On Foot to Constantinople

I retraced my steps to the railway station, resuming my journey towards the sea. Through the gaps between shops and houses, I could see a giant passenger ship slowly breaching the floodgates, like a great white palace sliding along the horizon. Linked by ferry to Britain, and by train to Paris, Brussels and Berlin, the small town of Hoek van Holland had long been one of the doorways to Europe. Today, however, the compact central square was deserted but for a few Lycra-clad cyclists shielding their sandwiches from a rowdy gang of seagulls.

Hungry from the walk and a long day of fresh air, I entered a slightly seedy café and ordered some traditional Dutch cuisine: a soft white roll stuffed with cheese and mustard, served rudely and wrapped in a greasy napkin. Perching on a folding chair on the pavement, next to an old couple savouring glasses of gloopy *advocaat* egg-nog, I opened a book I'd bought in Rotterdam a month or so before, a slim paperback with a drawing of a sunset on the cover. It told the story of how, some eighty years previously, one of my countrymen had travelled a similar route to me along the river in the opposite direction, making his way – as the book's subtitle put it – *On Foot to Constantinople: From the Hook of Holland to the Middle Danube*.

It was the winter of 1933, with Hitler ascendant and Europe on the verge of cataclysmic change, when Patrick Leigh Fermor set out to walk across the heart of Europe. Aged just eighteen, the precocious Leigh Fermor travelled 'like a tramp or pilgrim', sleeping in barns, beer halls and police cells. He completed his journey in 1935, but didn't get around to writing up the contents of his notebook until the 1970s. The resulting book, *A Time of Gifts*, became one of the classics of travel literature, a portrait of pre-war Europe as seen through the eyes of an adventurous young aristocrat. Leigh

Fermor, in turn, became something of a legend: a classicist and adventurer who swam the Hellespont, smoked up to a hundred cigarettes a day, and had – according to Freya Stark – the appearance of a Greek god and the sexual appetite to match.

Sitting outside the shabby café, I was mildly disappointed to read that Leigh Fermor had not lingered long in Hoek van Holland, although given the quality of the local cuisine I could hardly blame him. However, flipping through the pages of his book, I still found much that felt familiar after a day following the Maas, from his description of Dordrecht as a 'busy amphibian town... of weathered brick' to the rural church towers 'scattered haphazard across the landscape', and the 'geometric despotism of canal and polder and windmill'. With perfect timing, a horn sounded and I looked up to see the tip of a tall ferry gliding behind the shops and houses, just as I reread his lines: 'In the field a quarter of a mile away, between a church and some woods, serenely though invisibly afloat on the hidden Maas, a big white ship aflutter with pennants was apparently mooing its way across solid meadows under a cloud of gulls.'

Leigh Fermor's motto was *solvitur ambulando* – 'it is solved by walking' – and with that in mind I closed the book and left the café to complete my journey. A narrow road led away from the town centre towards the seafront, lined with toy-like retirement cottages and cheap hotels. The architecture was drab, but the air was filled with an exhilarating salty tingle and sand scuffed on the pavement under foot. Even here, a brisk ten minutes' walk from the sea, many houses were encircled by protective sea walls, with waist-high steel gates poised to swing shut in case of a sudden flood. On the edge of the town, four large apartment buildings stood high above the street on slender concrete stilts, like shoeboxes balancing on upright matchsticks. Built on the wrong side of the floodgates, they looked prepared for the worst.

The Threat of Climate Change

For all the Dutch efforts to keep the water out, the risk of flooding had not disappeared, and in some ways was only getting worse. In other parts of Europe climate change was a constant source of handwringing, but also a fairly abstract concern – something that would cause serious problems in the future, or elsewhere in the world, but was not yet having much effect at home. In the Netherlands, however, the effects were already tangible. Annual rainfall in the country had increased by nearly a fifth over the twentieth century, and the mean level of the North Sea had also risen significantly. Rivers like the Maas helped channel excess water out to sea, but as sea levels rose the rivers discharged less easily, making inland flooding more common.

Concern about the country's water defences was also growing – in 2010, almost a quarter of all dikes reportedly failed to meet official safety standards. After the 2011 Fukushima nuclear disaster in Japan, dikes around the Borssele nuclear reactor had to be raised. Drier areas of land were also sinking: the monument in Nieuwerkerk aan den IJssel describing it as the lowest point in the country was already inaccurate, the land having dropped several centimetres since it was installed. One popular website enabled concerned residents, or those hoping to acquire a sea view, to check how far under water their home might lie in the not-too-distant future. In my case, living some twenty miles from the sea, the answer was about a metre. Some Dutch politicians had taken to warning darkly that Amersfoort, a town about forty miles from the coast, would soon have to be renamed 'Amersfoort-on-Sea'.

The Dutch authorities had responded to these challenges in an unexpected way, retreating from land they had long fought to keep dry. A few years before my journey, the government launched the 'Room for the River' project, designating dozens of areas that could be offered up for sacrifice to the sea. The Noordwaard polder, for example, a large area of farmland outside Dordrecht, was in the process of being returned to the

Maas from which it had once been reclaimed. Several miles of dike had been removed or lowered, enabling controlled flooding of the surrounding area. More controversially, the government had also formally surrendered to the river part of the Overdiepse polder, an eye-shaped island in one of the main channels of the Maas. Some of the farmers who were asked to leave their homes were understandably less than thrilled, but eventually accepted a proposal to rebuild their farms on new artificial hills along the edge of the polder. Farmers not lucky enough to be allocated a hill were relocated to higher ground elsewhere. Many were surprisingly accepting of their fate, exhibiting the benign attitude to state intervention common among the Dutch. 'We came together and the government was very reasonable,' one farmer told the *New York Times*. 'These things are not easy, but they work if there is cooperation.' After centuries working to increase the size of their country, it remained to be seen how far the Dutch would go in the opposite direction.

The End of the Road

The light was fading by now and I stopped to take a photo of the sunset, a soft, warm glow spreading like a blush along the horizon. Except after taking my camera out and climbing onto a bench for a better view, I realised I was photographing not a sunset, but the artificial glow from an infinite canopy of floodlit greenhouses, just some of the hundreds carpeting the country. In recent years they had even begun to spread across the channel, with vast Dutch-owned greenhouses sprawling across parts of Kent. The beautiful Dutch tulips sold around the world came at a heavy cost to the environment.

Continuing along the road towards the sea, I came across a section of the Atlantic Wall, the network of coastal fortifications the Nazis built in the early 1940s. Once a heavily fortified barrier aimed at preventing a seaborne invasion from Britain, it was now a crumbling mass of black brick coiled among the grassy sand dunes like a slug. On top of a nearby sand dune sat four dilapidated satellite dishes, monstrous and skeletal, a relic of US army eavesdropping during the Cold War and a reminder that for all its current bleakness, this had always been one of the crossroads of Europe. A sign pointed with thick blue fingers towards distant megacities – New York: 5824 kilometres, St Petersburg: 1831, Shanghai: 8934.

The road ran out at the seafront, disappearing under the sand. Around were the usual distractions of a North Sea holiday resort: ice-cream and hot-dog stands, a children's fairground ride, shops selling sunglasses and wire baskets of beach toys. It did not quite feel like the end of the world, as the man on the train had suggested, more like the end of the pier. The vast car park next to the plaza was nearly empty and most of the shops were closed. An orange lifeguard tower stood sentry over acres of unoccupied sand and empty cafés, a single imported palm tree leaning precariously in the wind. I thought of Byron: 'Man marks the earth with ruin/ His control/ Stops with the shore.'

Down on the beach, the view was spectacular. To my left, the mouth of the Maas was marked by a long stone breakwater jutting out into the ocean. A small boat emerged from behind it, turning the corner of Holland, and I wondered where it had come from – Rotterdam? Dordrecht? Switzerland? Beyond the breakwater, the far side of the river was crowded with smoking chimneys, spinning wind turbines and tall cranes pecking at container ships like hungry birds. A gas flare glowed angrily in the gloom. Out at sea, perhaps a dozen top-heavy cargo ships queued to enter the port, hulking like tower blocks in a distant metropolis. It was strange to think that once, in the days of Doggerland, this point could have marked the dead end of the English Channel, and I could have kept walking all the way to Essex.

To my right, a thick belt of bleached white powder stretched all the way to the horizon, as flat and silky as a strip of fresh snow. A handful of surfers braved the failing light, zipping up each other's wetsuits before jogging tentatively towards the chilly sea. Further down the beach, a group of men with spades and brooms were digging like archaeologists in the sand dunes to uncover one of the temporary beach restaurants that would soon reopen for spring. In another eight months or so, the restaurants would have been dismantled and the sea would have reclaimed the area. I sat on the sand and watched the tide come in.

Two

The Religious Divide

Carnivals, Catholics and the War against Spain

In front of Maastricht's train station, a line of pandas was doing the conga. Across the cobbled street, a horde of Vikings in horned helmets and thick furs gathered around an iPad, searching for directions to the nearest bar. Nearby, four Roman centurions removed their red-feathered helmets, rested their shiny shields against a wall and opened a crate of beer.

They – and I – had travelled to the Netherlands' most southerly city for *Carnaval*, the annual carnival celebration, rooted in the Catholic faith, which offered a final opportunity for a blow-out before Lent's forty days and nights of piety. In northern Dutch cities like Amsterdam and Rotterdam the occasion passed almost entirely unnoticed, but in the south of the country, in the region known as *onder de rivieren* ('below the rivers'), it was widely celebrated. In the days leading up to Ash Wednesday, southern cities like Maastricht would be flooded with costumed parades, marching bands and street parties. Many workplaces were closed, and the normally down-to-earth Dutch embarked on an orgy of dancing, cross-dressing and above all drinking. Maastricht was temporarily renamed in the local dialect, becoming *Mestreech*, and thousands defied the cold in order to hold their own chilly Mardi Gras, ignoring stuffier northerners' traditional dismissal of the festivities as mere *Paapse stoutigheden*, or 'Popish naughtiness'.

The divide between the regions that celebrated carnival and those that did not had roots going back nearly five centuries. When the Reformation led to the creation of the Protestant church, the Low Countries – present-day Belgium and the Netherlands – were split between a largely Protestant north and a predominantly Catholic south. Given that the whole area was ruled by a Catholic King, the stage was set for a very ugly divorce. What followed would be described by one seventeenth-century diplomat as 'the biggest, bloodiest and most implacable of all the wars which have been waged since the beginning of the world'. After years of turmoil, the region eventually cleaved into two separate, independent countries: a Catholic-majority Belgium and a mostly Protestant Netherlands. However, even several centuries later, the political border between the two countries lay a significant distance south of the religious boundary between the two faiths, with the result that the Netherlands remained a subtly divided land. The south of the country retained a large Catholic population and traditions like carnival were firm fixtures on the social and religious calendar.

As someone born in an island nation, I was fascinated by how the Netherlands' borders had fluctuated over time, and by the way in which boundaries once fought over had now all but vanished thanks to European integration. I was also curious about how a country forged in religious conflict, and dominated until fairly recently by religious institutions, had evolved to become one of the most liberal, secular countries in Europe. A few weeks after my journey along the Maas, a tour of the carnival towns strung along the southern Dutch border offered an irresistible opportunity to learn more about this history – and to have some fun in the process.

The Deep South

The city of Maastricht sat at the southernmost tip of the Dutch province of Limburg, itself a peninsula dangling like an untied shoelace from the southeastern corner of the Netherlands between Belgium and Germany. I arrived there by train from Rotterdam after a long, slow haul across almost the entire width of the country. At a dreary time of year, carnival offered a welcome distraction for those tired of the North Sea winter, and the train was full of northern city-dwellers heading south to party.

The journey lasted almost three hours and many travellers used the time to assemble their costumes. As the train rumbled through mist-cloaked fields, black bin bags were opened to reveal an array of wigs, capes, face paints and hats, which gradually transformed a trainload of ordinary passengers into something resembling a mobile circus. In the seat next to me, a scruffy skateboarder donned a long red robe, black wig and bejewelled crown to become a medieval king. Across the aisle, a pair of grey-haired sisters metamorphosed into a giggling Batman and Robin. Ever eager to assimilate, I had brought a costume of my own – a fluffy orange tiger suit, complete with pointy ears and a tail, which my mother had sent unsolicited from Britain a few weeks previously. 'I saw this and thought you might like it,' the note in her parcel said, leaving me unsure whether to be flattered or offended. Studying my reflection in the grimy train window, I used a thick black marker to colour my nose and add whiskers to my cheeks.

After we arrived in Maastricht I left the station and walked past the pandas and centurions, down a narrow street of shops and restaurants, following a trickle of costumed revellers towards the sound of music. At first the streets were relatively quiet, but after a few minutes the road widened to reveal hundreds of people gathered on the banks of the Maas, which bisected the city in a wide channel the same slate colour as the sky. Stretching across the river was the ancient Sint Servaasbrug, or Saint Servatius Bridge, a long, low span of seven stone arches leapfrogging their way towards the historic city centre. The traditional Dutch drizzle had done little to deter a crowd from forming five or six deep on either side of the road. The carnival tradition supposedly took its name from the Latin *carne vale*, or 'farewell to meat', but here it looked like it was more about saying 'hello' to alcohol. The cafés and bars on the high stone riverbanks were overflowing with people dancing, singing and shivering over small glasses of beer.

On top of the bridge the carnival parade was in full swing. A long line of trucks crept across the water towards the old town, each decorated with jazzy flags and soggy paper bunting. On their flat backs, they carried giant speakers that blasted pounding music over the river and into the streets beyond. Between the trucks, squadrons of scantily clad young women marched in synchrony, wearing sparkly leotards, elaborate face paint and huge feathered headdresses, like American Indians in drag. They must have been freezing. Other, older marchers looked slightly warmer in more traditional carnival costumes: ruffled shirts, velvety suits and feathered hats that wouldn't have looked out of place on a Bavarian huntsman.

Among the spectators, the costumes were less traditional. The boisterous crowds spilling out of the riverside bars were dressed more for Fresher's Week than for an ancient religious celebration. I saw bananas, bridesmaids and ninja turtles, bishops bearing crosses, jockeys, an Elvis, a pair of skinny Shreks. One group of men had come as multicoloured Tetris blocks, their unwieldy cardboard outfits slotting neatly together when they posed side by side for photographs, but causing serious problems when they tried to enter a bar with a narrow doorway. A woman carrying a fake baby in a sling passed by, followed by a man carrying a real one, who looked terrified in a tiny green frog costume. I saw a convincing old man, in flat cap and baggy cardigan, being pushed across the bumpy brick street in a wheelchair by an even more convincing policeman in uniform. Then I realized it was actually a real old man, being assisted by a genuine helpful copper. My bright orange tiger suit had turned out to be the perfect camouflage. It clearly met the two basic requirements of any decent carnival costume: it was warm, and it looked ridiculous.

Maastricht was once considered one of the northerly outposts of the civilised world, lying close to the effective boundary of the Roman Empire. The Romans had built a bridge across the Maas somewhere close to where I now stood – the *mase trajectus* that gave the city its name. Maastricht's strategic location and fertile farmland meant it soon became an important garrison and trading point, but the Romans never fully gained control over those living north of the river, and were constantly harassed by rebellious local tribes, including the axe-throwing Franks of northern Germany. South of the Maas the dominant cultural influences were Roman, but to the north they remained Germanic.

In later years, as Roman influence waned, descendants of the Frankish axe-throwers eventually established a significant empire, the Merovingian, which covered much of the Low Countries. Around the end of the fifth century, the Merovingian king Clovis converted to Christianity and the faith spread slowly northwards, overcoming sometimes bloody pagan resistance. Later still came the Carolingian Empire, best remembered for the extraordinary Emperor Charlemagne. Born not far from Maastricht, in present-day Belgium, Charlemagne oversaw a series of military campaigns that expanded his empire until it covered much of Western Europe, from Denmark to the Alps and the Pyrenees. Charlemagne built a palace at Nijmegen, some eighty miles north of Maastricht, and had his court in Aachen, thirty-five miles to the east. Maastricht's location at the crossroads of these cities helped ensure its rise as a major trading hub.

Centuries later, the city retained a different flavour from the rest of the Netherlands. Even on the short walk from the station, it was apparent that compared with other Dutch towns like Dordrecht, Maastricht's streets were wider, its squares bigger and its buildings in a wider variety of architectural styles. Fittingly for the host of the 1991 negotiations creating the European Union, it had a cosmopolitan, international feel. Belgium was only a couple of miles away and Germany less than twenty-five; France and Luxembourg were both reachable in an hour and a half by car. Standing in the heart of the city, I was almost twice as far from Amsterdam as I was from Brussels.

The city's university attracted a large number of foreign students, and the budget airlines flying to the nearby airport brought a steady stream of British tourists in search of malty Belgian-style beers and other less wholesome entertainments.

As a result, Maastricht was a proverbial melting pot of cultures and cuisines. On the short walk from the train station to the river alone, I heard passers-by speak no fewer than six different languages, as well as the local Limburgish dialect of Dutch. A sign outside a café offered visitors *'LEKKERE BROODJES, PAIN FRANCAISE, TASTY CAKES'.*

The Carnival Parade

Following the flow of the parade, I walked over the St Servaasbrug towards the city centre. Halfway across, a statue of the saint himself stood sentry in cape and crown, his back turned to the passing marchers, staring stonily at the tourist cruise boats chugging along the river below. As I paused to inspect the statue, the carnival Prince appeared in the road behind me. A tall, grinning young man, he walked confidently amid a crowd of supplicants, doing his best to look regal in a royal fool's hat, wide ruff collar and gold-trimmed red velvet suit. By tradition, a new *Prins* was elected each year by the local carnival association. I saw more than one glittery dancing girl trying hard to catch the Prince's eye as he passed, the prettiest among them rewarded with a cheeky royal wink. A loud marching band romped past, dressed in Robin Hood–style suits, stomping to the beat of a tuba and oversized toy soldier's drum. I took a photo and – taking me for a tourist, which I suppose I was – a man of about sixty with absurdly over-gelled hair told me this was a *Zaate Hermenie*, a traditional Maastricht marching band. 'They are playing the instruments badly on purpose,' he said. 'Because it is funnier that way.' I wasn't sure this was true.

Although I had never been to carnival before, I had visited Maastricht some ten years previously, as a road-tripping student in search of the place nearest to Germany where one could legally purchase cannabis. Two friends and I had parked our rusting car in the suburbs and walked to the city centre, where we proceeded to enter a series of ordinary bars and cafés and offend genial proprietors by confidently demanding they sell us drugs. Given that we were entering not drug-vending 'coffee shops' but rather what the Dutch called 'brown cafés' – cosy, smoky watering holes where a kindly grandfather might nurse a beer and a newspaper – it wasn't surprising that our requests were met with scorn, and in a few cases outright hostility. Striding into one charming Italian bistro, my friend asked the proprietor: 'Can we please buy some weed?' Looking up from applying black pepper to plates of spaghetti, the moustachioed manager pointed at the door and yelled in fury: 'English tourists! Always only drugs! GET OUT!' We trudged back to the car and drove to Belgium.

Today, local residents were taking a more relaxed view of such excesses. Many revellers were drinking heavily – at least by the standards of the Dutch, for whom three or four thimble-sized glasses of beer constitute a heavy night out. The bars on either side of the river had turned the music up loud and opened their front doors wide, and scores of patrons were drinking al fresco. Outside several establishments, busty young women sold shot-sized bottles of drink from trays resting on their bosoms, to the general delight of the men in the crowd. Inside the bars the main focus was on the music, which was uniformly terrible. Drunken crowds linked arms and swayed like sailors, singing the much-loved carnival classics friends had warned me to expect, including 'Drink until we sink', 'A nail in my head' and 'Mother, where is my beer?' Song after song, everyone knew every word. I struggled to follow the slurred lyrics, but a common theme seemed to be meeting the girl of one's dreams and being struck by her beauty despite the costume and face paint she was wearing. 'In the south,' a friend had once told me, 'Everyone meets their wife at carnival.'

Picking a bar at random, I squeezed through a throng of merrymakers and ordered a beer from a barmaid wearing a candyfloss-coloured wig. In the usual Dutch fashion, she carefully filled a small plastic cup with one-third foam and two-thirds beer, expertly slicing the overflowing crown with a plastic spatula. Any less foam, or more beer, and the customers would complain. Around me the mob were holding their beers aloft like Olympic torches and singing lustily along to another carnival classic: '*Doe een stapje naar voren, en een stapje terug*', 'One step forwards, one step backwards'. It seemed an accurate summary of how the day was going. I carried my beer outside and rested on a wall with a view back across the bridge, against the flow of the parade. Next to me, a lantern-jawed young man in medical scrubs was using a surgical headlamp to gaze deep into the eyes of an attractive female soldier. Behind them, a grizzled man with a tea-coloured beard and dishevelled cowboy's outfit puffed happily on a large joint, in open defiance of the city authorities' recent attempts to clamp down on drug consumption.

Traditionally, the carnival season gave an often downtrodden population the freedom to indulge themselves in ways that were normally forbidden. Protected by the anonymity of masks and costumes, carnival goers felt free to behave badly, regardless of their day jobs. In 1445, a group of Parisian theologians complained that during the Dutch carnival, even local priests would 'dance in the choir dressed as women, matchmakers or minstrels and singing outrageous songs. They eat black pudding and fat sausages on the altar. They gamble and burn old shoes instead of incense... After mass they go out in their disguises... [and] incite filthy songs and obscene gestures.' The authorities had, at various times, attempted to stamp out the carnival tradition, but without much success. Following the division of the Low Countries, raucous carnival celebrations were officially discouraged and all but died out in many areas. Ironically, it was a foreign invasion – by the French, in the late eighteenth century – that helped revive what was now seen as a quintessentially Dutch tradition. Suspended again during the Second World War, carnival had since returned with a vengeance. Like a movie villain, it was impossible to kill off.

Past the bridge, the parade flowed on like a brightly coloured river. I jumped in and followed the crowd deeper

into the old city, a warren of cobbled streets and fancy bou-
tiques spreading west from the water. After a few minutes'
walk, the procession turned to cut across one side of a large
cobbled square lined with cafés and pretty trees. Open-sided
trucks sold an array of artery-clogging regional cuisine:
Belgian-style fries with mayonnaise, *kibbeling* fish nuggets,
bratwurst hotdogs and greasy *oliebollen* donuts. I bought
a paper plate of *poffertjes* – coin-sized pancakes slathered
with butter and icing sugar – and immediately regretted it.
Through the crowd I spotted two men in giant homemade
Lego costumes struggling to use a portable urinal, liquid spat-
tering on unwieldy cardboard boxes as their monstrous yellow heads rested on the ground behind them. Nearby, a pair
of Japanese tourists stared in amazement at another urinal,
a high-tech cylinder of polished steel that had just ascended
from beneath the pavement.

The Twin Towers

Set back from the chaos, atop a shallow flight of stairs in
a corner of the square, was the historic heart of the city: a
pair of great churches standing side by side like mismatched
twins, so close that they almost touched one another. On the
left was the ancient Sint Janskerk (St Jan's Church), the focal
point of the city's Protestant community, with its unmis-
takable scarlet clock tower. To the right sat its big brother,
the Catholic Basilica of St Servatius. A largely Romanesque
behemoth with square twin towers of grey stone, it looked
as if it could have been airlifted there from a hilltop in Sicily.
Even by the high standards of Dutch historic architecture, the
two imposing buildings, each honouring a different religion,
made an impressive sight.

With the carnival underway, the Protestant Sint Janskerk
was closed, its locked wooden doors providing a convenient
surface for a teenage couple to dry-hump against in the rain.
Leaving them to it, I rounded a corner and entered the neighbouring Catholic Basilica through a doorway decorated with

scores of small stone statues, lined up along the overlapping door frames like repeating reflections in a house of mirrors. Beyond the entrance was a low vaulted passageway running along three sides of a pretty internal courtyard, with large arched windows offering views of the neatly trimmed trees and fountain within. It reminded me of the Cambridge college where I had, as a nervous eighteen-year-old, been interviewed for a place to study Economics, and rejected when it became clear I didn't know what inflation was.

According to a book I'd read on the train, the Basilica had played an important role in the rise of Maastricht to regional prominence. In the fourth century, the bishop Servatius died while passing through Maastricht. A basilica was built in honour of the dead pilgrim and something of a cult developed around him, with Maastricht becoming an important stopping point for pilgrims on their way to other religious centres like Aachen and Liege. One fifteenth-century barber travelling through on his way from Venice back to Delft told excitedly of having visited a 'convent full of beautiful nuns... with uncovered heads, necks and breasts'.

Try as I might, I couldn't find any topless nuns. However, the tranquil atmosphere inside the Basilica provided welcome relief from the unceasing drizzle and the thump of the carnival bands. Skirting the courtyard, I pushed open a heavy door and entered the church proper. It was a cavernous space, with a high dome above the altar and stained glass windows that cast weak kaleidoscopic beams onto the rows of wooden pews. Thick stone pillars reached upwards all around me, giving the impression of being in a forest of exceptionally sturdy trees. Towards the rear of the nave, a tight spiral staircase led down to the crypt. I descended into a small, murky chamber containing a few rows of wooden chairs and a cloth-covered altar. On one wall, a frame contained a printed copy of a speech given by Pope John Paul II when he visited nearly three decades previously. At the rear of the chapel, in an alcove protected by a sturdy metal grate, was the man himself: St Servatius, resting under a thick stone slab. A generous bunch of red flowers lay on top of the tomb, between a pair of ivory candles with flickering golden tongues.

The Dutch Revolt

In medieval Europe there was often little distinction between Church and State. Kings, popes and bishops all claimed to be God's representatives on earth and were quick to suppress any religious dissent that might threaten their authority. Churches were frequently grossly corrupt, with religious leaders selling forgiveness for sin and living in finery while their congregations suffered in poverty. In the fifteenth and sixteenth centuries, however, these old certainties began to crumble. In 1517, the German priest Martin Luther nailed his Ninety-Five Theses to the door of a church in the German city of Wittenberg, rejecting the corruption of the Catholic religious authorities. Aided by the invention of the printing press, Luther's 'protest' against the Roman Catholic Church spread quickly across Europe, leading to the creation of a new 'Protestant' church.

In the Low Countries, Luther's ideas gained a wide following. Groups supporting the Protestant movement were bolstered by the arrival of refugees from other countries. As support for traditional Catholicism crumbled, religious denominations proliferated. Particularly popular in the Low Countries was Calvinism, a moderate branch of Protestantism that followed the teachings of the French theologian John Calvin. Also popular were the Anabaptists, perhaps because of their habit of encouraging their congregations to pray together naked.

To the authorities, the fracturing of the established religious order was deeply worrying. The history of the Low Countries' medieval rulers is rather too complicated to recount here, but suffice to say that after the death of the Emperor Charlemagne, his successors divided his empire into three parts, long strips of land that very roughly corresponded with the Low Countries, France and Germany. There followed a series of marvellously named leaders – Louis the Fair, Charles the Bald, Louis the Stammerer, Charles the Fat – each of whom ruled over various remnants of the empire. Eventually, in 1506, control of the Low Countries passed to Charles V, a fifteen-year-old who as the scion of several European dynasties held power over much of the continent. A decade later, when the Spanish King Ferdinand died, Charles was also crowned King Charles I of Spain. The new King was a devout Catholic, but the Low Countries he ruled over increasingly were not. Conflict was inevitable.

Like a modern-day dictator seeking to suppress a rebellion, the King rushed to eliminate the threat posed by the fracturing of the Catholic Church. In 1520, he declared Lutheranism a serious danger to the Low Countries, and three years later had his first Protestant martyr burned at the stake in Brussels. By 1550, anyone found in possession of a Protestant Bible in the Low Countries was liable to be condemned to death. Thousands of people were executed for their beliefs.

The persecution continued until 1556 when Charles, beset by gout and unable to sleep, stepped down from the throne and passed power to his son, Philip II. For religious dissidents in the Low Countries, this was decidedly bad news. Their new King had been born in Spain and spoke neither Dutch nor French, and exhibited little warmth towards his subjects. A cold and calculating man, Philip was described by one of his own ministers as having 'a smile that cut like a sword'. Centralising power in the hands of trusted Spanish officials, he stepped up persecution of those who questioned the authority of the Catholic Church, sending Spanish mercenaries to the Low Countries with orders to threaten, kill and torture his opponents.

In 1566, Calvinists who had been embittered by both the Spanish persecution and a harsh winter famine struck back against their rulers. Egged on by preachers who told them man-made idols were an insult to God, they ransacked Catholic churches throughout the Low Countries, destroying thousands of icons and pieces of religious art in a rampage that became known as the *Beeldenstorm* (the 'Storm of the Pictures', sometimes referred to as the 'Iconoclastic Fury'). Pictures were burned, faces smashed from statues and priceless religious figurines turned to rubble.

Monitoring these events from Spain, King Philip was infuriated. He sent thousands of soldiers to the Low Countries with orders to quash the rebellion. The force was headed by Fernando Alvarez de Toledo, better known as the Duke of Alva (or Alba), a sixty-year-old military veteran with a long Gandalf beard who was famed for his leadership in battles across the continent. On arrival in Brussels the Duke had established a 'Council of Troubles', a kangaroo court to prosecute those responsible for the destruction of the churches. More than 12,000 people accused of taking part in the rebellion were tried by what quickly became known as the 'Court of Blood'. Over a thousand were found guilty and executed or banished, and thousands more fled before they could be tried, to Amsterdam, Germany and the East of England. Catholic nobles who favoured taking a more moderate approach to the rebellion were also targeted. The Count of Egmont, for example, pledged loyalty to Philip but was tried nonetheless and sentenced to death. The battle-hardened Duke of Alva reportedly burst into tears as he watched his friend lose his head in Brussels' central square.

At first the heightened repression seemed to work, and the dissidents' attempts to raise a widespread revolt against the Spanish met with limited success. But as so often in history, increasingly vicious attempts to suppress the rebellion gradually emboldened it. Punished for their faith, the rebels came to see their fight against Philip as not only a struggle for religious freedom, but part of a broader tussle for the values of tolerance, dignity and liberalism that would later become the bedrock of Dutch identity. They would not give up without a lengthy fight.

The Meaning of Orange

Leaving Sint Servaas to his stony sleep, I climbed the crypt stairs and walked back out into the rain. After the tranquillity of the subterranean burial chamber, it was a shock to be back within earshot of the carnival's thumping music and cheering crowd. On the steps of the Basilica, a five-year-old Spiderman was showing his plastic six-pack to a pretty young woman, who announced to her friends that she wanted to adopt him. The boy's exhausted mother rolled her eyes but looked tempted to take up the offer. In front of the neighbouring St Janskerk, a wet dog wearing a plastic saddle with a miniature stuffed cowboy strapped to its back was posing for endless photographs.

At the far side of the square, the carnival parade flowed endlessly on. The rain had intensified and crowds clustered under leafless trees for protection, like cattle gathered around feeding pens. The junk food trucks were doing a roaring trade. In typical Dutch fashion, there were no queues, just crowds of people milling around the counters, ready to barge forwards whenever a gap emerged. Standing in line to buy a beer, I tried to make conversation with a group of Dutchmen with pointed false beards, long rapier swords and medieval cloaks. 'Are you having a good time?' I asked in Dutch. 'We are all Willem van Oranje,' came the reply. 'And we do not speak to commoners.'

As Spanish efforts to quell the Dutch rebellion intensified, the insurgents had needed a strong leader they could unite around. Thankfully, they soon had one. Willem van Oranje, or William of Orange, was born in Germany, lived outside the Netherlands for much of his life and spoke mostly French. He was, nevertheless, the closest thing the country had to a national hero. An ancestor of the ruddy-cheeked King I'd seen in Amsterdam, he was the reason for the predominance of orange in Dutch wardrobes, and his personal colours formed the basis of the national flag: three horizontal stripes of red, white and blue. He was even the inspiration for the country's national anthem, in which the first letters of each verse spelled out W-I-L-L-E-M.

In the time-honoured tradition of great historical figures, as a child William did not seem destined for particular greatness. All that changed, however, when a cousin died unexpectedly and he inherited the title of Prince of Orange, ruler of a principality surrounding the small town of Orange in southern France. At the age of eleven, he was catapulted into the highest ranks of the Dutch aristocracy. As a young man during the early years of the revolt against Spanish rule, he remained loyal to the Spanish court, a bashfulness that led to him being nicknamed *le Taciturne* or *de Zwijger* – 'William the Silent'. When the repression increased, however, he switched sides. As the Duke of Alva stepped up his campaign of repression, William was forced to flee to Germany, his landholdings confiscated and his eldest son taken in irons to Spain. Drawing on covert funding from sympathisers in France, England and Germany, William began recruiting men and building a rebel army. In 1568 he made his move, leading a ragtag militia across the Maas and into Spanish territory at Maastricht. Almost simultaneously, his brothers Louis and Adolph attacked Spanish forces in the north of the country. The Eighty Years' War had begun.

At first, William's efforts to assault the Spanish were disastrous. Towns that he had expected to rise up failed to do so, and King Philip's armies fought back fiercely, laying siege to northern Dutch towns such as Haarlem and Leiden. Desperate residents ate first their dogs, then rats, then leaves and grass. In time, however, the rebels scored a series of military victories, including the spectacular 1572 capture of the garrison town of Brielle on the Maas. In a final decisive break with his pro-Spanish past, William married a former Protestant nun and joined the reformed Church, pledging that in the areas he controlled everyone would be free to worship however they pleased. According to some historians, Dutch farmers who supported the rebels even began selectively breeding orange-coloured carrots, ensuring that these became far more common than the traditional brown, white and purple varieties.

Despite such propaganda, neither side scored a decisive victory. By 1573, the Duke of Alva had returned to Spain in disgrace after failing to end the rebellion. Three years later, several thousand Spanish troops whose salaries had not been paid embarked on a four-day rampage through Antwerp. In an orgy of destruction that became known as the Spanish Fury, the soldiers burned to the ground around a third of the city, raped scores of women and killed some seven thousand people. The chief consequence of this wanton destruction was to drive the forces opposing the Spanish even closer together. In 1579, the leaders of seven rebel northern provinces met in Utrecht to agree the terms of a closer union – a major step towards establishing the Netherlands as an independent country. Two years later, the United Provinces formally revoked their loyalty to the Spanish crown with the Act of Abjuration, perhaps the closest the Netherlands ever had to a Declaration of Independence. As Daniel Horst has written, the inscription on a popular medallion struck at the time provided a helpful summary of the rebel states' increasingly popular creed: 'When the King is a tyrant to his people, the people break away in accordance with divine and human justice.' Years later, settlers in North America would adopt similar language in declaring their independence from the British.

In 1580, King Philip formally declared William an outlaw and a traitor and offered a handsome reward for his death. Four years later, a twenty-five-year-old Catholic called Balthasar Gerard attempted to claim the reward. Working as courier for William's household under an assumed name, Gerard had gained the trust of courtiers, who failed to notice that the helpful young man was plotting to kill the leader of the Protestant revolt. When William gave him money to buy new clothes, Gerard invested instead in at least one small wheel-lock pistol. Such a gun was then at the cutting edge of weapons technology, but Gerard had little trouble obtaining one: he bought it from one of William's own men.

On Tuesday, 10 July 1584, William ate lunch with his wife and three daughters at his home in Delft. When he left the dining room, Gerard stepped from behind a pillar and opened fire, hitting William in the chest and stomach. The Prince fell and Gerard ran from the building, but was quickly captured. Several days of excruciating torture followed, during which he was propped naked next to a blazing fire, hung from a rack, beaten with rods, had boiling fat poured on him, burned with a hot grill, had salt rubbed in his wounds and had his genitals cut off. William, meanwhile, was carried by a servant to an adjacent room and laid on a couch, where he died. It was, according to the historian Lisa Jardine, the first time a head of state had ever been assassinated using a handgun. Legend has it that the Prince of Orange's final words were: 'my God, have pity on my soul; my God, have pity on this poor people.' He is believed to have said them not in Dutch, but in French.

The Spanish Armada

While the rebels reeled from the loss of William of Orange, help came from an unlikely quarter: the English. As part of the great game of empires playing out across Europe, the English formally allied themselves with the Dutch rebels in 1585, signing a treaty pledging a united front against the Spanish.

In response to this new alliance, Spain's King Philip began preparations for an all-out invasion of England, planning to send some 30,000 troops from the Netherlands, bolstered by a naval fleet from Spain. After nearly two years of preparation, the invasion fleet of around 130 ships – the Spanish Armada – sailed from Lisbon in May 1588.

In late July, the Armada was spotted passing Lizard Point in Cornwall and the English fleet was despatched to provide an unfriendly welcome. After skirmishes near the Isle of Wight and elsewhere in the Channel, the English attacked the disorganised Spanish fleet in the Channel in August, raking them with cannon fire and sinking or wrecking several ships. Prevented from linking with the land forces waiting to invade England from the Low Countries, the Armada was forced to flee back to Spain the long way, around the top of Scotland. Battle damage, bad weather and bad luck decimated what was left of the fleet, and only 60 of the original 130-odd ships made it home. Around 15,000 Spanish sailors had drowned, while the damage to the English fleet had been negligible. England had been saved from invasion, Spain humiliated and the rebels of the Dutch republic given a major boost.

Capturing the Castle

The carnival parade showing no signs of slowing, I walked away from the square and the two churches, hoping to see a little more of the city. The southern edge of Maastricht was laced with ancient fortifications and it was not long before I came across some: a thick stone wall rising high above the neat terraced houses around it, a narrow stone staircase leading up to the top. The thin dirt path along the battlements was unpleasantly exposed to the wind and rain, but the view was marvellous, with a prim little park on one side and the twin church towers bristling over slanted roofs on the other. At a corner in the wall-top path, a rusty cannon pointed menacingly at a sodden donkey in the petting zoo below. In the garden of one of the adjacent houses I could see a giant inflatable stork leering over the garden fence, a traditional Dutch decoration to celebrate the birth of a baby.

In Alexandre Dumas's novel *The Three Musketeers*, Maastricht was the setting for the siege that claimed the life of d'Artagnan. In real life, the city's fortifications had also played a role in several sieges, including a major one in 1632. By that time, the stop–start conflict between the Dutch and the Spanish had been subsumed into the Thirty Years' War, a rolling conflict between Catholic and Protestant Countries that engulfed much of western Europe. Recovering from the loss of William of Orange, the Dutch rebels had scored a series of significant victories over the Spanish, snatching control of key southern cities such as Venlo and Roermond. Maastricht, with its tough fortifications and location deep behind Spanish lines, was a bold next target for rebels seeking to strike a decisive blow. In June 1632, William's son Frederick Henry attacked the city, leading an army of more than 20,000 men along the River Maas. With perhaps 5000 loyal Spanish soldiers and armed civilians inside the city, the invaders dug a huge network of trenches and fortifications from which they could lay siege.

As reinforcements arrived, the Spanish inside the city fought back fiercely. Among the casualties was the Earl of Oxford, Robert de Vere, one of the many English fighting on the rebel side. More than two months of attack and counter-attack followed, until the ditches being dug by the rebels finally reached Maastricht's defensive walls. A mine was detonated beneath the main rampart, blowing a large hole in the walls. The Spanish quickly entered into negotiations to surrender, providing the rebels with a crucial victory. By 1648, the Spaniards had little option but to formally recognise the independence of the separatist northern provinces. Meeting in northern Germany, delegates from the warring parties agreed the Peace of Munster, one of a series of treaties known collectively as the Treaty of Westphalia that ended the Thirty Years' War. The seven United Provinces were definitively separated from the Spanish Crown, while the southern provinces (present-day Belgium) remained in Spanish hands. After decades of conflict, the Dutch struggle for independence was over.

Freed from the burden of war, the United Provinces boomed. Under the terms of the Treaty of Westphalia the river Scheldt, in present-day Belgium, was closed to international shipping. At a stroke, the city of Antwerp went from being one of the world's great trading hubs to a relative backwater. Amsterdam and Rotterdam were quick to exploit their rival's demise, and the United Provinces embarked on a period of extraordinary economic growth. Dutch merchants and explorers set off on long sea voyages that would create an empire spanning the globe. Canals were dug, windmills constructed and waterlogged fields drained. Wealthy merchants built grand canal houses, churches and civic buildings, and sponsored the careers of artists such as Rembrandt and Vermeer. Within the space of a few decades, the new country became a world centre of art, architecture, science and culture. The war with the Spanish had exacted a terrible toll, but its end marked the beginning of what came to be known as the Dutch Golden Age.

On towards Eindhoven

Tiring of Maastricht's rowdy charms, I walked back to the train station, ready to continue my procession through the cities of the south. It was early afternoon and the train heading north was quiet, only a few locals leaving in search of quieter climes. At least three people in the carriage were reading Disney children's comic books, sold in every train station in the Netherlands and inexplicably popular with even well-educated adults. In the seat next to mine, a curly-haired woman in a chocolate-coloured shawl opened a diary to that day's date and wrote, in English, 'TRIP TO EINDHOVEN'.

The train trundled up the narrow isthmus of Limburg, slowly gathering passengers from small stations like a trawler collecting fish. The province was roughly hourglass-shaped and just a few miles across in places, so the journey amounted to a brief sightseeing tour of its attractions. Compared to the rest of the Netherlands the landscape was strikingly varied, with not only the usual flat farmland but also thick patches of forest and countless small hills swelling from between the loops of the river Maas. In the distance I could see what looked like vineyards and grand country houses. I recalled something a Dutch friend had told me in astonished tones when she heard I was visiting the hilly south: 'In Limburg, the bicycles have three gears!'

The landscape was not all beautiful. In the distance I could see what looked like pitheads, great rust-coloured towers marking the entrance to some of the tunnels that pockmarked this part of the country. The mines had once been a major employer in the region, and their closure some half a century previously had helped tip it into an economic decline from which it had never fully recovered. Also less than scenic was the long string of strip clubs and brothels between the train tracks and the main road out of Maastricht – catering, presumably, to horny Belgians and Germans who couldn't be easily satisfied in their more prudish homelands.

The Dutch King of England

After about half an hour I changed trains in Roermond, a pretty town near the top of the Limburg peninsula. It was, I later learned, known for the neighbouring graves of a husband and wife of different religions. One Catholic and one Protestant, the couple had been buried in separate graveyards, but in graves that were topped with stone statues who held hands across the dividing wall. Less happily, the town had achieved notoriety in the 1980s when the Catholic dissidents of the IRA murdered three British soldiers in a machine-gun attack on an army base. A year later, two Australian tourists were also shot in the town after being mistaken for off-duty British soldiers. The perpetrators of these murders may well have been aware of the role the Dutch had played in Northern Irish and British history, in the years following England's 'Glorious Revolution' of 1688.

In 1677, Prince William III of Orange (the great-grandson of the William who launched the revolt against the Spanish) married Mary Stuart, the fifteen-year-old daughter of England's King James II. At the time such Anglo-Dutch royal marriages were not unusual, and for the Dutch Prince the union was more strategic than romantic – William assumed that his new wife would one day inherit the English throne. However, as so often in Dutch history, the best-laid plans were sent awry by yet another conflict between Protestants and Catholics.

The Prince of Orange was, of course, a Protestant, as was his English wife. Her father, however, was a Catholic. For the Dutch, the ascent of this Catholic King to the English throne had caused no end of anguish. Having won their independence from the Spanish, they were alarmed to see James building up his navy and developing a warmer relationship with his fellow Catholic King Louis XIV of France. The House of Orange naturally feared that England and France might soon join together in an anti-Dutch, anti-Protestant alliance.

Dutch concern peaked in 1688, when King James's wife gave birth to a son. The new arrival threatened to elbow Mary out of the line of succession to the English throne, establishing a Catholic dynasty that would rule England for generations to come. William responded decisively, with a plan to invade England. A high-minded declaration claimed that the Dutch were being forced to intervene in English affairs 'for the maintaining both of the Protestant religion and the law and liberties of these Kingdoms'. In practice, William hoped that an invasion would both secure his wife's claim to the English throne and secure England as a Protestant ally of the Dutch, rather than a Catholic friend of the French.

In early November 1688, a flotilla of more than 200 Dutch ships left a harbour near Hoek van Holland, carrying over 20,000 well-trained soldiers. Crossing the North Sea and turning south towards Kent, the ships made an awe-inspiring sight, stretching more than twenty deep across almost the entire width of the Channel. Crowds of nervous English people gathered on the cliffs at Dover to watch the Dutch approach – some of them supporters of plans to bring King James to heel, but others fearful of what a Dutch invasion would mean. The court in London was gripped by panic, with wild rumours circulating that Dutch soldiers had been seen on the Isle of Wight, in Poole, in Oxford. The King himself began suffering frequent nosebleeds.

Taking advantage of favourable winds, the Dutch sailed quickly southwest towards Devon. Trapped around the mouth of the Thames by an opposing headwind, the English navy could only watch in frustration as their enemy cruised past, including William on a ship decorated with orange flags and a banner reading 'For Liberty and the Protestant Religion'.

The Dutch fleet eventually made landfall at Torbay in Devon, horses and cannons splashing ashore through the cold winter surf. William stood high on the cliffs at Brixham to watch the rest of his fleet arrive, while some of his men made a quick trip to a pub to drink the local cider. Suitably refreshed, a huge convoy of Dutch forces headed northeast towards London. Arriving in Exeter, William rode through the city on a gleaming white horse, surrounded by hundreds of pages and gentlemen wearing suits of armour – including Protestant English and Scots who supported his attempt to reclaim England from Catholic rule.

Before the invasion, a group of leading politicians (known as the Immortal Seven) had written to William saying that they, along with many others, would support him if he invaded their country and overthrew King James. However, in reality not nearly as many locals rallied to William's cause as he had hoped. The Prince of Orange had expected thousands of people to join him in rising up against the King's corrupt and heretical rule, but in practice their reception was decidedly lukewarm. Many Protestant nobles were hesitant about being seen to support William too early, lest his attempt to seize the throne fail. As a result, as Lisa Jardine has written, the Dutch resorted to carefully stage-managing William's march on London, lining the streets with selected supporters in an effort to make his arrival seem more like a liberation and less like an invasion.

William's forces continued across the country almost unopposed, from Salisbury (where William, a great fan of gardening, stopped at Wilton House to admire the lawns and flowers) to Reading, Henley, Maidenhead and Windsor. In mid-December, with the Dutch closing on the capital, King James fled from Westminster to Vauxhall in a rowing boat, planning to head for the Catholic sanctuary of France. Destroying royal papers and famously tossing the royal seal into the Thames as he went, he hoped to make a legal take-over by William impossible and to force French intervention to prop up his own rule. This ruse failed, though, and on 18 December William of Orange arrived in London, parading down Knightsbridge in an eye-catching white cloak. Supporters lined the streets waving orange ribbons and handing oranges to the passing Dutch soldiers, while English soldiers fled from the capital to small towns like St Albans.

James, meanwhile, was captured by the Dutch and forced into effective house arrest in Rochester. A week or so later, his guards deliberately turned a blind eye and let him escape to France. Soon after, in early 1689, a special 'Convention Parliament' declared that because James had fled, the crown should pass to William and his wife Mary, who would rule the country jointly. The crown of Scotland followed a few months later. London remained effectively under Dutch military occupation and a Dutch Prince ruled from the English throne.

The Prince of Orange went on to rule England for nearly a decade and a half. (Mary died after roughly five years on the throne, after which William ruled on his own.) In Britain, his Glorious Revolution and the reign that followed had enormous consequences. As a condition of taking the throne, William had been compelled to sign a Bill of Rights, which was later seen as establishing the basic principles of British democracy. For Catholics, however, William and Mary's rule was less positive: they were denied the right to vote or stand for parliament, and British monarchs were forbidden from marrying Catholics until as late as 2011. Equally controversial were the couple's escapades in Northern Ireland, where King William and the former King James met for a rematch in 1690 at the famous Battle of the Boyne. Heavily outnumbered, James fled the scene and awarded William's largely Dutch and English army a victory that would be celebrated by some Northern Irish Protestants for centuries to come, many of them clad in the orange colours of their former leader.

The Dutch King of England died in 1702 after taking a tumble from his horse, which had stumbled into a mole hole.

His many enemies allegedly toasted the creature that had dug the offending hole, clinking glasses to 'the little gentleman in the black velvet waistcoat' who had rid them of their enemy. Buried in Westminster Abbey, William was commemorated by a statue in London's St James's Square. It depicted him on horseback, just about to trip over a molehill.

The City of Light

Wandering around a pretty square near Roermond station, I nearly missed my train thanks largely to the absurd Dutch method of telling the time, whereby 2.35 was not 'two thirty-five' but 'five past half before three'. After a hasty dash across the platforms, another near-empty train carried me some thirty miles northwest to Eindhoven, another of the south's major carnival cities.

A sprawling city of some 200,000 people, Eindhoven was best known to the Dutch as the home of the Philips electrical company. I had visited the city once before for a friend's birthday party and found it pleasant enough but rather forgettable, dominated by ring roads and modern office blocks. Philips was founded in the city in the late 1800s by a cousin of Karl Marx, and while the company thrived the city around it grew more than fortyfold. As in other industrial cities like Rotterdam, the presence of large numbers of factories and warehouses had helped give the region's inhabitants a reputation as no-nonsense, salt-of-the-earth types. One of the relatively few major Dutch multinationals, Philips was a source of considerable national pride, offering (along with Unilever and Shell) proof that the country's relaxed outlook and generous welfare state were not incompatible with profitability. Philips engineers were said to have played a major role in inventing technologies including the tape recorder, CD, DVD and Blu-ray. In recent years, however, Philips had fallen on harder times, announcing enormous job losses that hollowed out what had long been a one-company town. The signs on the ring roads welcoming visitors to the lightbulb-producing 'City of Light' now carried a touch of grim irony.

The disembodied voice of the train conductor wished passengers a fun carnival and I disembarked, stepping from the carriage into a steady stream of revellers flowing towards the city centre. I didn't plan to stay in Eindhoven for long, but was curious to see how the festivities there differed from those in Maastricht. The weather was still miserable, and people arriving from elsewhere were rushing to adapt costumes that had been funny or flirty at home but were now just cold. A young woman in a bikini top and hula dress was cutting armholes in a black plastic bin bag, while half a dozen burly male gymnasts were trying to fit winter jackets under their already overstretched leotards. I was again glad of my stupid tiger suit, which remained warm despite having absorbed several litres of water.

In the street leading away from the station, the parade was well under way. As in Maastricht, there were slow-moving trucks decorated with colourful bunting, sequinned girls dancing in the street, thumping music and hundreds of cheerful onlookers drinking beer in the rain. Compared to Maastricht, however, the crowd in Eindhoven was considerably more youthful. There were fewer green-suited marching bands and fewer older couples in elaborately feathered costumes, and more young people in comedy fancy dress, ignoring the parade in order to focus on drinking and flirting.

Eindhoven's carnival also had a rather Brazilian flavour – evidence, perhaps, of the long-standing Dutch affection for all things Brazilian, thanks to the Netherlands' colonial links with nearby Suriname. One patch of pavement opposite the train station was awash with green and yellow bunting, with tanned women in sparkling bikinis and elaborate headdresses dancing to staccato drum music. Dodging a young man in Brazilian football strip who was bouncing a ball on his head, I stopped to buy a caipirinha at a trestle table in front of a gold and green–decorated bar. The plastic beaker contained more alcohol than lime or sugar, and I couldn't help but gasp at the first sip. A beautiful dinosaur in a green suit laughed at me, her long blonde hair tangled in the spikes glued down her back. I tried to stroke her tail, but she snarled at me and slithered away.

A House Divided

Like much of the southern Netherlands, Eindhoven was traditionally a staunchly Catholic city. Following the conclusion of the war against the Spanish, the Netherlands' political boundaries were relatively stable, but the country remained divided internally along religious lines. In the early years of the new republic, Catholics were prohibited from holding public office and the southern province of Limburg was viewed by many as something of a geopolitical liability, a tempting morsel dangling within easy reach of the country's neighbours. In 1848, the prominent journalist J.G.H. Boissevain published *The Limburg Question*, arguing that the Dutch state should disown the province, calling it 'a strange appendix.... a pitiful piece of land, an outgrowth of our country, that consumes our best juices'. Further north, when the Catholic Limburger Pierre Cuypers won the competition to design the new Rijksmuseum in Amsterdam, his design was criticised for being more suitable for a Catholic cathedral than an art museum.

In an effort to manage these tensions, the Dutch developed a system of segregation along religious lines that now seems extraordinary in a country famed for its tolerance and diversity. Perhaps more than anywhere in Europe other than Northern Ireland, the Netherlands was a country where one's religious affiliation could be of as much consequence as one's nationality. Through a process of *verzuiling*, or 'pillarisation', the country was effectively sliced into neat social groups (*zuilen*, or pillars) based on religion, so clearly defined that they effectively represented distinct subcultures. Nearly every aspect of social and professional life – education, healthcare, housing, unions, banking – was then decided according to which group one belonged to.

To understand how the system worked, one might consider the example of two hypothetical boys born into different pillars of the Netherlands in the 1950s. Jan's parents are Catholic, so he is born in the hospital for Catholics. Justin's family live in the same street but are Protestants, so his mother gives birth at the local hospital for Protestants. Jan's father, who works in a warehouse at the local harbour, is a member of the Catholic trade union. Justin's father, who works in the same warehouse, joins the Protestant trade union. When the children grow older, they prepare to attend school – Jan will go to the local Catholic school, while Justin will attend the one for Protestants. In the evenings after school, the boys may be allowed to listen to the radio or watch some television: Jan enjoys the programmes of the Catholic broadcaster, while Justin sticks to those aired by its Protestant rival. Once the children have been put to bed, their fathers may sit down to read the paper – Justin's father reads the Protestant paper, while Jan's takes a Catholic one. When an election comes round, Jan's father inevitably votes for the Catholic party, while Justin's parents back the Protestants. Both boys like playing football so join a local club, but unfortunately they never get to play at one together: Jan plays for a Catholic club on Sundays, but Justin plays with the Protestants on Saturdays. After a year or two at junior school, the boys will go on to Catholic and Protestant middle schools and high schools, and eventually to Catholic and Protestant universities. Jan and Justin both marry their university sweethearts, who are of course members of the same religious denomination. They both find jobs in their home town, join the appropriate unions and send their children to the same schools, hospitals and sports clubs they themselves once attended. Eventually reaching old age, Justin moves into a home for the Protestant elderly, while Jan relocates to the Catholic home across town. When they die, a Catholic or Protestant undertaker buries them in a Catholic or Protestant graveyard. Born a few yards apart, they have lived their entire lives on separate parallel paths, from the cradle to the grave.

This story is, of course, a caricature. In practice people strayed across religious boundaries, and some aspects of Dutch society stayed unpillarised. Large companies, for example, often hired workers without regard to their religion. Yet for much of the early twentieth century, the Netherlands remained starkly segregated along religious lines. Until as late as 1960, for example, just one in twenty of all Catholics who married did so to a non-Catholic spouse. Ironically for a country forged out of Protestant dissatisfaction with Catholic rule, the system put particular power in the hands of the Catholic community, with a single political party operating all but unchallenged as the political wing of the Catholic Church. On both sides of the divide political parties were tight and disciplined, able to rely on a strong base of support without much competition for votes. However, the endless need for different religious groups to reach a compromise made Dutch governments unstable, with frequent disputes over issues such as abortion. In 1952, a bizarre situation arose during negotiations to form a new coalition government when a Catholic party claimed the right to appoint the foreign minister, despite objections from Protestants who pointed out that every other foreign minister in the European Community was already – as they saw it – a Catholic taking orders from Rome. In a typically Dutch compromise, the dispute was resolved by appointing two foreign ministers, a Catholic and a non-Catholic, who both represented the country overseas for the next four years.

By the 1950s the pillars were already beginning to crumble. Economic development and increasing personal mobility drove the so-called *nivellering*, or levelling, of Dutch society. As the Catholic magazine *Tablet* reported in 1954, in southern cities like Eindhoven employers such as Philips had a tendency to 'attract workers and technicians from other parts; men with enquiring, searching minds, the setting of their own lives... often sundered from the family tradition'. These migrant workers were, the magazine noted with a sigh, 'men sometimes ready to describe themselves as agnostics when it comes to religion'. The Second World War also did much to undermine the pillars. Wartime occupation by the Nazis forced the Dutch to cooperate with one another in order to survive, and when the conflict was over the idea of breaking apart into neat columns again seemed rather outdated. The post-war rise of the welfare state also meant that people no longer had to depend on their social networks and religious institutions for services like education. Perhaps most importantly, the elites who had once sustained the pillars began to lose the will to fight for them. In 1967, a Catholic bishop took the revolutionary step of announcing on television that party choice should be a matter of individual conscience, not religious denomination.

The result was a sea change in the way the Netherlands was run. Between the 1950s and the 1990s, the proportion of practising Catholics who voted for a Catholic party almost halved. Three successive general elections saw unprecedented turnover in parliamentary seats and the political parties themselves began to fracture, with new smaller parties breaking away from the established majors. After the 1948 election seven parties were represented in the Dutch national parliament; by 1972 there were fourteen. As elsewhere in Europe, an increasingly liberal younger generation rebelled against the conservative values of their parents, while the arrival of thousands of Turkish and Moroccan 'guest workers' further eroded the traditional Catholic/Protestant divide. Many organisations that had previously defined themselves in religious terms merged, with newspapers and television channels ditching their religious affiliations in favour of a more neutral stance. Church attendance also declined rapidly: in the 1950s around nine out of ten Dutch Catholics attended mass regularly, but by the early 2000s this had fallen to under one in four.

By the time of my visit to Eindhoven, the idea of separate football leagues for Protestants and Catholics seemed at best old-fashioned and at worst faintly ridiculous; an example of the kind of balkanised politics usually associated with failing states. However, the Dutch pillars had left a clear legacy, much of it positive. The system of *verzuiling* enhanced stability in a country that was overcrowded and wracked by war. Along with the need for cooperation to maintain flood defences, pillarisation was one reason the Dutch tended to resolve political disputes through negotiation and compromise. The fact that even small minorities were given a voice in political debates also helped guarantee the rights of groups such as homosexuals. Years after the pillars crumbled, the emphasis in Dutch politics remained very much on what political scientists called the 'politics of accommodation', with little space for consensus-shattering Thatchers or Reagans to challenge the equilibrium.

As a recovering political hack, I was routinely amazed by the lack of political rancour around even the most controversial issues in the Netherlands. Coverage of politics on Dutch television was limited, and most cabinet ministers could walk down the street not only unguarded but completely unnoticed. It was exceedingly rare to hear a Dutch person express a strong opinion about any political issue, and unusual to hear current affairs discussed in a bar or over dinner. When the former health minister Els Borst was found dead in early 2014, the news barely merited a mention on the front pages of national newspapers – even after the police said they thought she had been murdered. Vigorous political protest or public rallying was almost unheard of, and at election time many people were genuinely unsure who to vote for – perhaps because coalition governments meant it was impossible to be sure a party would deliver on its promises. The choice available to voters seemed overwhelming: at the 2014 European elections, no fewer than 19 parties were listed on the ballot sheet, with a combined 345 candidates competing for just 26 seats. Even if the Prime Minister gave a major speech about a contentious issue – immigration, say – the response from most of his political opponents would be polite agreement, with perhaps a few mild suggestions for improvement. The next day newspapers would report the speech on perhaps page seven, in a brief column summarising what was said, with little opinionising or speculation about its impact on his political future. People generally thought that politicians were decent and hard-working, and free from the taint of corruption or self-interest.

In recent years there had been a slight trend towards a more combative style of politics, fuelled by the rise of populists such as Geert Wilders, but Dutch politics was still far from a blood sport. Watching anaemic debate programmes and reading pallid newspapers, I could never quite decide whether the Dutch determination to agree to disagree was a mark of civilised society, or just very tedious.

Catholic Neighbours

Short of time and weary of the rain, I decided I had already seen enough of Eindhoven's carnival. I walked back to the station and boarded yet another train, heading west towards Breda. The double-decker carriage was uncrowded and I took a seat in the low-ceilinged upper floor, opposite a sturdy blonde woman doing what Dutch people usually did on trains: eating a homemade cheese sandwich from a small plastic bag. The train slid quickly through the open farmland, raindrops chasing one another across the windows. I noticed several small Catholic shrines hidden among the farmhouses and narrow lanes, brick chapels about the size of a garden shed, each with a cross above the door and a carefully tended garden. Consulting a map, I realised we were travelling roughly parallel to the Belgian border, which lay perhaps six miles to the south behind damp grassy fields filled with monochrome cows. As a Brit usually forced to board a flight or ferry to travel abroad, I still found it strange to think that another country lay just a short walk away.

Following the Dutch victory over the Spanish, Belgium and the Netherlands had remained intricately linked. After a period of political uncertainty, French forces invaded the

United Provinces in 1795, establishing a client state known as the Batavian Republic. A few years later, Napoleon installed his brother as King. To say that the Dutch were unhappy with this return to colonial rule would be an understatement. One French diplomat described them as 'a people more rebellious than in any other country'. In 1814, when European leaders met in Vienna to gloat over Napoleon's downfall, they agreed to form the Kingdom of the Netherlands, with the latest William of Orange as King, uniting the Netherlands and Belgium in a single state for the first time since they had split during the war with Spain.

Finding himself in charge of the reunified Low Countries, William of Orange gamely attempted to build the trappings of a unitary state, but the new kingdom was yet another uneasy marriage between a Catholic, largely French-speaking south and a Protestant, Dutch-speaking north. The Belgians were particularly opposed to what they saw as one more round of foreign oppression. In 1830, a performance of a nationalistic opera in Brussels sparked an anti-Dutch riot in the city, with Belgian mobs looting shops and smashing factories. In a strange reversal of earlier Spanish actions, the Prince of Orange despatched Dutch troops to quell the rebellion. In 1839, the Dutch belatedly recognised the independence of Belgium, formalising the existence of the Netherlands and Belgium as separate countries. William was officially appointed the first King of the modern-day Netherlands. He would, however, not remain on the throne for long – he abdicated soon after and married a Belgian Catholic.

Nearly two centuries later, relations between the Dutch and their southern neighbours had settled to a level that could only be described as boring. While the Netherlands' relationship with Germany was sometimes fraught, tinged with both competitiveness and post-war recrimination, the Netherlands' relationship with Belgium was as flat and unthreatening as the landscape. There was no great rivalry between the two countries, and no real interest in developing one. The Dutch thought of Belgium roughly how the British viewed France: it was a nice enough place with some good food and drink, but also slightly backward and old-fashioned, a country of bad roads, failing businesses and late-sleeping gastronomes. 'It's nice to go to Belgium for the beer,' a colleague once told me. 'But I could never do business there. They just don't really know what they're doing.' The Belgian people, meanwhile, were viewed by many Dutch as Tintin-reading simpletons. Belgians appearing on Dutch television were often shown on screen with subtitles, so the Dutch could understand their accents. 'What does it say on the bottom of Belgian beer bottles?' a popular joke in Rotterdam asked. 'OPEN AT OTHER END.'

With a map open on my lap, I tried to follow the train's progress relative to the border, but the lack of landmarks made it difficult. Where other countries had mountain ranges, deserts or encircling oceans to define their boundaries, the Netherlands had only endless marshy farmland. In previous generations the roughly 300-mile border with Belgium might have been marked with border posts or checkpoints, but EU integration had rendered it porous to the point of invisibility, detectable only by careful examination of the fonts on road signs or the potholes in under-maintained Belgian roads. Through the rain-streaked windows of the train it was impossible to tell where one country ended and another began.

Perhaps the most extreme example of the porous border lay a few miles south of the train track, in a small town (or towns) I had visited a few months previously. Baarle-Hertog/Baarle-Nassau's hyphenated name indicated what made it unique: straddling the border between the Netherlands and Belgium, it was neither here nor there. When the modern boundary between the two countries was settled in the mid-nineteenth century, negotiators decided the nationality of thousands of parcels of land on a case-by-case basis. In most instances the decisions were fairly sensible, but around twenty parcels of land were granted to Belgium despite the fact that they were isolated not only from the 'mainland' of

Belgium but from one another, encircled by land belonging to the Dutch. Amazingly, some of these enclaves even had other enclaves within them – small islands of Dutch territory sitting inside islands of Belgian territory that were themselves surrounded by Dutch territory, like bulls-eyes on a dartboard. Zooming in on a Google map of the area revealed a bizarre archipelago where it was possible to plot a straight line that passed through an international border a dozen times within a single mile.

For those living in the enclaves, this geography had sometimes bizarre consequences. Like air hostesses, residents of Baarle-Hertog and Baarle-Nassau traversed international borders almost continuously, sometimes travelling from Belgium to the Netherlands and back again just to cross the street in front of their homes. Within the towns many services were duplicated, with two electrical systems, two postal services, two police departments, even two mayors. Each house apparently paid taxes in the country where its front door was located, so – as *The Ultimate Guide to Offshore Tax Havens* advised moguls – houses on the border needed only to move their front doors in order to cut their tax bills. For Dutch people used to shops remaining closed on Sundays, living a few metres from Belgian stores was another obvious advantage. According to one legal textbook, police officers had sometimes even used buildings on the border to interrogate witnesses, who could sit in the same room as their questioners but in another country, safe from fear of arrest.

Recognising the ridiculousness of the situation, the Dutch and Belgian governments made repeated attempts to swap parcels of land and agree a more rational border, although without much success, and the enclaves endured as what one legal scholar called 'indestructible legal fossils'. When I visited I found a bustling little town much like any other in the region but for the string of white stone crosses laid flat in the pavement, with a 'B' on one side and an 'NL' on the other. The narrow streets were jammed with Belgians stocking up on Dutch Edam cheese, and Dutchmen loading their cars with strong Belgian beer. I couldn't resist joining the hordes of tourists posing for photographs straddling the equator-style white lines curving through the town, one foot in a Dutch-speaking land of beer and bicycles, and the other in the Netherlands.

Beer in Breda

As the sun slouched towards the horizon, the train neared Breda. The city (pronounced, to the confusion of the few tourists who ventured there, to rhyme with 'fader' rather than 'feeder') lay just six or seven miles north of the Belgian border, roughly halfway between Eindhoven and Rotterdam. Breda had played an important role in the revolt against the Spanish, passing back and forth between the two sides repeatedly before finally settling in Dutch hands. Home, at various times, to England's King Charles II, Daniel Defoe and Oliver Cromwell, the city was well off the usual Netherlands tourist trail, but had a reputation as a place where carnival was taken seriously.

I walked south from the train station towards the city centre through a sprawling circular park. 'A pleasant, easygoing place to while away a day' was what my Rough Guide travel book said about Breda, and the description already seemed accurate. The park was generously endowed with statues and water features, and dotted with children splashing through puddles in rubber boots. One side of the park was overlooked by a squat military fortress with red brick walls and sharp grey turrets. Encircling it – and the rest of the city – was a river: the *breede* (or wide) river Aa that gave Breda its name.

Behind the park and the fortress lay the heart of the city, dominated by the soaring gothic clock tower of the fifteenth-century Grote Kerk, or cathedral. I walked through a warren of narrow cobbled streets leading around the cathedral to the main square, where the carnival celebrations were once again in full swing. Loud music boomed from the bars and restaurants lining the square, which was filled with revellers in the by-now familiar elaborate headdresses, braided suits and top hats. Opposite the cathedral, on a stage in front of what I assumed was the town hall, a moustachioed ringmaster in top hat and red tails was waving, for some reason, a giant skull and crossbones. Tragically, I had missed one of the highlights of the day, the *Boerenbruiloft*, or Farmers' Wedding, a farcical fake marriage between an honorary bride and groom, both of whom were probably already married to other people.

Compared to those in Maastricht and Eindhoven, the crowd in Breda was raucous. The celebrations held further to the south and east had attracted mostly local revellers, including many older people, families and children. Breda was closer to the urban centres of Rotterdam and Amsterdam and so had drawn a less local, more youthful crowd, including many teenagers and Dutch university fraternities looking for a riotous night out. In my early thirties, I felt more than a little old. In front of the cathedral a group of teenage girls dressed as nuns were grinding provocatively below the stained-glass windows as toilet rolls catapulted over their heads, streaming like comets. There was, I noticed, a clear gender divide when it came to costumes. The men had mostly chosen outfits that maximised the likelihood of making young women swoon, while requiring minimal effort to put together: soldiers, pilots and SWAT team members. For the women, meanwhile, the primary aim was to reveal as much leg and cleavage as possible. Everywhere I looked there were sexy vampires, sexy pirates, sexy schoolteachers and sexy nurses.

Many of the bars around the square had erected crude wooden extensions to increase their capacity, in some cases removing their front walls altogether to offer unimpeded access to the festivities. The one I chose to enter had adopted a ski hut theme, with fake snow blanketing the roof, white spray paint on the windows and a row of skis standing upright by the front door; a taste of après-ski in one of the flattest places on earth. Inside the packed bar, three men in furry bear suits were dancing on a table, surrounded by a baying crowd. The music was a mixture of whomping carnival tunes and beloved Dutch chart toppers: Anouk, Blof, Nick and Simon. At the bar itself, an Arab sheikh in headdress was throwing geopolitical caution to the wind and buying a drink for a moustachioed Latino dictator in gold sunglasses and military epaulettes. Finding that my euro notes were not an accepted currency, I was directed to an impromptu bureau de change next to the ski rack and bought a small pile of plastic *muntjes* – drinks tokens – at a grossly inflated exchange rate. Back at the bar, a busty blonde in a Bavarian barmaid's outfit exchanged a few of them for a foam cup of *jagertee*, a kind of hot rum mixed with black tea, which tasted about as good as it sounded. Struggling to keep the drink down, I couldn't help but admire the legs of the slender nurse in a long blonde wig standing beside me, who promptly turned around to reveal his hairy chest and slurped a Heineken through his stubbly brown beard. At the front door, a team of bloodied surgeons pushing a gurney were turned away by a shaven-headed security guard. Crossing the street, they padlocked the stretcher to a lamppost and came back to buy a round.

A Nation of Atheists

It was strange to think that the carnival celebrations were rooted in Catholic traditions of piety, moral conservatism and restraint. However, the abandonment of traditional values was perhaps less surprising when one considered the rapid decline of organised religion that had taken place following the collapse of the pillars. At the time of my visit to Breda, roughly 30 per cent of the population of the Netherlands was Catholic, compared with about 20 per cent who were Protestant. A further 6 per cent were Muslim. Around 40 per cent were atheist, and according to the national statistical authorities, only one in six Dutch people attended church or mosque regularly. Research by one Dutch thinktank claimed that the Netherlands passed a notable tipping point in 2015 when the number of atheists in the country exceeded for the first time the number of people who believed in some form of god. For a nation that a generation previously had been organised along sectarian lines, this was a striking change. As one sociologist put it, the twenty-first-century Netherlands had become 'one nation, without God'.

Even as an atheist from sin-loving London, I was often struck by the absence of religious moralising in the Netherlands. The prevailing liberal attitudes to issues such as abortion, same-sex marriage and drug consumption, together with the endless pornography and condom adverts on tele-vision, made it easy to see the country as a quintessential post-religious society. I was also struck by how many lead-ing Dutch politicians unashamedly declared themselves to be atheists, in a way unheard of in Britain or the United States. Religious rituals and habits that had been absorbed into mainstream culture in my home country – weddings, funer-als, christenings – in the Netherlands were either treated as purely legal procedures or went unmarked. I didn't know anyone who went to church, and most of my Dutch friends and colleagues remained unmarried well into their forties. On one occasion I learned that a colleague who I thought I knew quite well had got married only when he casually mentioned it in conversation: 'Oh, I almost forgot to tell you – I got mar-ried last weekend...'

In some areas, however, one could detect traces of the country's more observant past. The fabled Protestant work ethic was alive and well, and the Dutch retained a tendency to frown on anything that smacked of frivolous spending or excessive luxury. The whole country ground to a halt around religious holidays like Easter, and even in the centre of siz-able cities like Breda it was difficult to buy milk on a Sunday morning. In other parts of the country the situation was even more extreme. In 2013, newspapers reported a measles out-break in the central Dutch 'bible belt', where fundamentalist Protestant parents had refused to allow their children to be vaccinated.

For all their liberal attitudes towards homosexuality and drug use, my Dutch friends also held some fairly conservative ideas about the primacy of family and the duty they had towards their parents. In Britain, visiting one's relatives was usually seen by young people as a chore to be endured, often in the hope of a compensatory cash gift. In the Netherlands, family visits were a pleasure to be seized at every possible opportunity. Many families would regularly schedule a 'Family Day' or 'Family Weekend' on which large numbers of distant relatives would gather for a pre-arranged set of fun activities. Dutch men in particular often exhibited traces of a strange kind of Mediterranean Catholic macho, never prouder than when complimented on their tidy house, tidy car or tidy wife. Most Dutch bathrooms included a calendar pinned to the wall carefully listing the birthdays of every distant relative, all the better to celebrate with them. Woe betide anyone who forgot to send a card, or who failed to clink beer glasses with each and every guest around the table at the inevitable drinks party. A common complaint among expats was the frequent recurrence of Dutch 'circle parties', at which a vast array of relatives and acquaintances would sit in a circle in someone's living room, drinking cup after little cup of strong black coffee and gossiping for hours. If, say, a twenty-five-year-old man wanted to celebrate his birthday, it was common to do so not by getting drunk in a bar with friends, or dancing with girls in a nightclub, but by having coffee with his aunts and uncles and grandparents. 'I can't come to the party on Tuesday,' I once heard a fashionable young Dutchman tell a friend. 'Tuesdays are when I have dinner with my mama.' 'Dinner with your mama?' the friend replied. 'Cool!'

In need of some traditional Dutch courage, I moved on to another bar, a low-ceilinged dive crammed with costumed students drinking watery lager from plastic cups. The place had been painstakingly decorated with coloured streamers and balloons, but the smoking ban was being flouted so flagrantly it was difficult to see them. A barmaid carrying a tray of drinks offered me a *Flügel*, a small glass bottle of poison decorated with neon colours and googly cartoon eyes, which I drank quickly and regretted immediately. Then came a *boswandeling* ('forest walking') shot, a milky fruit liqueur served in a thin plastic thimble, which I proceeded to spill down the front of my tiger suit. I could sense my efforts to understand Dutch culture – or indeed anything else – slipping away from me.

After mopping up the mess, I struck up a conversation with a female strawberry in red face paint and green hairspray. 'Carnival's great, isn't it?' I slurred in clumsy Dutch. 'It's not as good as it used to be,' she pouted. 'Too many northerners coming down on the train just for the party, when they don't really live here. It was better when it was just for Brabanders.' Yes, I agreed, it's terrible. We really should keep it just for us people from the south.

Homeward Bound

It was raining quite heavily again, but outside the bar the party was just getting started. In the main square, the still-growing crowd chanted favourite carnival songs, including one with – as I carefully recorded in my notebook – the ingenious lyrics '*heli, heli, heli, heli, helicopter*', repeated ad infinitum. There was not a policeman in sight, but – as usual at such booze-soaked events in the Netherlands – the atmosphere was entirely peaceful. Empty plastic beer cups cobbled the floor. In the lee of the clock tower, a fat Batman was wrestling with a very drunk Super Mario, to the delight of the cheering teenagers looking on. A single fancy restaurant remained immune from the festivities, an island of decency amid the carnage. Behind the large front windows, a grey-haired couple sat hunched over plates of pasta looking bemused, like a goldfish in a bowl at a student party.

I entered a final bar that was as packed as an airport terminal bus and joined the queue for yet another drink, behind a Power Ranger and the back half of a pantomime cow. The DJ shouted something unintelligible over the sound system and thumping Dutch house music shuddered through the room. A hundred sweaty hands thrust skyward. It was six o'clock in the evening.

Feeling utterly defeated by the three carnivals, numerous beers and uncounted sticky shots, I returned to the station and boarded a train heading north out of carnival country. A disembodied voice announced the train's departure in three languages; signs on the carriage walls added a couple more. The train itself was unexpectedly quiet and comfortable, an extension of the high-speed line running from Amsterdam towards Belgium that had been constructed at great expense in partnership with the Italians as a flagship of European unity and innovation. Unfortunately, the service had proved an abject failure, beset by technical problems and delays. Toilets flushed directly onto increasingly smelly tracks, and marginally faster journey times generally failed to compensate for the extreme delays to the service. The farce had descended into predictable political mudslinging, characterised in the press as yet another conflict between lazy, underperforming southerners and high-tech, high-paying northerners. The Dutch, if one believed the newspapers, had once again been screwed over by their unscrupulous southern neighbours. Some things would never change.

A round little man in a round little hat entered the compartment, calling: '*Kaartjes alsjeblieft! Billettes s'il vous plait!* Tickets please!' I flashed him my ticket, then pulled up the hood on my tiger suit and closed my eyes for a minute. When I opened them I was in Rotterdam.

Three

The Golden Age

Empire, Slavery and the Rise of Amsterdam

It was nearly midnight and the museum was filled with people dancing. The subterranean courtyard of Amsterdam's Rijksmuseum (National Museum) had been converted into a temporary nightclub, with a DJ set up in front of the gift shop, pulsing dance music echoing off the marble walls and a cocktail bar near the cloakroom. Shielded from the night sky by a high glass roof, the courtyard was packed with revellers, most of them the kind of people who wore sunglasses indoors.

Museumnacht, or museum night, was an annual event when museums throughout the capital threw caution to the wind and stayed open into the early hours, attracting a youthful crowd with a uniquely Dutch blend of high culture and house music. Around two dozen of the city's museums were taking part, but the Rijksmuseum was the undisputed highlight.

The most famous gallery in the country had recently reopened following a refurbishment that had closed its doors for a decade. Originally intended as a Dutch answer to France's Louvre, its reputed one million artefacts included everything from paintings to ancient tapestry, furniture, porcelain and blunderbusses. A vast repository of Dutch culture, it was as if London's national gallery, national archives and history museum had all been rolled into one. The collection spanned several centuries, but the most significant examples were from the Golden Age – the period of exceptional dynamism and growth, roughly the length of the seventeenth century, during which the Dutch led the world not just in the production of fine art but also in trade, science, philosophy and architecture. At a time when much of the rest of Europe was mired in crisis, one of its smallest countries had managed, within a relatively short period, to produce Rembrandt and Vermeer, inspire Locke and Voltaire, build the canals and townhouses of Amsterdam, and establish an empire that stretched around the world. The Netherlands, as British Ambassador William Temple wrote in 1674, was 'the envy of some, the fear of others, and the wonder of all neighbours'. More than 300 years later most of that fear had dissipated, but the wonder remained, much of it hanging on the gallery walls.

The museum had opened at this location in 1885, a neo-gothic palace of red and white brick, topped with spindly turrets, triangular slate roofs, weathervanes and statuary. From the outside it was strikingly similar to the city's central train station; unsurprising given that it had been designed by the same architect, the Catholic church-painter's son Pierre Cuypers. Inside, the recent renovation project had aimed to restore some of its original grandeur while adding the kind of features now deemed essential for any major gallery: disabled access, a modern art wing, an oversized gift shop and an overpriced café. The scheme had been bedevilled by disputes and technical problems, with workmen at one point floating through the atrium in boats after a serious bout of flooding. (In Amsterdam, the museum's director grumbled to a reporter, 'you cannot dig a hole in the ground without getting wet'.) Another major delay had occurred when an argument broke out about whether cyclists would retain the right to ride through the museum on a cycle path that punctured the ground floor. A lengthy public inquiry eventually concluded that if one was to have a museum of Dutch culture, recklessly speeding bicycles would have to be a part of it. The internal courtyard that was now filled with dancers was sunk some thirty feet below ground level so that cyclists could pass over the top of it.

Thanks to such compromises, the renovation had been completed some five years late, the final bill running to a reported €375 million, far more than originally planned. It was, nevertheless, a triumph. The museum's reopening had been a major national event, with the soon-to-retire Queen

Beatrix walking the orange carpet and crowds lining the streets to cheer the return of Rembrandt's 'Night Watch' to its rightful home. The changes had received rave reviews in the local and international media, and *Museumnacht* was something of a coming-out party: an opportunity for the grand old dame of Dutch art to flaunt her assets to Amsterdam's many hipsters. For me it offered a convenient way to learn more about the Golden Age, and probably resurrect my post-carnival hangover in the process.

On the Brink of Change

Reluctantly leaving the party behind, I threaded my way through the crowd towards the entrance of the museum proper. A security guard in tight trousers stopped me at the doorway, and watched with a smile as I downed the milky cocktail I had just bought from a passing waitress. Reeling from the five-second piña colada, I passed through a high stone arch and into the first of many galleries.

After the airy, noisy atrium, entering the museum was like walking into a crypt. A labyrinth of small rooms had low, vaulted ceilings and walls painted the colour of charcoal. There were no windows, and the gallery was dimly lit by scores of crystalline LED lights hanging from the ceiling in circular hoops. The spaces under the low stone arches were filled with statues and paintings, many of them on religious themes: virgins, saints, monks and sinners. A white marble bust of Jesus watched over the entrance like a nightclub doorman, near a painting depicting the execution of St Lucy, serene amid an angry crowd as flames licked at her feet and a long sword was thrust through her throat.

I stooped to examine an oak statue, well over 500 years old, which showed an elfin St Roch in a ruffled cap, long cape and boots. The patron saint of plague victims, he pointed with a wooden hand to an ugly sore erupting from his upper thigh like a volcano. Nearby, a beautiful triptych of the raising of Lazarus hung in long strips on the wall. Five centuries old,

Why the Dutch Are Different

it showed a colourfully dressed crowd gathering on a rocky hillside around a rather worried-looking Jesus, his arm outstretched as he woke an ungrateful Lazarus from his slumber. A caption explained that the painting had been commissioned from the artist Aertgen Claesz by a married couple, who were included kneeling piously at the fringes of the scene. Stepping forward to examine them, I narrowly avoided tripping over a drunk teenager sitting on the floor, holding his head in his hands, in need of a resurrection of his own.

It was apparent that many of the artworks were intended to convey a strong moral message. Peter Aertsen's painting *Egg Dance*, for example, from 1552, depicted a small child gazing in wonder at a group of adults drinking, fondling one another and playing ridiculous egg-rolling games. The artist's message was clear: pointless amusements and lustful behaviour were misleading the young, their debauchery an insult to accepted moral codes. It was hard to imagine what he would have made of the events now taking place just around the corner, as the polished wooden floor trembled with the echo of hundreds dancing Gangnam style.

These moral themes reflected the fact that at the time these artworks were completed, on the cusp of the Golden Age, the Low Countries were devout but also riven with religious strife. For much of the sixteenth century, the largely Protestant Northern provinces had been engaged in a bitter war of attrition against the Catholic Spanish authorities that ruled over them. In that climate, art was acceptable only if it demonstrated the appropriate morality, discouraging the population from such wanton activities as egg rolling. A turning point came in 1585, when the port city of Antwerp, in present-day Belgium, fell into Spanish hands after a long siege. It had long been one of Europe's great trading centres, but the Spanish takeover sparked an exodus of Protestants, many of whom fled north in search of a more tolerant religious climate. Antwerp's loss was Amsterdam's gain, and the Dutch capital prospered as artists and skilled craftsmen flooded in. The British ambassador to Amsterdam, Dudley

92

Carleton, wrote in 1616 that while Antwerp 'was a town without people', the Dutch capital was overflowing with 'people, as it were, without a town'. Amsterdam, he said, 'goeth up apace'. The stage was set for an explosion of artistic licence and an era of unprecedented innovation and growth.

Wandering on through the labyrinth, I passed under a low archway and into the Navy Models Gallery. This contained exactly what its name would suggest: dozens of elaborate model ships, lighthouses, cannons and other nauticalia. It felt like entering a pirate's cave, stacked with precious plunder. At the centre a vast display case contained perhaps thirty model ships, many of them as big as a man, each decorated with papery sails, cobwebbed rigging and thumb-sized brass cannons. Many of the models, a sign explained, were decorations made for the boardrooms of the old Dutch Admiralty – the equivalent of a Newton's cradle on a corporate go-getter's desk.

Next door was another crypt-like gallery, with another self-explanatory title: the Armoury. This contained what looked like hundreds of pistols and long rifles, suspended in mid-air between thick sheets of glass dividing the room. A pair of petite brass cannons squatted on the floor between ivory-handled pistols, cutlasses and swords with blades almost as tall as I was. Given the swords' immense weight, a sign explained, soldiers were paid double to fight with them.

By the time of the conflict with Spain, the Netherlands had already established itself as one of Europe's greatest seafaring nations. The Dutch were accomplished shipbuilders, mapmakers and navigators, and had used their expertise to achieve a powerful position in European trade. The Low Countries were the birthplace of the atlas, the globe and the principles of triangulation, and many Dutch nautical terms found their way into the English language – yacht, schooner, jib, skipper, bow, boom, sloop, cruise, deck, wreck, blunderbuss. Located between the powerhouse economies of Britain and Germany, with a long seaboard at the crossroads of major trade routes, Dutch merchants made handsome profits ferrying goods like wine north from the Mediterranean and grain south from the Baltic. Waterborne traffic went not only past the Netherlands but through it, Dutch rivers and canals providing a convenient means of avoiding the stormy North Sea.

However, Dutch trading prowess was largely confined to Europe, and the country had effectively been a bystander of the great period of colonial expansion, preoccupied with the fight for its independence during the years when the Spanish, Portuguese and English laid claim to much of the world. The Portuguese in particular had established a formidable monopoly over the trade in East Asia, earning handsome profits from the import of spices such as pepper and nutmeg. When Dutch domestic strife eased, that began to change.

The Moses of Dutch Colonialism

Among the first Dutchmen to recognise the opportunities outside Europe was Jan Huyghen van Linschoten. Little known today, he was, perhaps more than anyone else, responsible for launching the Golden Age. Van Linschoten was born in 1563 in the Dutch city of Haarlem, near Amsterdam. At a young age he moved with his family to Enkhuizen, a small fishing town some fifty miles north of the capital. Watching local fishing boats unload their catches in the compact harbour, he nurtured dreams of escaping his modest roots and exploring the high seas, later writing of his yearning to 'see and travel into strange countries, thereby to seek some adventures'. When he was still in his early teens, van Linschoten followed an older brother to the Spanish city of Seville, where he spent four years before moving on to the Portuguese capital, Lisbon.

By the age of twenty he had become fluent in Portuguese and, on the strength of these language skills, managed in 1583 to get himself appointed as an assistant to the Catholic archbishop of Goa, a Portuguese colonial city on India's west coast. For a curious young man who dreamed of seeing the world, it was a perfect job. Goa was a major hub for the Portuguese empire in Asia and Africa, with thousands of merchants and seamen passing through the colony's port each year. As a trusted record-keeper for the influential archbishop, van Linschoten had access to reams of information about Portuguese activities, including reports from traders who had achieved huge profits trading in distant, mysterious countries such as Japan. He made careful copies of many of the papers that crossed his desk.

In 1587, disaster struck: the archbishop died suddenly during a trip home to Portugal. His powerful patron gone, van Linschoten had little choice but to leave Goa and return to Europe. However, his journey home was seriously interrupted when he was shipwrecked in the Azores, another Portuguese colony far out in the Atlantic. He ended up being stuck on the islands for two years. For anyone else being stranded in such a place might be something of an inconvenience, but the ever-resourceful van Linschoten soon turned the predicament to his advantage, studying closely the movements of Portuguese vessels heading to and from the Americas.

Eventually he made it home to the Netherlands, but did not rest for long, soon joining an expedition led by the famous explorer Willem Barentz in search of the fabled Northeast Passage offering a shortcut over the top of the globe to Asia. Curving around the northern edge of Scandinavia, the expedition reached the arctic archipelago of Novaya Zemlya, but was forced to turn back after finding its way blocked first by marauding polar bears and then by enormous icebergs. (A disastrous later expedition to the same area ended with Barentz dying, icebound, in the sea that would later bear his name.)

As a result of these exploits, van Linschoten was, by the time he reached his early thirties, an unusually well-travelled man. In 1595 he published a book, snappily titled *Reys-gheschrift vande Navigatien der Portugaloysers in Orienten* ('Travel Accounts of Portuguese Navigation in the Orient'), which drew on both the accounts of sailors, missionaries and

traders he had met, and on the papers he had copied while
working for the archbishop. Published at a time when relatively few Europeans had travelled outside the continent, the
wealth of detail in the book is astonishing. There are elaborate descriptions of Madagascar and Mozambique, Aden
and Arabia, Bengal, Burma and Borneo. As the historian Giles
Milton has related, the book is packed with colourful features
van Linschoten had either seen himself or heard about from
others, from the curious lifestyles of Hindus and Muslims,
Ethiopians and Jews to the elephants that could be found
roaming Burma and the Indian widows who burned themselves alive on their husbands' funeral pyres. The catalogue
of weird and wonderful sights sometimes strays towards fantasy, with descriptions of loose women, rats as large as pigs
and fish as big as dogs, but most of the material is remarkably
accurate. Eventually running to five bulky volumes, including
beautiful illustrations, this was one of the world's first great
travel books.

More importantly, the work was also a treasure trove of
practical advice for those seeking to expand trade in Asia. It
amounted to an encyclopaedia of Portuguese empire trade
routes, including detailed nautical maps, information about
the weather and tides, descriptions of the languages spoken
by merchants in different ports, and the types of goods available for trade. The book identified quicker sailing routes from
southern Africa to the East Indies, and explained the secret to
breaking the Portuguese hold on the narrow straits between
present-day Malaysia and Indonesia: by approaching from
the south, Dutch ships could sneak through unnoticed by
their rivals. The overall impression given by the book was of
a Portuguese empire that was highly lucrative but also ripe
for the taking.

Among Amsterdam's mercantile classes, van Linschoten's
book was a sensation. It became a bestseller and was translated into several languages. The book also had a real practical
impact, with merchants clamouring to prepare expeditions
following van Linschoten's advice. Almost single-handedly,

the young author spurred a burst of exploration that was to end the Portuguese monopoly on Asian trade and build the foundations of the Dutch empire. It was not for nothing that the historian E.M. Beekman later called him 'the Moses of Dutch colonialism'.

Old Spice

One of the first expeditions to draw on van Linschoten's findings departed the Netherlands in 1595. A convoy of four merchant ships set out from the North Sea island of Texel with the aim of reaching the Moluccas, an archipelago on the western side of present-day Indonesia that was famous as a source of hotly demanded spices like pepper and nutmeg. To lead the expedition, the investors who funded it chose Cornelis Houtman, a sailor from Gouda whose brother was a famous sea captain and who had lived in Portugal for several years. With the expedition in Houtman's capable hands, the merchants were confident of earning a handsome return.

Houtman, however, proved to be a disastrous leader. As Giles Milton has described, the convoy carried a copy of van Linschoten's book, but reportedly no other maps. Perhaps as a result, the four ships took a huge circular route to Asia, travelling first to the Cape Verde islands off West Africa, then south to the equator, across to Brazil, and then back towards Africa before heading for Asia. One ship sank, killing more than half of its crew, and a lack of provisions meant that many others died from scurvy. After months at sea, the expedition eventually reached the East Indies, only to discover that the local Malay traders they encountered found the goods the Dutch offered for trade – mostly cloth and blankets – unappealing, and were reluctant to do business.

Houtman's behaviour only made matters worse. A tactless and authoritarian leader, he had a brusque manner that insulted many of the island traders he should have been doing business with. He also treated his own sailors harshly. According to Milton, any sailor found causing a fight would have one hand nailed to the mast and the other tied behind his back, and be left there until he managed to tear himself free. Local traders who declined to do business with the Dutch were shown even less mercy. In the Indonesian trading city of Bantam, Houtman became enraged at the high price of the spices offered for sale and – according to Milton's translation of a sailor's diary – 'decided to do all possible harm to the town'. Cannons were fired and locals captured, tortured and murdered in an orgy of destruction. Moving on to the next town, the Dutch crew were cheered when a local prince rowed out to welcome them in a flotilla of ships, until Houtman ordered them to open fire with dozens of cannons. Almost all of the welcoming party were massacred, including the prince. 'I watched the attack not without pleasure,' said one Dutch sailor, 'but also with shame.'

Unsurprisingly, the Dutch crew became increasingly mutinous, and eventually forced Houtman to return to the Netherlands without ever reaching their destination. Arriving back in Amsterdam after more than two years away, the fleet made a sorry sight. Only three of the four vessels that originally left the Netherlands had made it home, and nearly two-thirds of the 240 expedition members had died. The merchants who financed the expedition, gathered on the Amsterdam quayside in expectation of a triumphant home-coming, watched the ships' arrival with a sense of impending doom. When the hatches were opened, the backers were hor-rified to see that most of the cargo consisted of the same silver they had loaded onto the ship roughly two years before.

There was nevertheless some good news. Despite its many catastrophic mistakes, the expedition had managed to procure a small quantity of spices, including nutmeg, and these were to prove its salvation. As Milton explains, demand for spices in Europe was high, thanks in part to widespread belief in their medicinal effects – cloves were said to cure earaches and pepper to alleviate colds. Some people were even convinced that saffron, if mixed with wine, could bring back the dead. Most popular of all was nutmeg, prescribed by physicians in late sixteenth-century Amsterdam as a remedy for upset stomachs and bad breath, and even as a cure for the plague. In Asia a pound of nutmeg cost the equivalent of an English penny or two, while in Europe it was so valuable that Samuel Pepys could write of swapping a small bag of nutmeg and cloves for a considerably larger bag of gold. Thanks to this disparity, even the small amount of nutmeg and other spices that Houtman's expedition brought back was enough to ensure that it turned a small profit. His backers were disappointed, but realised that larger cargoes could be hugely valuable.

Investors quickly assembled a second expedition. Needless to say, its leader was not Houtman but the rather more competent Jacob Corneliszoon van Neck, an experienced Amsterdam merchant. In 1598, seven ships left Texel for the East Indies. They were heavily armed in case of encounters with the Portuguese, but took a kinder approach to dealing with Asian traders than the previous expedition had, and were rewarded with considerably more success. Relying again on van Linschoten's book for advice, they reached the southern tip of Africa in excellent time. A storm divided three ships including van Neck's from the others, but after restocking their supplies in Madagascar they proceeded towards the 'Spice Islands' of today's Indonesia. Arriving roughly seven months after leaving the Netherlands, van Neck's men quickly managed to procure an enormous quantity of nutmeg and other spices before heading home.

When the second expedition arrived back in Amsterdam it made quite a splash. Dozens of small boats sailed out into the harbour to meet the returning ships and a huge crowd assembled on the quayside, eager to discover what riches van Neck had obtained. They were not disappointed. One observer famously recorded that 'as long as Holland has been Holland there have never arrived ships so richly laden as these'. With the promise of Eastern riches finally delivered, the city's merchants were ecstatic. Van Neck and his crew were given as much wine as they could drink and paraded through the city to the sound of trumpets and church bells ringing in celebration. For Van Neck himself, the celebrations ultimately proved rather short-lived, however: the gold cup he was rewarded with later turned out to be gold-plated.

The nutmeg, pepper, cloves and cinnamon proved so popular that the expedition's investors quadrupled their money. Other merchants quickly began organising their own expeditions, and the race to build Dutch trade links in Asia was on. By the beginning of the seventeenth century, the stage was set for the creation of a new global empire.

The Birth of an Empire

Leaving the underground galleries, I ascended a narrow modern staircase to the second floor of the Rijksmuseum. The Dutch King had refused to attend the institution's opening in the 1880s on the grounds that the sumptuous décor chosen by its Catholic architect made it seem more like an 'archbishop's palace' than a museum. Arriving upstairs, I thought he may have had a point. The modest stairway emerged into a cavernous hall that had stained-glass windows covering almost an entire wall, its floor tiled with thousands of fingernail-sized coloured tiles. On the walls hung dozens of large oil paintings of saints and sinners, and the lofty ceiling – painstakingly restored as part of the recent renovation – was decorated with scores of delicately painted green leaves and yellow flowers. The whole space was lit by circular constellations of LED lights as large as dining tables, hovering over the room like visiting spacecraft. Improbably, a Buddhist monk in orange robe and sandals stood near the top of the staircase, taking a close-up photograph of a coloured window with an iPhone. The contrast with the labyrinthine, crypt-like galleries I had seen downstairs was striking.

Following the signs on the walls I passed into an adjoining gallery, a large square room with a high ceiling and a window offering a view of the park behind the museum. Another sign near the doorway explained the theme of the room's contents: 'The Netherlands Overseas'. On the other side of the doorway, a lively oil painting by Hendrik Cornelisz Vroom depicted the triumphant return to Amsterdam in 1599 of van Neck's successful spice-trading expedition. It showed four immaculate ships bobbing in the teeming harbour, church spires jostling for attention with the hundreds of masts crowding the background. The hulls were gleaming in the sunlight, their rigging lined with agile crewmen and topped with colourful flags and ribbons as their cannons fired in celebration. In the choppy sea around the ships, dozens of small boats had come to greet their return, each packed to the gunwales with gentlemen in tall hats, trumpeters, and sailors drinking toasts.

Within a few years of van Neck's expedition, so many independent trading companies had sprung up that the Dutch authorities were concerned the country's early lead in the spice trade risked being squandered. Given the dangers of piracy, scurvy and shipwreck, international exploration was a risky business, and companies often survived only as long as a single expedition. Bitter competition between merchants in Amsterdam and Rotterdam kept driving spice prices down, and the establishment of Britain's own East India Company meant that competition was set to intensify. By the early 1600s, the government had decided that in order to retain the country's competitive advantage, the numerous Dutch companies trading in Asia would have to pool their resources. A meeting in The Hague set down strict conditions for the merger: a single company would be granted a 21-year monopoly on all Dutch trade east of the Cape of Good Hope in southern Africa. Anyone who resisted the takeover would not be allowed to trade, but the rewards for joining in were potentially enormous, with participating merchants earning a share of huge revenues while paying only negligible taxes. The new company's geographical focus would be reflected in its name: the *Vereenigde Oost-Indische Compagnie*, or Dutch East India Company.

Formally established in 1602, it quickly became known by its more easily pronounceable initials: the VOC. It was, according to modern business school textbooks, the world's first major joint-stock company and first multinational corporation. The Company even had what its modern equivalent might call an in-house thinktank or intelligence unit, collecting reams of information from outposts around the world and analysing it to produce new maps, charts and trading schedules. Given a free hand to fight wars, dispense justice, establish forts and agree treaties in the countries where it traded, the VOC was almost as powerful as a sovereign state. It even had the power to issue its own currency, decorated not with a head of state but with the company's nifty logo.

This logo was visible in a painting hanging opposite Vroom's picture of the returning ships in the Rijksmuseum. The picture, by Jeronimus Becx, was oval and about the size of a large dining plate. Painted in 1651, it depicted the company's coat of arms: a bearded Neptune standing with his trident opposite a busty mermaid with waist-length blonde hair, both of them knee deep in a layer of coloured seashells. Between them was a small picture of a ship, as well as an array of brass navigational instruments and weapons. And above that was the logo: an interlocking 'V', 'O' and 'C' of brilliant gold, the seventeenth-century equivalent of McDonald's golden arches.

Just a few weeks after the VOC was formed, the first ships set sail. The crews' orders were threefold: to buy prized spices, woods and silks in present-day Indonesia and Sri Lanka; to explore the coast of China; and to seize control of Spanish and Portuguese trading posts across the East Indies. The early expeditions were successful on all counts. Within a few years of its creation, the VOC had eclipsed the Portuguese and other rivals in the East Indies, forcing them to surrender trading stations with ruthless efficiency. Rivals were not treated kindly: the East India Company briefly gave the Dutch a run for their money in the Spice Islands, but capitulated after the Dutch massacred ten Englishmen they were holding hostage in Ambon. Giles Milton reports one unlucky trader's account of being stripped naked by Dutch sailors in Indonesia, who cut his flesh open and then rubbed it with lemon and vinegar.

The Dutch, for their part, were also not always received warmly by the locals they visited – one skipper arriving in Australia reported one of his sailors being torn limb from limb, and nine of his colleagues killed with a variety of arrows and spears or clubbed to death with oars.

Other exhibits in the Rijksmuseum testified to the growing reach of the company. Above the VOC coat of arms, a set of three large paintings offered aerial views of different Dutch colonies: in India, in China and in Indonesia. Attributed to Johannes Vinckboons, each showed lush green islands populated by star-shaped military forts and neat spice plantations, ships offshore vying for space with oversized fish and other fantastical sea creatures, like treasure island maps from a fantasy board game. A pair of tipsy thirtysomethings stumbled briefly to a halt in front of the picture and paused just long enough for one of them to pronounce it '*erg fucking cool*', 'very f**king cool'.

While the VOC thrived, Dutch traders and explorers laid claim to lands covering an enormous area of the globe. In 1619 the Company captured Jakarta, renaming it Batavia. The base they built there would form the keystone of Dutch control over Indonesia for more than 300 years. Efforts to infiltrate China were less successful, but the VOC established a lucrative trading post in present-day Taiwan, and built a lucrative opium trade in India. In Japan the Dutch set up a trading post on the island of Dejima, which would remain Japan's only window on the western world for roughly 200 years. Further south, in 1606, a Dutchman called Willem Janszoon became the first European ever to set foot on Australian soil. Encountering the first Aborigine ever to encounter a white man, he promptly shot him dead. Dutchmen who followed Janszoon to Australia were largely unimpressed by his discovery, complaining that the barren landscape was 'inhabited by savages' and surrounded by fish that were 'unnatural monsters'. Nevertheless, they were swift to claim as much land they could, and within a few years the whole country was known to the world as 'New Holland'.

Further east, the Dutchman Abel Tasman became the first European explorer to reach New Zealand, his homesick crew naming it after their home in the southern Dutch province of Zeeland. Another island they discovered was christened in honour of their captain: Tasmania. In need of a staging post for ships on their way to Asia, the Dutch also established the Cape Colony settlement that would later become South Africa, a country speaking an adapted version of Dutch and planted with acres of vineyards to help combat sailors' scurvy. In Mauritius – named for the Dutch Prince Maurits – sailors entertained themselves riding bareback on giant turtles; in what is now Sri Lanka, they made enemies of local Hindus by butchering and eating sacred cows.

With the promise of such adventures, it was little surprise that Dutchmen clamoured to join the payroll of what they commonly referred to as 'Jan Company'. According to a count ordered by the VOC's directors in the 1680s, in Asia alone the Company had more than 11,000 employees on land, as well as around 4000 sailors. Many were Dutch, but a large proportion were recruited from elsewhere in Europe: England, Germany, Poland and Scandinavia. Some of these men shared in the Company's success, but many were less fortunate – around two-thirds of those who went to sea would never return home. VOC ships were deeply unpleasant places: freezing cold in winter and stiflingly hot in summer, infested with vermin and rife with yellow fever, malaria, typhus and dysentery. Sailors slept, worked and ate in tiny spaces stinking of vomit and urine, with little to eat other than dry biscuits and tough salted meat.

As news of these conditions spread, it unsurprisingly became harder to recruit enough men to fill the ships. VOC representatives toured Amsterdam's orphanages and workhouses looking for recruits, promising great riches that would rarely be delivered. As the historian Geert Mak recorded, the VOC sometimes even relied on 'soul sellers' for recruitment in Amsterdam, unscrupulous agents who provided room and board for unemployed men, only to sign them up as involuntary crew members when the Company came calling.

At War with the English

By the middle of the seventeenth century, the VOC had grown to dominate seagoing trade across much of Asia, effectively controlling an empire on which the sun never set. For a while the Dutch fleet was bigger than the English and French fleets combined, and the Netherlands imported more from Asia than did Portugal, France, England, Denmark and Sweden combined.

The rapid growth of the Netherlands' trading links naturally concerned its rivals, including the English. Like the Dutch, the English had arrived late at the empire-building game, for many years only watching with envy as the Portuguese constructed a lucrative global trading network. Under Queen Elizabeth I, however, the English began building a serious naval force. At first the Dutch and English were allies. In 1585, Elizabeth signed the Treaty of Nonsuch with the United Provinces of the Netherlands, the two countries agreeing to unite against Spanish attempts to cement the Catholic dominance of northern Europe. English sea captains such as Francis Drake did a fine trade in capturing Spanish loot.

As Dutch sea power grew, however, relations between the Dutch and English became increasingly strained. In the seventeenth century, King Charles I signed a series of treaties that had the effect of gradually switching sides, so the English were aligned with Spain against the Dutch. During and after the English Civil Wars, leaders including Oliver Cromwell continued to invest heavily in building up the English navy, and became increasingly keen to challenge Dutch dominance of the seas. In 1651, the devoutly Calvinist Cromwell even attempted a barely disguised takeover of the Netherlands, sending a delegation to The Hague that offered the Dutch the chance to join the English Commonwealth. Rebuffed by the Dutch, the English attitude hardened, and English ships began regularly hassling Dutch fleets in the North Sea, claiming they had the right to seize whatever they wanted under laws banning foreign ships from importing goods to England.

The year after Cromwell's failed Dutch takeover, war broke out, the first of a series of four conflicts between England and the nascent Dutch Republic during the seventeenth and eighteenth centuries, which later became known as the Anglo-Dutch Wars. The first conflict consisted of a run of marvellously named scuffles at sea – the Battle of the Kentish Knock, the Battle of Dungeness, the Battle of Leghorn, the Battle of the Gabbard – in which both sides won some battles but neither managed to win the war. A peace treaty was eventually agreed in 1654, but the rivalry between the two nations had not been laid to rest, and they continued to jostle for control of the seas that divided them.

Within a decade or so of the peace treaty being signed, war had broken out again. England won an early victory off the coast of Lowestoft, but in this second Anglo-Dutch war the Dutch generally had the upper hand. The conflict was later best remembered for the embarrassing defeat of the English at the 1667 Raid on the Medway, in which a flotilla of Dutch ships sailed up the Thames, smashed through the chains that were meant to blockade the river, and burned much of the English fleet moored at Chatham. Coming within a few years of the Great Fire of London (which many English suspected the Dutch of igniting), the Medway raid was traumatic for the English, and panicking Londoners made plans to flee the city when rumours spread that full-scale invasion was imminent. London diarist Samuel Pepys wrote: 'All our hearts do now ache; for the news is true, that the Dutch have broken the chain and burned our ships... and, the truth is, I do fear so much that the whole kingdom is undone.'

Ultimately, fears of a Dutch invasion proved ill-founded. Having wreaked havoc in small towns along the Thames, the Dutch eventually withdrew, but not before sinking almost every ship they could find and taking with them the pride of the English fleet, the *Royal Charles*. Their navy in tatters, the English had little option but to accept defeat. 'In all things, in wisdom, courage, force, knowledge of our own streams, and success, the Dutch have the best of us,' wrote Pepys, 'and do end the war with victory on their side.' The Dutch remembered the war rather more fondly, and the admiral who humiliated the English, Michel de Ruyter, became an enduring national hero.

Five years after the Raid on the Medway, the conflict ignited yet again. Like a playground bully ganging up with others, the English had secured an important ally this time – the French. In 1672, Louis XIV of France invaded the Dutch Republic with support from the English navy. The French quickly seized control of much of the country, but the tables turned when the Dutch opened dikes around Amsterdam, flooding a huge area of land to create a 'Water Line' blocking the path of the invaders. The Dutch navy, meanwhile, fought fiercely to hold off the English ships that were attempting to attack from the sea. Further afield, the Dutch even managed to seize New York City briefly from the English, renaming it 'New Orange'. A peace treaty returned it to English hands, and to its previous name, in 1674. After three wars in a little over twenty years, the English and the Dutch would remain at peace for another century.

Go West

Moving on from the paintings of India and Indonesia, I passed into another gallery, and another hemisphere. A small square room with a high ceiling contained a series of small paintings by Frans Jan Post, all landscapes of sugar plantations controlled by the Dutch in Brazil. Commissioned by the Dutch authorities in the mid-seventeenth century, they depicted idyllic tropical scenes. Neat colonial bungalows were held in the gentle embrace of wide curving rivers; a ruined cathedral crumbled amid exotic wildlife, including an armadillo, an anteater and a monkey dozing in the sunshine.

These South American scenes demonstrated how, as trade in the East flourished, the Dutch turned their attention westward. Some traders had grown frustrated with the monopoly exercised by the VOC and now sought to circumvent it, by creating new trade routes offering access to Asia from the opposite direction. Other motivations also came into play: the Spanish empire had been busily getting fat on South American silver and gold, and the Dutch were keen to seize a piece of the action. A European fashion for furs and an increasing demand for salt to cure fish also offered lucrative opportunities for imports from North America.

In 1621, the *Geoctroyeerde Westindische Compagnie*, or Chartered West India Company, was established. Modelled closely on its eastern counterpart, the WIC (as it is usually referred to in English) aimed to replicate the VOC's successes in the Americas. Like the VOC, it had the power to establish colonies, build fortresses, sign peace treaties and attack European rivals. Compared to its predecessor, the WIC's successes were rather limited – the new Company quickly became embroiled in battles against the Spanish and Portuguese and it struggled to turn a profit. It did, however, succeed in expanding the Dutch sphere of influence in the western hemisphere, establishing Dutch trading posts in Curaçao, Aruba and Sint Maarten, Suriname, Brazil and Guyana. The Netherlands would remain a significant colonial power in the Caribbean for centuries to come.

Perhaps the most notable Dutch outpost in the Americas was founded in 1609. The explorer Henry Hudson, an Englishman working for the Dutch, had been searching for the fabled Northwest Passage to Asia when his ship, *De Halve Maan* ('The Half Moon'), landed on the east coast of North America. Hudson's weary part-English, part-Dutch crew thought they had arrived in paradise. 'The meadows are rich with grass and flowers and trees and lovely fragrances are wafted around,' wrote one, while another focused on the 'beautiful rivers, bubbling fountains flowing into the valleys... [and] agreeable fruits in the woods'. 'There is considerable fish in the rivers, good tillage land,' he wrote, and little to fear from the 'naked natives of the country'. Just as important as the attractive water features were the beavers who lived there: beaver pelts were highly prized in Europe as a material for making waterproof hats, and juices from the animals' anal glands were thought to create a fine perfume. Building a base at the mouth of a river named after Henry Hudson, Dutch traders soon developed a profitable trade exchanging European goods with beaver pelts from local tribes.

In 1624, the threat of attack from other European powers encouraged the Dutch to establish a more permanent colony and a fort – later known as New Amsterdam – was constructed to protect the mouth of the river Hudson. Land surrounding the fort was purchased from the local Lenape tribe for what legend records as the equivalent of $24 in trinkets and beads. Over the next few decades the new colony flourished, until the Dutch ill-advisedly swapped it with the English for the Caribbean outpost of Suriname in 1667. Its new owners promptly gave it a new name: New York.

Eleven years after Henry Hudson's arrival in North America, another set of travellers also crossed the Atlantic. The Pilgrims, a group of religious radicals who were pressing for reform of the Church of England, had been persecuted in England for their beliefs. In 1608 they fled, and like many other religious minorities found safe haven in the Dutch city of Leiden. However, they didn't like their new home much either, with John Robinson and William Brewster complaining that the Netherlands was 'a strange and hard land'. In 1620 they moved on, travelling by canal from Leiden to the port of Delfshaven in Rotterdam, where they allegedly spent the night in the church on the quayside.

On 22 July, the Pilgrims sailed in a stubby little ship called the *Speedwell* to Southampton, where they switched to a ship with a more famous name: the *Mayflower*. Two months later, 102 travellers arrived at Plymouth Rock in present-day Massachusetts. Anchored offshore, they drafted a document they called the Mayflower Compact, setting out basic principles of democracy and equality, based on ideas they had heard discussed in the Netherlands. The Plymouth Rock colony would go on to be celebrated as the birthplace of the United States, and the ideas the Pilgrims had ferried from Leiden, together with the documents the Dutch had published declaring their independence from Spain, eventually helped inspire the Declaration of Independence. When future President John Adams later visited the Netherlands to raise funds for the American Revolution, he was struck by the influence Dutch culture had had on his home country. 'One nation is a copy of the other,' he said.

The Gallery of Honour

At the Rijksmuseum, I ducked back through the overseas gallery and into another room leading off it, a smaller square space with charcoal-coloured walls and an arched glass ceiling. There was a long cushioned bench in the centre and a security guard was shaking awake a young man who had fallen asleep stretched along it, using his own battered skateboard shoes as a pillow. The room was largely empty, but a group of perhaps half a dozen people were clustered against one wall, examining closely a painting I recognised from posters and postcards. It was a delightful winter landscape by Hendrick Avercamp, the mute painter famous for his early seventeenth-century depictions of skaters on frozen lakes and rivers. Compared to many landscapes of the time, Avercamp's work was colourful and lively, and crammed with detail. Four not entirely sober young women in cocktail dresses had gathered in front of *Winterlandschap met schaatsers* ('Winter landscape with skaters') and were playing a high-brow form of 'Where's Wally?', racing to spot humorous details hidden in the picture – the couple kissing on the ice, men skating in baggy trousers, the dog gnawing at the corpse of a frozen horse, the man watching his hat slide away after falling face first on the frozen river. A grey-haired woman in a floral dress peered closely at the lefthand side of the painting, where a bare backside was visible poking out of a cracked toilet door.

Museumnacht had attracted a curious mixture of visitors, divided between well-educated middle-aged couples for whom the event was an opportunity to compare and contrast van Goghs over a decent glass of Merlot, and young hipsters for whom it was an opportunity to hit on the maximum number of potential partners in the minimum amount of time. As the evening progressed I could sense the balance tipping in favour of the latter group, with older art-lovers bowing out and the youngsters becoming drunker. While the party in the atrium downstairs grew louder, the galleries upstairs got quieter. A minute passed and I was left almost alone with the Avercamp, accompanied only by a tall young man with a polar explorer's beard and a black sweatshirt emblazoned 'TOO DUMB FOR NEW YORK, TOO UGLY FOR AMSTERDAM'. He had his flies undone; I wasn't sure whether it was by accident or was a new fashion I hadn't heard of yet. We stared silently at the painting together for a few seconds, and then wordlessly went our separate ways.

I retraced my steps to the cathedral-like hall at the top of the staircase and passed through a pair of high wooden doors into the most famous and popular part of the Rijksmuseum. The *Eregalerij*, or 'Gallery of Honour', was another cavernous space, a long, nave-like hall that stretched into the distance, lined on both sides with deep alcoves in which the artworks were displayed. The high arched ceiling was painted with green leaves and red stars, giving the room a gothic flavour that made me feel once again that I could be in a cathedral rather than a museum. Even a cursory glance at the walls revealed how the gallery had got its self-promoting name: a dusky self-portrait of a rumpled Rembrandt here, Vermeer's homely milkmaid with her breadbasket over there. Stormy grey walls drew the eye to rich still lifes of fruit and cheese, lively portraits by Frans Hals, sweeping landscapes by Jacob van Ruisdael and bawdy domestic scenes by Jan Steen. Amid such competition, an alcove of priceless Vermeers went all but unnoticed by the dozen or so visitors ambling through the chamber. 'Everybody loves Vermeer, except me,' Francis Bacon once said.

The works displayed here represented the epitome of the Dutch Golden Age. As the VOC and WIC helped make Dutch merchants rich, artists in turn benefited from the patronage of those who – in keeping with their Calvinist faith – believed that wealth should be used to support meaningful cultural pursuits. Keen to keep their customers happy, the artists often focused on themes reflecting the sources of their wealth: the sea, the windmills and the fertile farmland. Newly affluent merchants were also keen to document their own successes, commissioning self-portraits that kick-started the careers of portraitists such as Hals and Rembrandt. Nevertheless, owner-ship of fine art was not restricted to the wealthy. Visitors from other countries often expressed amazement that even sim-ple farmers in the Netherlands owned beautiful works of art. As a result of this varied market, Dutch painters produced high-quality works covering an unusually wide range of genres, from portraits to landscapes to still lifes.

An Inventory of the Possible

Of course, Amsterdam's flourishing mercantile classes did not invest only in art. Trade also financed the construction of the concentric canals encircling the city. Each of these was given a name indicative of the class of resident it hoped to attract: the Gentleman's Canal (*Herengracht*), the Prince's Canal (*Prinsengracht*), the Emperor's Canal (*Keizersgracht*). A northern Venice was born, albeit with colder weather and worse food. Along the canals, handsome townhouses were built in classical or neo-Renaissance style, complete with orna-mented façades, large windows and high-ceilinged rooms for entertaining guests. The houses were taxed according to their width at the front, so a unique shape of building evolved: narrow fronted but very tall and surprisingly deep, often with a sizable garden hidden Tardis-like at the back. Many included what the Dutch called *doorzonwoningen*, individual rooms running the whole length of the house, so that sunlight could shine all the way through from the windows at either end. Steep staircases saved valuable space inside, with elaborate systems of ropes and pulleys enabling front doors to be opened from upstairs by tugging on a loose end. Building smaller rooms on the upper floors than on the lower ones helped enhance the sense of perspective when one looked up from the street, exaggerating the height of the buildings. Gabled rooves were topped with flagpole holders pointing out like fingers, together with cranes and pulleys for lifting in furniture that would not fit through the narrow interior staircases.

Majestic churches also appeared throughout the city, together with ornate civic buildings like the grand Town Hall on Dam Square, complete with its sculpture of a Dutch Atlas carrying the world on his back. Keen to protect his beautiful city from accidental damage, Herengracht resident Jan van der Heyden developed one of the world's first fire engines.

Amsterdam grew quickly to become – after London and Paris – the third largest city in Europe, a magnet for the innovative and audacious. For the time the Dutch capital was strikingly cosmopolitan. Signs at the harbour announced the destinations of ships leaving for ports all over the world, and the surrounding streets thronged with Germans, English, French, Spaniards, Norwegians, Poles and Turks. Wharves and marketplaces were a riot of colour and noise, with live armadillos and elephants jostling for space among exotic spices, woods, fabrics, fruits and vegetables.

Visitors from other countries were astonished. After touring a Dutch trading ship, Samuel Pepys wrote in his famous diary of having seen 'the greatest wealth in confusion that a man can see in the world'. Daniel Defoe, the author of *Robinson Crusoe*, described the Dutch as 'the carryers of the world, the middle persons in trade, the factors and brokers of Europe'. Moving to live in Amsterdam, the French philosopher René

Descartes reputedly called the city 'an inventory of the possible', marvelling at the 'ships arriving laden with all the produce of the Indies and all the curiosities of Europe'. 'Where else in the world,' he asked, 'could one choose a place where all life's commodities and all the curiosities one could wish for are as easy to find as here?'

New industries sprang up to process the exotic imports: sugar refining, pearl polishing, tobacco processing, wool washing and diamond cutting. The country was enveloped in a brief craze for blue-and-white porcelain imported from China (used as a prop in many Golden Age paintings), until imitators in Delft mastered the technology and began to sell their superior knock-offs back to the Chinese. Imports also introduced new variety to Dutch diets, although some people might argue that the local cuisine failed to develop much in subsequent centuries. As the historian Simon Schama has written, one French visitor was amazed to see common workers and fishermen in the Netherlands eating fresh meat, vegetables, fruit, eggs and cheese. Another English traveller reported that salmon was so readily available that servants used to beg their masters not to be given it more than twice a week.

Within a few years, tea and coffee had also become major imports, replacing the old favourite of warm beer with nutmeg and sugar, particularly after doctors Nicholas Tulp and Cornelius Bontekoe recommended tea as a treatment for almost every illness. Charles Dickens wrote that Bontekoe 'thought two hundred cups daily not too much even for a moderate drinker', also noting snidely that 'The Dutch East India Company is said to have made it worth his while to uphold this opinion'. Bontekoe may, however, have overdone it: another observer reported later that his prodigious consumption of tea had so affected his joints that they 'rattled like castanets'.

Opportunities for investment abounded. New windmill pumping technology enabled vast tracts of valuable farmland to be drained outside the city, while wind-powered sawmills facilitated the construction of yet more of the ships needed to increase trade. Peat provided a cheap energy source, while the establishment in Amsterdam of a commodity exchange, public exchange bank and lending bank drew capital from across the continent. The city produced financial innovations such as the direct bank transfer, and the Dutch guilder was, for a time, the dollar of its day, a currency accepted by traders around the world. Dutch traders were even credited with inventing the art of short-selling, the type of high-risk stock market speculation that would later be blamed for helping crash stock markets worldwide. Early Dutch speculation led inevitably to excesses, most famously a 1637 bubble in the price of tulips, which saw prices rise more than twentyfold in just one month, with a single onion-sized bulb costing roughly the same as a decent family home. When the price collapsed, thousands of people who had been hugely rich on paper were suddenly ruined.

The progress the country had made was nevertheless astounding. 'In the conversations of wise men,' Englishman William Aglionby famously wrote, 'almost no topic features so frequently as the wondrous ascent of this small state, which has risen within no more than a hundred years, to a height which does not only infinitely exceed the standing of all the old Greek republics, but in some ways is not even shamed by the great monarchies of our time.'

As Amsterdam thrived, it became a magnet for not only the entrepreneurial but also the persecuted. Just as later generations of Afghans and Iranians would flock to New York or London, persecuted minorities such as Sephardic Jews and French Huguenots fled to Amsterdam from France, Spain and Portugal. Swelled further by the ranks of Dutch farmers moving to the city in search of wealth, the population more than tripled between the 1580s and 1620s. The arrivals included prominent scientists and thinkers such as Baruch de Spinoza, a philosopher whose parents had fled from Portugal to Amsterdam, and the French philosopher Pierre Bayle, who immigrated to Rotterdam. It was in Amsterdam that Descartes published his *Discourse on the Method of Rightly Conducting One's Reason and of Seeking Truth in Sciences* (in which he wrote 'I think therefore I am'). 'In what other country could you find such complete freedom,' he asked, 'or sleep with less anxiety?' Thomas Hobbes had his books printed in the Netherlands and Voltaire visited seven times, even setting part of his famous novel *Candide* in Amsterdam. The Dutch scholar Hugo Grotius established many of the basic principles of international law, including that of 'Freedom of the Seas', while the philosopher John Locke did some of his best work in Amsterdam. The latter's diary praised the Dutch for their cheap bookshops, but complained bitterly about 'the hardest winter in the memory of man' and recommended warming up with hot tea mixed with eggs and sugar. The University of Leiden, established by William of Orange as a sign of his gratitude for the city's support in the struggle for Dutch independence from Spain, became one of the finest in Europe. When Galileo's claims that the sun rather than the earth lay at the centre of the solar system were banned by the Catholic Church, it was in Leiden that he was able to publish them. As Bertrand Russell wrote in his magisterial history of philosophy: 'It is impossible to exaggerate the importance of Holland in the seventeenth century.'

Amsterdam residents also made discoveries with important practical implications. Christiaan Huygens invented the pendulum clock and discovered the rings around Saturn. In 1673, Antonie van Leeuwenhoek ground his own magnifying lenses and peered through them at pond water, seeing microscopic life forms that he called 'animalcules', later considered the first ever description of bacteria. The Dutchman Cornelius Drebbel even invented the world's first navigable submarine, demonstrating its safety by taking England's King James on an underwater tour of the Thames. Empire building and scientific discovery were two sides of the same coin, both aimed at stretching the boundaries of the known world.

Rembrandt's 'Spectacular Failure'

If the Rijksmuseum was a cathedral, its undisputed altar was at the rear of the Gallery of Honour. In a large annexe with a high glass ceiling sat the star attraction around which the whole museum was said to have been designed: Rembrandt's *The Company of Captain Frans Banning Cocq and Lieutenant Willem van Ruytenburch*, better known by its nickname, 'The Night Watch'. Walking through the long gallery towards the painting and seeing it suspended amid golden statues and marble pillars, I almost felt I should drop to my knees and pray.

Rembrandt's colossal group portrait of a group of Amsterdam civic militiamen was considered revolutionary not just for its size – roughly four metres across – but for its use of light and shade, and because it depicted its subjects actually doing something interesting rather than merely sitting and posing. Surrounded by men loading rifles and beating drums, the bearded leader in black gesturing towards the viewer managed to be both dynamic and brooding. The painting was certainly popular: although the other galleries were emptying fast, half-drunk hipsters had still traipsed their way upstairs in order to upload photos of themselves posing with the musket-wielding militiamen. When Barack Obama visited a few months later, he did much the same thing.

Ironically, the painting suffered from a persistent myth that it had been a flop, received poorly by the customer who had commissioned it, although scholars have debunked this. 'See Night Watch,' said a 1967 advert for the Dutch national airline, 'Rembrandt's spectacular failure.' The painting was not universally loved – velvety ropes now kept the public well back from the canvas after incidents when it was slashed with a bread knife and sprayed with acid. However, perhaps the greatest vandalism of all had been at the hands of its curators, who once cut large strips off it in order to display it between two pillars in Amsterdam's city hall.

The painting's popular name was also rather misleading. For many years the picture was so darkened by layers
of dirt and varnish that it was widely believed to be a night
scene, but restoration in the 1940s revealed that the artist had
included bright beams of golden light to highlight the main
features, including a young girl in the foreground wearing
an eye-catching yellow dress. A poem written by John Eisum
in 1700 summarised well Rembrandt's smudgy, smoky style:
'Rembrandt! Thy pencil plays a subtle part,/ This Roughness
is contriv'd to hide thy Art.'

The Dark Side of Empire

Turning my back on the guns of the 'Night Watch', I went
in search of something rather less honourable, an aspect of
the Golden Age I had read about but seldom heard mentioned in the Netherlands. After searching several adjoining
galleries, I found what I had been looking for, high on the
walls of the mosaicked hallway leading to the Royal Gallery.
Hidden in a gloomy archway above the level of the chandeliers was a small painting of a virginal figure in a blue robe
and white headdress. To her right stood a large, pelican-like
white bird with two younger birds at its feet; and to her left
was a winged angel with curly golden hair, one of his legs
raised, gazing intently at the woman in the centre. At each
breast she nursed an infant child, one of them black and the
other white. A printed caption explained that the black child
clutching hungrily at her breast 'personified the protection of
the overseas colonies'.

The picture probably goes unnoticed by almost everyone
who traipses past it on their way to the 'Night Watch', but it
points to an important fact about the Golden Age that is rarely
acknowledged: the Rijksmuseum's treasures, together with
Amsterdam's beautiful canals and townhouses, were paid for
in part with the blood and sweat of those who were unfortunate enough to live under Dutch rule overseas. Walking
around tolerant, easy-going Amsterdam, most visitors remain

unaware of a national dirty secret: the Netherlands was one of the world's leading slave-trading nations.

Despite their early dominance of many aspects of European trade, when it came to slavery the Dutch were late starters. The beginning of the slave trade in Europe is generally put at some time in the 1440s, when the Portuguese began ferrying captives from northern Africa across the Mediterranean. Within a century the trade had spread across the Atlantic, again led by the Portuguese – thanks partly to a blessing from the Pope, who confirmed their right to enslave 'Saracens, pagans and any other unbelievers'. The Dutch, however, seem to have lacked the appetite for trading in human cargo. Some Dutch sea captains did trade slaves when the opportunity arose – Captain John Smith's famous history of the first permanent European settlement in North America recorded that in 1619, 'About the last of August came a Dutch man of Warre that sold us twenty negars.' However, the ever-sensible Dutch generally frowned on the idea of profiting from the export of people. In 1615, the Dutch poet G.A. Berderoo captured the prevailing mood when he condemned the practice of selling people into 'horselike slavery', damning it as 'inhumane custom! Godless rascality!' In 1596, the Rotterdam skipper Pieter van der Haagen brought more than a hundred African slaves to the southern port of Middelburg, and according to the historian Johannes Postma sparked a lengthy debate at the town council, which eventually concluded that no slave trading would be permitted there and that all the slaves should be set free. A natural opportunity to take up the trade arose when the transatlantic WIC was formed in 1621, but after consulting religious scholars the Company's directors decided that to do so would be immoral.

Over time, the profits the Portuguese were making from the slave trade became difficult for the Dutch to ignore. A decade or so after the WIC's decision, the company reversed course and took the trade up with gusto. One reason for this change of heart was the growth of the new Dutch colonies in South America and the Caribbean. Dutch plantations in places like Suriname were soon satisfying much of Europe's demand for sugar, a crop that was hugely labour intensive to harvest. It became apparent that if the plantations were to be profitable, large numbers of workers would have to be imported, against their will if necessary. Postma records that the governor of the Dutch colony in northern Brazil told his superiors: 'it is not possible to accomplish anything in Brazil without slaves.'

In 1637, a Dutch fleet sailed to Ghana and snatched the slave-trading castle of Elmina from the Portuguese. Within a little over a decade, the Dutch had built or captured a string of fortified slave stations along the hook of western Africa, matched with similar transit points on the opposite side of the Atlantic. Once the necessary infrastructure was in place, major slave trading could begin. According to the historian J. W. Schulte Nordholt, within twelve years the Dutch had transported over 23,000 slaves from Elmina and Luanda alone. Another source estimated that within a decade, some 25,000 slaves were shipped in irons from Africa to Brazil. The Dutch became significant players in the famous 'triangular trade', whereby guns, ammunition and other factory-produced goods travelled from Europe to Africa; slaves were carried from Africa to the Americas; and slave-produced goods such as sugar, tobacco and rum were sent from the Americas back to Europe. To a nation of traders, black Africans had become simply another commodity to be bought and sold. Amsterdam, in the words of the historian Richard Oluseyi Asaolu, was 'the European capital of slavery'.

The Dutch claimed they treated their slaves well, but of course this was all relative. Slave cargoes included many babies and children, and starvation and disease meant that death rates were high. Both on board the ships and in the plantations, suicides and hunger strikes were common. It was not unheard of for disobedient slaves to be burned alive; records told of one slave dying after his testicles were bitten off. When the Dutch slave ship *De Leusden* began to sink off the coast of Suriname in 1738, the crew nailed the hatches shut before escaping, leaving more than 600 slaves to drown. Slaves who did survive the long Atlantic crossing had yet more to fear from the inhuman conditions in Caribbean sugar-processing mills, where naked slaves were beaten severely and suffered terrible burns while being forced to stir vats of boiling syrup. Europe's sweet tooth was fed at a very heavy price.

Late to take up slaving, the Dutch were also late to give it up. Almost a century after the abolitionist William Wilberforce vowed to end slavery, and decades after the parliament in London abolished the slave trade on British ships, the Dutch were still going strong. The British officially abolished slavery in 1833, France a few years later. The Netherlands did not do so in its main slaving colony, Suriname, until 1863, and even then the ban was not fully implemented for another decade. As Postma wrote, with typical Dutch understatement, while the seventeenth- and eighteenth-century Netherlands is generally remembered as an incubator for the arts, 'for some half a million unfortunate Africans who were transported across the Atlantic, the Dutch must have been remembered in a more negative way'.

In the UK, discussion of the British Empire in books, in schools or on television often retained a jingoistic flavour, but also generally acknowledged the negative consequences of empire and the heavy price paid by the inhabitants of many British colonies. When the Dutch slave trade ended, it was quickly forgotten and the darker side of the Golden Age was rarely acknowledged. The horror stories were, perhaps, too much of a challenge to the national self-image of the Dutch as a kind, tolerant, liberal people. According to a survey by the American sociologist Melissa Weiner, less than a quarter of Dutch school history textbooks mention slavery in the country's overseas colonies, and even those that do usually focus on the hardships endured by Dutch colonists rather than the suffering of the slaves. There are notable exceptions, including the admirable National Institute for Study of Dutch Slavery and Its Legacy, but I found it difficult not to read something into the fact that while London's monument to slavery was situated in the very heart of the city, a few metres from the Houses of Parliament, Amsterdam's sat largely unnoticed in a park outside the city's historic centre. On formal state occasions, the Dutch King and Queen still rode in a golden carriage whose sides were decorated with paintings of shirtless black slaves bowing at the feet of angelic white colonisers.

Empire's End

The decline of the Dutch slave trade was mirrored by the decline of the nation's trading empire in general. For tourists the delights of the Rijksmuseum's Royal Gallery epitomised the Dutch Golden Age, but by the time Rembrandt was buried in an unmarked grave in Amsterdam in 1669, the country's status as a global power was already fading.

The reasons for the Dutch decline were complex, but included the fact that the monopolies on trade enjoyed by the two great trading companies were actually not always profitable. Large fleets and numerous forts and trading posts were hugely expensive to maintain, and as the VOC and WIC expanded they began to prove Benjamin Franklin's dictum that great empires, like great cakes, tend to crumble at their edges. As spices such as nutmeg declined in popularity and competition from other European powers increased, merchants' profit margins grew ever thinner.

England also played a significant role in the Company's decline. Following the three previous Anglo-Dutch Wars, a fourth conflict broke out in 1780, after the English discovered that the Dutch had secretly been supporting the rebels who were fighting for independence in the American Revolution. The Dutch colonies in the Caribbean, in particular, were doing a roaring trade with the rebels just as the English were trying to starve them out. Ironically, the only real fighting of the war took place off Dogger Bank, the vast sandbank that was the last remaining relic of the land bridge once linking England and the Netherlands. That skirmish was won by the Dutch, but they proved unable to rally enough of a naval force to build on their victory, and the English launched fierce attacks against Dutch colonies around the world. In 1784 the Dutch were forced to admit defeat – a humiliating move that was later seen as the beginning of the end of their time as a major world power.

Buffeted by such geopolitical currents, the two great Dutch trading companies became trapped in a downward spiral. The VOC struggled to service its large debts and unwisely cut spending on essential areas like mapmaking. By the late 1700s the WIC had gone bankrupt and the VOC was struggling to stay afloat, eventually going bust in 1798. It was disbanded a few years later, an ignoble end for a once mighty institution.

With the VOC gone, the Dutch crown assumed responsibility for all its overseas possessions and debts, including the colony of present-day Indonesia. It would cling to them for nearly another 150 years. The story of Dutch decolonisation is too long to recount here, but suffice to say it was not an edifying spectacle. Colonial power had routinely been abused in places like Java and Sumatra, and many of the local inhabitants lived in abject poverty. In the mid-nineteenth century the Dutch writer Multatuli wrote a famous book about the corrupt administration of the Dutch colonies, *Max Havelaar*, one of the first publications to advocate what later became known as 'fair trade'. The ensuing publicity shamed the government into adopting a more ethical policy, but did little to address the underlying injustices.

During the Second World War, the East Indies were occupied by the Japanese. When that conflict ended, nationalists seized the opportunity to issue a declaration stating: 'We, the people of Indonesia, hereby declare the independence of Indonesia. Matters relating to the transfer of power etc will be in a conscientious manner and as speedily as possible.' The 'etc' ended up taking another four years, including bloody fighting between the Dutch army and local rebels. There were some terrible acts of repression by the Dutch, who initially refused to let go of the jewel in their colonial crown. International pressure finally forced their hand when the United Nations Security Council intervened and the Americans threatened to cut off post-war financial aid to the Netherlands. In 1949 the Dutch reluctantly agreed to transfer sovereignty and a few days after Christmas the Indonesians celebrated their independence. With the exception of a handful of small islands in the Caribbean, the Dutch Empire was no more.

Imperial Echoes

Some three centuries after the Dutch Golden Age drew to a close, its physical legacy was clear to see – most obviously in the Rijksmuseum itself and in Amsterdam's wonderfully preserved canals and townhouses. Yet it seemed to me that the Golden Age had also left an enduring imprint on the national culture and outlook. The VOC may have been long gone, but the Netherlands remained a confident and prosperous place, enjoying a degree of geopolitical influence and self-assurance on the world stage that was disproportionate to its size. The Dutch themselves were well travelled and well informed about the world, with an outward orientation that would put many insular Brits to shame. The country's maritime heritage was still evident, with enormous docks remaining Europe's largest gateway for seagoing trade. Furthermore, for its size, the Netherlands retained a formidable military footprint, with Dutch forces playing a significant role in the conflicts in Afghanistan and Libya, for example. An airbase in the south of the Netherlands even housed a small arsenal of nuclear weapons. The city of Den Haag (The Hague), once home to scores of Golden Age merchants and diplomats, still hosted numerous international institutions, including the International Criminal Court.

The Netherlands had also retained a good deal of its Golden Age cosmopolitanism. Walking down the street outside the Rijksmuseum, one was still as likely to hear English, Spanish, French or Chinese being spoken as Dutch, and for a Dutch person to speak three or even four languages was considered entirely normal. (I once saw a promotional survey seeking to drum up publicity for a language school in the Netherlands that included three options: 'My English is OK / Great / Fantastic.') The home of Rembrandt and Vermeer remained proud of its status as a global leader in design and architecture, even if boutique bicycles and chairs had replaced oil paintings as the creative output of choice. In a country where the Prime Minister cycled to work and the wealthy paid high taxes without complaint, one could perhaps even detect enduring traces of the guiding philosophy of the Golden Age: that one had a duty to work hard, but that gains should be invested for the common good.

More tangibly, the colonial legacy was evident in an abundance of imported Asian street names. Amsterdam and other major cities were filled with the likes of Javastraat, Sumatrastraat, Bataviastraat and Borneostraat. Conversely, names exported by the Dutch were still in use (often in bastardised form) in many other countries. Perhaps the most famous examples were in New York City: Harlem was named after the Dutch city of Haarlem, Brooklyn after the small town of Breukelen, and Flushing after the southern Dutch city of Vlissingen. Wall Street was originally De Waal Street and Broadway was once better known as Breede Weg. Several other Dutch words also made it into the American vocabulary: cookie, waffle, noodles, brandy, coleslaw. A form of Dutch was spoken in New Jersey until as late as the 1920s, and the Dutch accent was said to be the source of the famous Brooklyn drawl. Elsewhere in the US were numerous small towns called Holland, an Amsterdam in upstate New York, a Rotterdam, a Dutch Harbor, a Nassau and a Nederland, and at least four Batavias. Further afield, South Africa had Delft, Gouda, Middelburg and Utrecht; Suriname Nieuw Amsterdam, Groningen and Lelydorp; and Australia Arnhem Land, Groote Eyland and Cape Leeuwin. The Dutch port of Hoorn lent its name to Cape Horn, near the southernmost tip of Latin America, while Easter Island, home of Chile's famous giant stone heads, was christened thus by the Dutch explorers who arrived there on Easter Sunday.

Closer to home, the Netherlands' colonial history was evident on the country's dining tables and restaurant menus, with Indonesian cuisine offering a rare bright spot among otherwise dire food options. It was common for family celebrations or corporate events to involve a *rijsttafel* ('rice table'), a lavish banquet consisting of dozens of gelatinous Indonesian dishes displayed on a vast table. Just as no British town could be complete without an Indian curry house, most Dutch towns had at least one restaurant offering peanut soup, chicken satay and spicy noodles. *Nasi goreng* (fried rice) and *bami goreng* (fried noodles) were as well known to Dutch diners as chicken masala and naan bread were to the British. After centuries of trade with Indonesia, the Dutch had developed an abiding obsession with coffee, with an expensive coffee machine an essential feature of even the scruffiest student house. Surinamese food, which I'd never even heard of before moving to the Netherlands, was also popular. The Dutch had left their mark on the world, and the world had returned the favour.

The museum would close in half an hour and I needed another drink. Leaving behind the stained glass and tiled floors, I descended a grand, Harry Potteresque stone staircase and returned to the party in the courtyard downstairs. The music had got louder and the crowd had got bigger, and drunker. Kanye West was playing on the sound system and perhaps 300 people were jumping energetically to the music, many of them still with their sunglasses on. It didn't seem like many of them had looked at the art, although I did see one girl in a 'FUCK WARHOL' T-shirt. Nervous security guards loitered at the gallery entrances, battling to maintain a cordon between the heaviest drinkers and the priceless antiquities beyond. Near the entrance to the new Asian art pavilion, a man with a long beard and a thick sleeve of tattoos passed a small plastic bag of white pills to his girlfriend. I put away my notebook and bought another cocktail.

Four

Fire and Ashes

The Nazi Destruction of the Netherlands

By the time the war was over, the fifteenth-century Sint Laurenskerk, or St Lawrence Church, was one of the few buildings left standing in central Rotterdam. Half a decade of conflict had reduced the city to a sea of rubble and ash. Only the shell of the church remained, its hollow clock tower pointing accusingly at the sky from where the bombs had rained.

Some seventy years later, on the anniversary of the air raid that destroyed much of the city, I sat inside the church and waited for the remembrance service to begin. The building had been lovingly restored not long after the Second World War, its resurrection a symbol of the rebirth of the Netherlands' second city. For an ancient Protestant church it was surprisingly light and airy, a titanic space with a curved wooden roof resembling the upturned hull of a boat. The slender pipes of an enormous organ towered over a nave lined with candles and statues. Orb-like golden chandeliers hung from the high ceiling, and the shadows of the trees outside danced on the stained-glass windows.

It was not my first visit to the church, but it was the first time I'd been there sober. My previous trip had taken place during Rotterdam's *Museumnacht*, the local rival to that in Amsterdam, when the church served beer and snacks on rough trestle tables and kept its doors open till midnight. Today, the beer had been locked away and perhaps seventy people had gathered to mark the anniversary of the building's improbable survival. Too few to fill the rows of chairs in the nave, congregants were compressed into wooden pews near the altar, facing each other across the tiled floor like commuters on a subway train. Collecting a prayer sheet and memorial booklet from a mournful usher, I sat on a folding wooden seat in the choir stalls and did my best to look sad.

Most of the others in attendance were far older than I – old enough, perhaps, to remember the war themselves. Wearing a hooded sweatshirt and with a full head of hair, I couldn't help but feel self-conscious in a sea of rumpled wool and shiny pates. I also couldn't help noticing that in a city where almost half the population were ethnic minorities, all but one of the people in the church were white. An old gent with round glasses and a walking stick squeezed into the stalls next to me, wheezing like a steam train. '*Ben je een journalist?*' he asked me, wondering why I was scribbling in a notebook. 'No, I'm not a journalist, just writing a little,' I replied in Dutch. 'Yes,' he said, 'it is good to write about these things.'

The clock tower above us struck twelve, and a balding pastor wearing sand-coloured robes climbed the steps to the lectern and welcomed the congregation. In the vast echoing space I found it difficult to understand his Dutch, but I picked up enough phrases to understand his message – 'a city destroyed, but come back again stronger'; 'wars still going on in other countries, other cities'; 'wherever you come from, this city welcomes you'. There were even a few phrases in English – 'peace and reconciliation' was repeated several times – and a tribute to the people of Coventry, the English city that had also been destroyed from above and had partnered with Rotterdam for the purposes of remembrance. The old man with the walking stick caught me scribbling notes on a prayer sheet, and frowned.

For the Netherlands, as for many other countries in Europe, the Second World War remained by far the most significant event of the twentieth century. The impact of the conflict on a small, close-knit country – bombed and invaded by the Nazis, occupied and then painfully liberated – was devastating. As a proportion of the population, Dutch war deaths were far higher than those in Britain, France or Belgium. In the colony of the Dutch East Indies (present-day Indonesia) perhaps four million more died under Japanese occupation. The Holocaust, the most barbaric element of a barbaric conflict, had one of its epicentres in the Netherlands, with Dutch Jews less likely to survive the war than those in almost any other country.

Coming after centuries of relative peace, the war had a transformative effect on Dutch society. Physically, the conflict changed the shape of cities such as Rotterdam completely, leaving it with few of the pretty canals and townhouses common in that part of the world. Dutch experience of (and sometimes complicity in) repression and persecution also had a profound effect on the country's political culture, ensuring that the greatest civic virtue was intolerance of intolerance. In political debates about interventionism, peacekeeping and war-making, the country's wartime experiences were a constant benchmark. The Dutch famine of the 'Hunger Winter' of 1944 had helped spur the creation of a beneficent welfare state that provided cradle-to-grave security for citizens, and perhaps helped shape Dutch attitudes to work and family. Even the Dutch love of bicycles was rooted partly in the planning decisions taken during post-war reconstruction. To understand the Netherlands, then, one had to understand the war.

The Destroyed City

The church service dragged on. With the exception of a couple of wedding ceremonies, I hadn't been to one for years and had forgotten how repetitive they could be. Short speeches and bible readings were punctuated by bursts of music from an enormous organ, the congregation singing lustily in Dutch as I mumbled awkwardly along. I remembered again why I usually avoided such occasions.

Proceedings livened up a little when a new speaker approached the lectern, a curly-haired man of about thirty wearing a smart dark suit. Speaking Dutch with the faint buzz common among those of North African or Middle Eastern descent, he told a long story about how his parents and grandparents had fled a civil war in Morocco, come to Rotterdam and struggled to assimilate in an alien land. There was a happy ending, however, when his mother came to accept his choices and adore her new half-Dutch grandchild: a metaphor for a welcoming, tolerant city risen from the ashes. He was an engaging speaker and I found his story rather moving, if a touch long-winded, but clearly not everyone agreed. Across the aisle from me, a woman of about sixty harrumphed visibly at the mention of a Moroccan man who had more than one wife. Another flinched at the mention of 'Allah'. When the young man finished his speech and sat down beside the pastor, no one applauded and no one congratulated him.

The pastor led the congregation in the Lord's Prayer – '*Onze Vader, die in de Hemel zijt...*' – and the service drew to a close. I shuffled with the crowd towards the doors at the rear of the building, passing a couple of framed photographs of the church in the ruined city and a small gift shop selling bottles of fair-trade wine. It had been grey and cloudy when I entered the building, but the small square outside was now bathed in sunshine, and the clock tower cast a long shadow over the brick floor.

I followed the crowd across the square towards one of the city's many small harbours, near where the next phase of the memorial service would take place on a small plaza next to the maritime museum. The site had been chosen because of the monument to the bombing that stood there. *De Verwoeste Stad*, or 'The Destroyed City', was created in 1951 by the French-Russian sculptor Ossip Zadkine, who had himself been injured in the First World War. The bronze statue of a misshapen figure was perhaps four times my size, with arms raised in despair and a mouth gaping wide with horror. Stylistically similar to Picasso's famous painting of war-torn Guernica, the statue was – I later read – built after the rejection of an earlier proposal to construct a replica of Nelson's Column with a statue of Winston Churchill on top. At the centre of the torso was a gaping hole, through which a small slice of sky was visible. Like the city around it, Zadkine's statue had had its heart ripped out.

By the time the group from the church arrived, a crowd of perhaps 200 people already encircled the memorial, lined up four deep like children watching a playground fight. Behind the memorial, the tip of the Erasmusbrug, the great white bridge over the Maas, was just visible in the distance over cranes and the masts of old sailing barges. In front of the statue, three rows of chairs were filled with minor dignitaries, and a local TV news cameraman was enjoying shooting close-ups of a leggy blonde sitting among them. A smattering of proud military veterans wore ancient uniforms weighed down with medals and ribbons, together with perhaps a dozen serving soldiers and sailors in crisp jackets and caps. A brass band warmed up while a choir waited patiently nearby, three rows of grey-haired men in black suits and bow ties. The sunny, cheerful weather seemed slightly inappropriate for the occasion. '*Dit is leuk!*' a woman standing next to me exclaimed loudly to her husband. 'This is fun!'

The mayor arrived, resplendent in a silver medallion as thick as a boxer's belt, sparking a Mexican wave of mobile phones held aloft to take his picture. A trim man of about fifty with salt-and-pepper hair, he was the first person of Moroccan descent ever appointed to run a major Dutch city. He began to tell the story of the bombing of Rotterdam: the winds that had fanned the flames, the subsequent loss and starvation, the church that was struck by bombs but somehow remained standing. The statue of 'a man without a heart', the mayor said, symbolised a country that had lost almost everything but still believed in a better world; a world without war. '*Het leven moet verder gaan,*' he said, 'life must go on.' A tall young woman standing next to me lit a cigarette, sending smoke curling across the crowd like a ribbon, providing a convenient excuse for all the men with watery eyes.

Watching the ceremony, I was struck by the differences in the way Dutch people commemorated the war compared to the British. In the UK, the Second World War was remembered largely in heroic terms: Winston Churchill flashing a V-sign or wielding a Tommy gun; Spitfires soaring over the white cliffs of Dover; plucky islanders keeping barbaric invaders at bay thanks to their indefatigable 'Blitz spirit'. Major anniversaries were an opportunity to remember the fallen, but also to glory in the military triumphs of our 'brave boys', to the accompaniment of brass bands and air force fly-overs. In Britain, the war could even be a source of comedy, the inspiration for much-loved television comedies such as *Blackadder, Dad's Army* and *'Allo 'Allo*.

In the Netherlands, the war was commemorated in a rather different way. As a small country squeezed between Germany and the Allies, it had been crushed by the boot of history, suffering years of invasion, occupation and oppression. Many thousands of Dutch had lost their lives, and many people of my father's generation still had clear memories of the post-war 'Hunger Winter' when mass starvation set in. As a result, anniversaries were commemorated not with patriotic pageantry, but with deep feelings of sorrow, regret and even a hint of shame. The Second World War was remembered in the Netherlands similar to how the First World War was in Britain – as a tragedy of unimaginable proportions. Anniversaries were widely observed and using the war as a setting for a comedy programme would be unthinkable. When a man next to me at the ceremony in Rotterdam took advantage of a pause in the proceedings to quietly take a photograph of the wreaths, several people angrily told him to either stop being so disrespectful or leave.

An Island of Tranquillity

Such attitudes prevailed partly because before the war, the Netherlands had been a rare island of tranquillity in an otherwise rough neighbourhood. Throughout the nineteenth and early twentieth centuries, the Dutch had maintained a strict policy of neutrality with respect to their larger neighbours, abiding by Erasmus of Rotterdam's principle that 'the most disadvantageous peace is better than the most just war'. In contrast with heavily militarised France and Germany, and oft-trampled Belgium, the Netherlands had hardly seen a shot fired in anger since Napoleonic times.

Even as the First World War engulfed Northern Europe, the Netherlands had avoided the conflict. At least one Dutch citizen – Margaretha Zelle, the *femme fatale* better known by her stage name of Mata Hari – took advantage of the country's neutral status for nefarious purposes. However, the Dutch authorities were generally scrupulous in maintaining their impartiality, even looking the other way when German forces passed briefly through Dutch territory on their way to invade Belgium. When the First World War ended, it was to the peaceful Netherlands that the defeated German Kaiser was exiled, billeted in a manor house in Doorn until his death in 1941. Rising at seven every morning, he spent much of his time tending the extensive gardens – in 1929, he told a visiting interviewer he had felled his 20,000th tree, but asked that this not be reported lest critics ask: 'What are twenty thousand trees compared with twenty million German lives?'

As Hitler consolidated power in neighbouring Germany, many Dutch remained remarkably sanguine about the threat to their own country. Concerned about the growing 'red peril', many officials in the Netherlands saw Hitler as a reliable ally in the fight against communism, and offered him their support. In 1935, the Amsterdam police commissioner reassured the Gestapo that the Dutch would cooperate in the fight against 'Communist and Marxist machinations', while the city's Attorney General called for 'the establishment of concentration camps where all undesirable communist elements could be sheltered'. Even as tensions increased, many Dutch leaders refused to believe that a second global war would be much different from the first, believing that they could sidestep the conflict. Dutch neutrality, the Prime Minister said, was 'a beacon in a dark world'.

Hitler had other ideas. In September 1939, Germany invaded Poland, and France and Britain declared war on

Germany. To the Nazis, the Dutch coast offered vital staging posts for the planned invasion of Britain. An attack on the Netherlands looked inevitable. The Dutch, moreover, were ill-prepared to defend themselves. While other countries had relentlessly built up their armed forces in the 1930s, until as late as 1940 the Dutch possessed not a single tank, and had a collection of weapons mostly dating back to the 1800s. In a rare exception, the country had established a new regiment of 3000 soldiers after the First World War ended: a regiment of cyclists, with the motto 'Swift and Nimble – Composed and Dignified'. As Pete Jordan later wrote, their firepower included a military band equipped with bikes with special handlebars that could be steered while playing a horn. When Nazi invasion looked imminent the Dutch Army was belatedly mobilised, but the country's defensive strategy remained largely as it had since the seventeenth century: in the event of an invasion, a 'waterline' of land would be flooded to create a liquid barrier protecting major cities. If things got really bad, they could rely on a second Cyclist's Regiment created in March 1939, with gleaming new bicycles and a corporal who served as a mechanic.

On the evening of 9 May 1940, Hitler authorised the invasion of Western Europe. The codeword 'Danzig' was flashed to German forces and the following morning they attacked the Netherlands, ignoring the Dutch foreign minister's protests that his country had no quarrel with anyone. The invaders were so confident of swift victory that one of their commanders, General von Sponeck, had brought with him a formal dress uniform to wear when he accepted the Dutch surrender from the Queen. For the Dutch, more than a century of peace was over.

At the remembrance ceremony, the mayor's clichés – walls breaking down, great sacrifices being made – had become almost overwhelming. In comparison, I found the scene at the statue quite moving. This was partly because of the diversity of the crowd in attendance. Elderly congregants from the church mixed with office workers on their lunch breaks and teenagers leaning against bicycles; Indonesians and Moroccans and Turkish gents in baggy suits stood nobly alongside tattooed toughs from the harbour. Next to me, an elderly veteran in a sailor's cap stroked his tremendous grey moustache while his small granddaughter played with his shoelaces. Behind them, a bearded man with holes in his shoes removed his baseball cap and stared solemnly at the ground.

At a nod from the mayor, the choir began to sing, a sweet hymn that was unexpectedly tender coming from such a burly group of men. They reminded me of a Welsh male voice choir. A succession of dignitaries stepped up to lay huge wreaths before the statue, several of them struggling to balance the coffee-table-sized garlands on the upright wooden trestles. A red-haired woman standing in front of me let out a strangled sob and dabbed at her eyes with a tissue. At 13:29, the time when the bombing raid on Rotterdam had started, a military trumpeter played the Last Post. A two-minute silence was declared. In the centre of one the Netherlands' largest cities, on a weekday afternoon, it was briefly quiet enough to hear birds' wings flapping overhead.

The Nazi Invasion

When invading the Netherlands the Nazis relied on a combination of overwhelming force and trickery to get around the Dutch defences. At one key bridge in Gennap, on the eastern Dutch border with Germany, a group of Nazi soldiers dressed in the uniforms of Dutch military police and escorted another group across the bridge as their 'prisoners'. Safely past the Dutch checkpoint, they removed their disguises and quickly overwhelmed the defenders. In the town of Grebbeberg, a Dutch army officer described for *LIFE* magazine how 'young fanatical Nazi troops climbed up into the trees at night and, like monkeys hopping from tree to tree, stole across no-man's land until they were up in the trees surrounding our trenches'.

The Dutch put up a spirited resistance. Many German planes were shot from the sky, and others were prevented from landing by burning wreckage scattered on the runways. Numerous Nazi paratroopers were captured by Dutch solders and shipped to Britain as prisoners of war. In an effort to identify other invaders, some Dutch allegedly carried out random checks on strangers, asking them to pronounce the name of a seaside town near The Hague. If anyone fluffed the pronunciation of *Scheveningen*, they were presumed to be a foreign spy. As Pete Jordan recorded, the Cyclists Regiments were deployed at key points along the defences. One of their members, Roelof Keppel, wrote to his wife: 'Cyclists have a dangerous job. They seek danger and they find it.' The next day he was killed.

As the invasion proceeded, the strength of the Dutch resistance began to concern the Nazis. German paratroopers had successfully seized control of several strategic locations, but the Nazi leadership was becoming concerned that a failure to seize Rotterdam could slow the march south towards Paris. On 13 May 1940, Nazi pilots received their orders by radio: 'Resistance in Rotterdam is to be broken by all means available. If necessary, the destruction of the city is to be threatened, and conducted.' The following day, Dutch military leaders were told that a hundred bombers were already flying towards the city, and would destroy it within the hour if the Dutch forces failed to surrender. Unknown to the Dutch, the incoming pilots had been warned that their mission would likely be aborted once the city surrendered. If they saw red signal flares, they should attack the Belgian city of Antwerp instead.

After a short debate, the Dutch signed the terms of surrender a few minutes before the three o'clock deadline. German radio operators ordered the incoming planes not to bomb the city. Not all the planes received the message. While many turned back, others continued, unaware that the mission had been aborted. 'For God's sake!' the furious leader of the Nazi ground troops exclaimed. 'There's going to be hell to pay!'

Desperate to halt the raid, a German officer picked up a flare gun and began firing red flares into the sky. 'We believed we could prevent the attack up to the last minute,' another officer later wrote. However, flying through a cloudy sky and distracted by flashes from Dutch anti-aircraft guns, most of the remaining pilots did not see the flares. The first group of planes dropped their bombs. In the second group, the lead pilot ordered his planes to drop theirs, and seconds later spotted two red flares. 'Abort! Abort! Don't drop!' he ordered. It was too late. The planes had already released their cargoes, and hundreds of bombs were falling towards the city.

On the ground, Nazi soldiers rushed for shelter. Some of the first bombs to land hit Rotterdam's water main, cutting the supply to fire hydrants. Others hit a margarine warehouse, sparking an enormous fire that quickly spread through the centre and north of the city. As a German soldier on the ground later explained, 'Rotterdam was a sea of flame', surrounded on every side by 'an impenetrable wall' of fire. 'Shop windows exploded about our ears,' he said. 'Burning decorations and clothed mannequins presented an unearthly picture... the heat was unbearable.' Thousands of people fled the city centre with singed hair and blackened faces. One resident, Elisabeth de Graaff, later wrote of how the walls of the zoo had been destroyed by bombs, leaving wild animals free to wander the ravaged streets. Years later, when she was living in the United States, the 9/11 attack on New York reminded her of how patients had jumped from the windows of Rotterdam's burning hospital.

By the time the fires were finally extinguished, over 600 acres of the city had been destroyed. Most of Rotterdam's historic core – once said by a *New Yorker* correspondent to be as idyllic as Oxford's Cherwell – had been obliterated. Tens of thousands of houses had been destroyed, as well as scores of factories, schools and hospitals. Around 900 people were killed, although early news reports dramatically exaggerated the death toll, claiming that twenty, thirty or forty thousand people had died. Official records listed the grim inventory of destruction: 31 department stores, 13 banks, 19 consulates, 2 museums, 4 churches, 22 cinemas, 517 cafés and restaurants. According to one magazine correspondent, parts of the city were still burning more than four months after the bombing. In London, an outraged Winston Churchill told Parliament: 'the peaceful city of Rotterdam [has been] the scene of a massacre as hideous and brutal as anything in the Thirty Years' War.'

With the destruction of Rotterdam, any remaining hope that the Dutch might hold out against the Nazis was lost. The Dutch commander-in-chief, General Henri Winkelman, travelled through the burning city to the Maas, where he signed an unconditional surrender on 15 May. Elsewhere in the country, Queen Wilhemina avoided capture and fled to Britain, accompanied by what remained of the Dutch navy. ('I fear no man in the world,' Winston Churchill said, 'except Queen Wilhelmina.') Despite a spirited resistance, the whole of the Netherlands fell to the Nazis in less than a week. In late May Belgium fell too, and four weeks later France.

For the Dutch, the surrender marked the beginning of five years of hardship and suffering. In this respect their experience was hardly unique – similarly tragic litanies of invasion, occupation and oppression filled the first few pages of tourist guidebooks to almost every country in Europe. What was unusual about the Netherlands was the depth of suffering experienced by the country's Jewish population, which was among the worst in the war. According to Hannah Arendt, three-quarters of all Jews living in the Netherlands would be killed. A Jew in the Netherlands was less likely to survive the war than those almost anywhere else in Europe.

North to Westerbork

The remembrance ceremony ended and the crowd dispersed. I left too, headed for Camp Westerbork, a Nazi transit camp located in the far northeast of the Netherlands, close to where the border with Germany ran into the North Sea.

Although not well known today, the camp played a crucial role in the destruction of European Jewry, transporting more than 100,000 people to concentration camps including Auschwitz, where most of them were killed. Their number included a young girl who had spent years hiding above her father's office in Amsterdam, an experience she recorded in her diary.

I had arranged to rent a car to make the trip, which I collected from a small office a few minutes' walk from the statue. The curly-haired Dutch-Moroccan man collecting signatures and distributing keys at the hire centre expressed amazement when I told him where I would be driving. Why would a young Englishman, presumably on holiday, spend considerable time and money to reach a distant corner of the country where something unpleasant had happened three-quarters of a century ago? *'Wat je wilt'* – 'Whatever you want' – he eventually shrugged, with the air of someone accustomed to hearing ridiculous requests.

Driving towards the camp, I began to wonder if he was right. For such a small country the Netherlands could be surprisingly slow to get around, and I'd forgotten what a chore driving could be. In the 1950s, the country's first ever traffic jam had been celebrated as proof that the Dutch had joined the modern age, and they had apparently decided to create as many more of them as they could. Roads were usually heavily congested and punctuated by endless unnecessary roundabouts and stop signs. Traffic lights were not only frequent but carefully positioned so that a driver waiting for the lights to change couldn't actually see them. It was, I thought, not a coincidence that the inventor of the speed camera, Maus Gatsonides, was a Dutchman.

Thanks to such obstacles, it took nearly two and half hours to reach Westerbork, heading northeast through miles of patchy forest and polder. The tiny red car I'd rented was a triumph of Japanese accountancy over engineering, and its lawnmower engine complained noisily at the almost imperceptible inclines as it rattled across the country. I spent an hour flicking through radio stations in search of one that wasn't playing terrible Dutch house music, before eventually settling on a British armed forces radio station, presumably broadcast from some military base in Germany. The news bulletin offered a strange mix of the parochial and the exotic: a jumble sale in Suffolk, a ministerial visit in Cyprus, a reminder to take malaria medicine in Afghanistan.

The fleeting mentions of Camp Westerbork in travel guidebooks had reinforced my fears of a wasted day, but I arrived to find that the area around the camp was almost indecently attractive. Leafy forests backed onto wide green pastures sprinkled with pink blossoming trees, small farms and boxy black-and-white cows. This was as close as the Netherlands ever came to unspoilt nature. As I squeezed the car into a narrow space among the trees, a Dutchman in a white sun-hat eagerly marshalled his unenthusiastic sons towards the nearby museum, promising loudly that it would be '*heel interessant*', really interesting. The cheerful atmosphere was abruptly dispelled when I spotted a reproduction railway sign as I got out of the car: 'Westerbork-Auschwitz'. My mobile phone buzzed in my pocket; about twenty-five miles from the border, I was close enough to Germany for it to switch automatically from a Dutch service provider to a German one.

I crossed the busy car park and entered the squat museum building. A friendly woman with hair like muddy candyfloss sold me an entrance ticket, flattering me by pretending to understand my rudimentary Dutch. 'From England? And you speak Dutch already?' she cooed. 'Fantastic!' I flattered her back by buying a translated guidebook I didn't really want. The museum itself was depressingly similar to those found at memorial sites across Europe: jerky black-and-white films of people being loaded onto trains like livestock, and sad displays of the shoes, suitcases, violins and comic books they had left behind. Some of it was deeply moving, but much of the display information was in Dutch and I struggled to translate the terminology, my ability to understand only the present tense turning out to be something of an obstacle to historical study. Yet the translated biographies of a few of those who had passed through the camp were enough to tell the terrible tale. Fourteen-year-old Samuel Bobbe was sent from Rotterdam to Westerbork, held there for seven months, and then put on a train to the gas chambers at Auschwitz-Birkenau. Margaret van de Horst, sent from Westerbork to the death camp at Soribor in 1943, left behind her seventh birthday present, a book called *New Year with Grandma*.

Camp Westerbork itself lay a mile or two from the museum, hidden deep within a thick forest of tall fir trees. A large tour bus shuttled tourists through the forest from the museum to the camp, its sides tastefully emblazoned with decorative flames and key facts about the site (102,000 dead! 120 Roma killed!). I preferred to walk and set out along a winding path through the trees. In the late 1960s, the area adjoining the camp had become an important site for radio telescopy and the path passed close to a long row of enormous white satellite dishes, each the size of a five-storey building, pointed through the forest canopy at the sky. There was something unsettling, I thought, about a place where thousands had been sent to their deaths now being used to look for life on other worlds.

After perhaps half an hour's walk, I reached what remained of the camp: a huge grassy clearing in the trees, studded with long, grave-like mounds where wooden huts had once stood. Neatly mowed and fenced, it reminded me strangely of the sprawling suburban sports fields where I had jogged on weekends when I lived in London. However, a few token reconstructions helped imagine what the camp must have been like in its terrible prime. Long strings of rusting barbed wire led to crumbling concrete walls, overlooked by a hulking black watchtower perched on tall wooden stilts. At the far side of the field, surrounded by tourists with cameras, was a memorial to those who had been ferried here: a set of train tracks that had once brought prisoners to and from the camp, now abruptly severed and twisted skyward like a monstrous rusty ski ramp.

The Destruction of Dutch Jewry

Amazingly, Camp Westerbork was built not by the Nazis but by the Dutch government in 1939 to house some of the thousands of Jewish refugees who had fled to the Netherlands from German oppression. The first group of refugees transported there were anxious at being kept so near the German border and uneasy about the camp's isolation. 'A vast and desolate area of bare heathland and sand,' was how one described it. 'We were very depressed, but we had to accept it,' said another.

In the early years of the Nazi occupation, Dutch Jews were at first able to live in relative peace. Between 1940 and 1942, however, conditions both inside and outside the camp deteriorated rapidly. Jews were obliged to wear a Star of David on their clothes and to register with the authorities, each paying a fee for their own registration form. A timeline of just some of the rules introduced during that period made grim reading:

> August 1940: Jewish religious rituals outlawed
> October 1940: Government employees forced to sign
> declarations saying they are of Aryan descent
> November 1940: Jews banned from holding jobs as civil
> servants
> January 1941: Jews banned from attending cinemas
> February 1941: Jews forbidden from attending college
> and banned from donating blood
> March 1941: Jewish companies seized by the authorities
> April 1941: Jews forbidden from going to cafés
> And so on.

Among the victims of the new rules were a family of German Jews who had fled to Amsterdam before the outbreak of war. At first they found life in the Dutch capital peaceful, but that soon changed following the Nazi invasion. The father of the family, Otto Frank, was forced to hand his business over to a non-Jewish owner, while his two daughters had to leave the schools they loved to attend a Jews-only high school. In May 1942, they had to pin yellow stars to their clothes so they could be identified as Jews. The following month one of the girls, Anne, received a thirteenth birthday present: a diary.

In January 1942, a few weeks after declaring war on the United States, Nazi leaders met at a villa in the Berlin suburb of Wannsee and agreed on the *Endlösung der Judenfrage*, or 'Final Solution to the Jewish Question'. Within a few months, Camp Westerbork had been taken over by German authorities, fortified with watchtowers and sentry posts, and designated the key transit hub for Dutch Jews being transported to the East. For most, it would be a one-way journey.

The day was gloriously sunny, a bright midday sun framed neatly in a rectangle of blue sky punched through the forest canopy. The sensitivity of the nearby satellite equipment meant that cars and mobile phones were banned around the camp, and the only sounds were those of people talking and laughing and children playing. An overheated dog lolled in the grass near the amputated train tracks. A young woman sitting next to a gnarled barbed-wire fence carefully rolled up the legs of her jeans and lay down to catch some sun. Nearby, a family of four sat on a red blanket and had a picnic in the long shadow of a reconstructed watchtower.

Sitting under a tree and watching them happily share crisps and sandwiches, I had the same conflicted feeling I'd had at other places – Bosnia, Cambodia, Rwanda – where ethnic and geopolitical rivalries had been played out to their terrible conclusion. The scene was unsettling not simply because of the evil once carried out there, but because of how completely the place had been reclaimed by normal life. Was it distressing to see people picnicking and playing football in a place of remembrance, or reassuring to see happy memories being made in a place that had generated so many bad ones? I wasn't sure. I sat and scribbled in my notebook while a young couple kissed passionately in the dappled shade.

As the population of the camp grew, conditions deteriorated. 'What we saw defies any description,' one prisoner wrote in 1942. 'Approximately 17,000 Jews came to the camp at the beginning of October... They arrived pushed along like cattle, some of them buried under their luggage, others with no luggage at all, not even properly dressed. Sick women, lifted from their beds, dressed in thin nightshirts. Barefooted children still in their pyjamas, old people, sick people, lame people; the stream of newcomers went on and on.' Prisoners worked long days in the kitchens and gardens or in workshops, where they sewed clothes and shoes for despatch to Germany or sorted scrap metal from destroyed aircraft.

Sitting on the neatly trimmed grass, I read a booklet I'd picked up in the museum that told the story of Michael, a premature baby born in the camp at the height of the horror. With the infant struggling to breathe, the camp commandant sent for a professor of paediatrics to discuss how to keep him alive, and ordered an incubator from a hospital in the nearby city of Groningen. In a rare show of compassion, the commandant himself visited the baby regularly to check on his progress, and with expert medical care the child slowly gained in strength, his weight creeping up to five and half pounds. Eventually he was strong enough to be taken out of the incubator and put in an ordinary cradle. For the inmates, the baby's survival offered a rare sign of hope. 'This proved there was something good after all,' said one survivor. 'There was hope, there was a future.' The camp authorities had other plans. As soon as Michael weighed six pounds he was put on a train to a labour camp, where he very likely died.

Once a week, a train would leave Camp Westerbork with around 1000 people on board, most of them making what would be their final journey. As Adolf Eichmann recalled when he stood trial in Jerusalem after the war, the deportations were conducted with impressive efficiency. 'The trains from Holland – it was a delight,' he said. For the individuals being deported, it was rather less delightful. Marched through the camp to the train platform, deportees were packed into bare wooden wagons that would carry them to Auschwitz, Bergen-Belsen, Theresienstadt or Soribor. The journeys to Auschwitz usually lasted three days; most who made it were gassed immediately on arrival. The last train left the camp in September 1944, headed for Bergen-Belsen, carrying a cargo of 279 people including 77 children who had been caught hiding from the authorities. The camp remained in operation until the spring of the following year, when the Germans fled from the approaching allies. It was liberated on 12 April 1945 by Canadian soldiers, who found nearly 900 starving prisoners inside. By that time, over 100,000 people had passed through Camp Westerbork. Only 5000 survived.

Feeling thoroughly depressed, I left the camp and walked back through a forest of lengthening shadows to the car park. Next to my car stood a sign I hadn't noticed when I arrived, a quote from a camp survivor posted between the rubbish bins and a map of the car park. '*Kom vanavond met verhalen, hoe de oorlog is verdwenen, en herhaal ze honderd malen, alle malen zal ik wenen,*' it said. 'Come tonight with stories, of how the war has gone by. Repeat them a hundred times, and every time I'll cry.'

The Hunger Winter

Even for those who avoided being sent to Camp Westerbork, life in the occupied Netherlands was grim. Rotterdam, which had suffered heavy bombing raids at the hands of the invading Nazis, now had to endure further raids from the allies seeking to liberate the city. British and American bombers visited well over a hundred times, bearing gifts that destroyed further swathes of the city and left thousands homeless.

In Amsterdam, the young girl with the diary, Anne Frank, had moved with her family into a secret annexe hidden behind a bookcase in her father's office building. They would stay there for more than two years, during which time she wrote diligently about the miseries of life in hiding and the experience of growing from a girl into a woman. In August 1944, the Franks were betrayed and arrested. The family feared for their lives, but for Anne even the train journey to Camp Westerbork was a source of interest: after years trapped indoors, she couldn't tear herself away from the windows offering views of meadows and forests. At the camp the Franks were assigned to barracks and set to work breaking old batteries apart with hammers and chisels. On 2 September, the camp authorities read out the names of the next thousand people to be sent to Auschwitz, including the eight former inhabitants of the secret annexe. Only Anne's father Otto survived.

By mid-1944, the tide had turned against the Nazis. In the space of a few months, the allies liberated Rome, landed at Normandy on D-Day and captured Paris. In early September, Brussels and Antwerp were liberated and the Dutch Prime Minister, Pieter Gerbrandy, mistakenly announced that the liberation of the Netherlands was already underway. Scores of people rushed to the outskirts of Rotterdam carrying bunches of flowers to throw to their saviours, but Gerbrandy (known to Churchill as 'Mr Cherry Brandy') was mistaken. A group of 'liberators' spotted in Breda turned out to be a British patrol who had crossed the border by accident. In September, an attempt by British parachute troops to capture a key bridge over the river Rhine at Arnhem – Operation Market Garden – ended in ignominious defeat, the crossing proving to be the famous 'Bridge too Far'. Asked by Gerbrandy if the Netherlands would be free by October, a senior US military officer replied with a single word: 'impossible'.

The Germans, however, were already preparing for defeat. Scores of Nazi soldiers fled the Netherlands, often taking with them whatever they could carry. One witness reported the scene at Amsterdam Central Station as looters stacked 'all sorts of things; furniture, desks, typewriters, stoves, even chicken coops with and without chickens'. In the eastern city of Arnhem, one resident told of finding a note requesting the theft to order of a dinner set and Persian carpet, 'as if the place was a department store'. By the end of the war, the Red Cross had recorded the theft or destruction of 30,000 beds, 20,000 cooking stoves, 60,000 chairs and 80,000 blankets in the city of Arnhem alone. Nationwide, the government estimated that two-thirds of the country's cars had been stolen. Bicycles also proved particularly tempting: over the course of the war, roughly half of the Netherlands' around four million bicycles were either destroyed or confiscated; a war crime many Dutch would never forgive. As a Nazi army officer wrote in a report to his superiors: 'no German measure has caused such bitterness in all ranks of society as the confiscation of the bicycles.'

The fleeing Nazis also took people. Desperate to end a shortage of manpower in Germany's factories and eager to undermine the Dutch resistance, the occupiers arrested tens of thousands of Dutchmen and took them to Germany, where they were held in squalid barracks and forced to work in factories. Even household pets weren't safe. In The Hague, authorities announced they would confiscate all large dogs. Ever entrepreneurial, local residents quickly established a dog rental facility, where an owner of a large dog could hire a smaller one that had already passed official inspection, enabling them to obtain the papers to protect their pet from dognapping.

What the Nazis couldn't take with them they often destroyed. One writer in Amsterdam recorded the consequences: ripped-up quays and sunken docks disappearing under thick black smoke, tall cranes collapsing like 'constructions of reed', as 'the barbarians revelled in the destruction of... the source of prosperity of this merchant city'. In Rotterdam, Nazi demolition experts blew up many of the city's enormous quays, as well as ships, warehouses, cranes and offices. Reporting this latest wave of destruction, the London *Times* called the suffering of the Dutch 'worse than those so far inflicted on any other country in Europe'. A letter from a clergyman published in the same newspaper proposed replacing the gongs of Big Ben on the evening news with recorded prayers for the Dutch.

By autumn 1944, basic supplies in the Netherlands were running desperately low. With gas and electricity cut off, some residents had resorted to pedalling on stationary bicycles to generate power. The American newscaster Walter Cronkite, parachuted into Arnhem, recorded that the Dutch were 'near starvation... They looked like children in their parents' clothing.' But the worst was yet to come. While the war dragged on into December, one of the coldest winters on record descended on the country. As the survivor Henri van der Zee recorded in his remarkable book *The Hunger Winter*, supply routes that had been established on rivers and canals ground to a halt as the waterways froze over. Without access to fuel or electricity, people were forced to scavenge for wood to burn. Leafy parks were razed to the ground, large trees stripped of their branches, and wooden fences and benches ripped up. Amsterdam's Vondelpark was closed to the public after enterprising locals repeatedly attempted to auction off its trees, promising home delivery of harvested wood at exorbitant prices. According to van der Zee, the Dutch Bible Society was dismayed to discover that a sudden increase in sales of the good book had occurred not because of an outpouring of religious faith, but because black marketeers were selling bible pages for use as cigarette paper. Even walking became problematic due to a shortage of shoes. City dwellers conducted excursions into the countryside by bicycle, trading – if they were lucky – jewellery and cutlery for milk, eggs and potatoes. If they were luckier still, they might find a horse killed by bombing and take home steak for dinner.

A sense of impending doom was heightened by heavy rain, which drenched the cities and turned fields into mud. For much of the war, many people had been able to go about their normal lives relatively undisturbed, providing they were not Jewish, or members of the resistance, or residents of the bombed areas of Rotterdam. The famine, however, affected almost everyone. Children dug in rubbish heaps for food and starving old people collapsed in the street. The problem was not simply that people were poor, but that even those who had money could not find any food to buy with it. One writer in Amsterdam told of searching in vain for a meal for his family, and buying instead a bunch of flowers for his living room.

By spring 1945, Dutch food-supply lines had been cut completely. In one of Europe's wealthiest countries, millions of people were in the grip of famine, surviving on a single slice of bread and a handful of vegetables a day. In March, *The Times* put the number of deaths in Rotterdam at forty per day. In Amsterdam, a visitor reported seeing piles of corpses stacked outside the ancient churches.

One girl, half Dutch and half English by birth, was trapped in Arnhem during that winter. After an uncle was murdered by the Nazis she joined the Dutch resistance, carrying messages through checkpoints hidden in her shoe and helping to save a British paratrooper who had become stranded during the disastrous invasion of Arnhem. When food supplies ran out, she drank glasses of water in place of meals and spent much of every day lying in bed. 'It was human misery at its starkest,' she later told a reporter. 'Masses of refugees... some carrying their dead babies, born on the roadside, hundreds collapsing in hunger.' Eventually the girl's life was saved by the timely delivery of a Unicef food parcel, but the experience left its mark. Some fifty years later, visiting a refugee camp in Sudan, she would compare the stretch marks on her ankles caused by childhood starvation with similar marks on the swollen limbs of a famished boy, and cheer when another Unicef truck fortuitously arrived just in time to save his life too. Her slight frame and prominent eyes had by then helped make her world famous: she was Audrey Hepburn.

The Allied powers were well aware of the unfolding tragedy. At one stage American military leaders even proposed that much of the population of the Netherlands should be relocated to Britain. In one of Churchill's last letters to Franklin Roosevelt, in April 1945, the Prime Minister called for urgent intervention to save the Dutch 'if we can', saying 'we may soon be in the presence of a tragedy'. A few days later Roosevelt, who was descended from Dutch emigrants to the United States and had taken the oath as President on a Dutch bible, died. For the Dutch, the President's death was another bitter blow.

In early 1945, relief for the starving finally arrived. The Red Cross distributed Swedish white bread and Allied air drops finally began, delivering crates of food to the village of Terbregge as part of the biblically named Operation Manna ('The Lord said unto Moses: I will rain down bread from Heaven for you').

By mid-April the Nazis were facing defeat, but the war in the Netherlands was not quite over. One notable engagement took place on the island of Texel, off the Dutch coast, where the Nazi occupying force included a group of roughly 600 Red Army soldiers from the Soviet Republic of Georgia, who had been captured as prisoners of war and forced to serve alongside the Nazis. One dark night, the Georgians rose up against the Nazis, killing hundreds of German soldiers and taking control of almost the whole island. A Dutchman and three Georgians set out in a lifeboat across the North Sea to seek help from the British, but after landing in Norfolk they found their pleas for assistance ignored. The expected reinforcements for the Texel mutineers never came. It took thousands of German soldiers more than a month to regain control of the island, after which all the surviving Georgians were executed. The uprising, now all but forgotten by most historians, was to be one of the last battles of the war in Europe.

Liberation

On 30 April 1945, Hitler committed suicide in his bunker in Berlin. Despite a ban on owning radios, the news spread quickly through the Netherlands and crowds of people gathered to dance around bonfires lit in the street. The following week, Germany formally surrendered to the western allies and liberating troops, mainly Canadian, swept into

Dutch cities. Cheering residents lined the streets to welcome them. Houses were decked with red, white and blue flags and orange streamers, the roads carpeted with tulips and flowers. As Winston Churchill later told the British Parliament, the Netherlands was like 'a community which had been gripped and compressed in the enemy's clutch. The grip is released and once food has flowed in, the people spring forth, strengthened by the compression they have endured.' As elsewhere in Europe, the liberators drove through ravaged cities throwing chocolate, cigarettes and soap to cheering crowds. In Arnhem, a teenage Audrey Hepburn was woken by the smell of foreign cigarettes drifting through her bedroom window. 'We crept upstairs to the front door, opened it very carefully and to our amazement the house was completely surrounded by English soldiers, all aiming their guns at us,' she remembered. 'I screamed with happiness, seeing all these cocky figures with dirty bright faces and shouted something in English.' She later told the *Daily Mail* that the corporal outside apologised for disturbing her. 'I laughed and said: go right on disturbing us! Then a cheer went up that they'd liberated an English girl. I was the only one for miles.'

Inevitably, some showed gratitude to their liberators in the most traditional way. Soldiers were showered with kisses from grateful Dutch girls. Eventually, a staggering 40,000 Dutch war brides would move to Canada with their new husbands. 'Whatever you do, don't fall in love with any of them,' young Margriet Blaisse's father told her as she set off to welcome liberators to the Dutch capital. 'They're all going back to Canada and you're staying right here in Amsterdam!' She went on to marry the first soldier she had seen.

A City Reborn

I drove back to Rotterdam, returned the car to the bemused rental agent, and walked through the city centre to the harbour. The sun was setting behind the harp-like Erasmusbrug, and I sat with my legs hanging over a high wall above the

Maas, close to the spot where I had disembarked from the ferry a couple of months earlier. After a sombre few hours in Westerbork and the memorial service before that, it felt strange to be back in the energetic heart of the city. On the opposite bank of the river, cranes were busily completing the final stages of the construction of a triptych of office towers designed by local 'starchitect' Rem Koolhaas. Cloaked in gunmetal-coloured glass, the upper floors of each tower were slightly offset from the vertical, like stacks of Jenga bricks with the top layers shuffled carefully out of alignment. I thought the buildings fairly hideous, but they were perfect examples of the post-war school of Dutch architecture that emphasised concept over context. To my untrained eye, the rule seemed to be: design something provocative, and then build it anywhere you can find a gap, without worrying too much about whether it fits in with its surroundings or matches its neighbours. In Rotterdam, anything was permitted as long as it included a quirky twist, strangely angled wall or precarious overhanging roof. The city had not only been rebuilt, but continued to expand and evolve.

When the conflict in the Netherlands ended, the departing Germans left behind them a ravaged country. An estimated 210,000 people had been killed, including many civilians, and another 70,000 had died due to starvation and the hardships of war. The economic impact was also devastating: between 1940 and 1945, Dutch real GDP had fallen by some 40 per cent. Economists later estimated that more than a quarter of all the country's capital stock – houses, machinery, factories and railways – had been destroyed. Within a few years would come the wrenching loss of the Dutch colonies in Indonesia, begrudgingly granted independence by a Dutch government that had neither the capacity nor the willpower to keep fighting for them. Rebuilding the country would be a formidable task. In one telling example, the minister of economic affairs explained that it would prove difficult to resume production of bicycle tyres, because factory workers had no tyres for the bicycles they needed to get to the factory.

Overseas aid would play a critical role in the recovery. The Netherlands received well over a billion dollars from the European Recovery Program (ERP), the post-war aid initiative better known as the Marshall Plan. Relative to the size of the Dutch economy this was an enormous sum: the Netherlands received roughly ten times as much aid per capita as Belgium. As well as financing the country's physical reconstruction, the ERP aimed to put the Netherlands on a path towards mass production and consumption on the American model – exemplified by the programme's US-produced slogan, 'You Too Can Be Like Us'. The Dutch government deviated from capitalist orthodoxy by building a generous welfare state, but even decades later the Dutch still had a noticeable love of all things American, from fast food to fashion, from TV comedies to holidays in Florida and New York.

The subsequent economic recovery was close to miraculous. According to some estimates, Dutch GDP increased by almost 20 per cent a year between 1945 and 1950. Currency devaluation helped spark an export boom, while a post-war baby boom saw the country's population increase by more than a third from 1950 to 1970. The discovery of enormous natural gas reserves in the north of the country also provided a huge boost to its coffers. By the mid-1950s, industrial production was nearly double what it had been immediately before the war.

The economy healed and Dutch companies thrived. Barriers to global trade were crumbling, and the country's international outlook, trading links and thrifty business sense proved a perfect recipe for profitability. Heineken, for example, grew from a modest Amsterdam brewery into the world's third largest beer company, while Royal Dutch Shell became one of the world's largest energy companies, generating revenues in excess of a billion dollars a day. Unilever, founded in the 1850s by a pair of Dutch brothers seeking to export the butter produced in their dairy, grew into a sprawling conglomerate of some 500 companies, headquartered in London and Rotterdam, selling everything from nappies to chocolate bars under brand names including Dove, Ben & Jerry's, Hellmann's, Wall's and even Marmite.

Many Dutch companies became household names across Europe: Philips electronics, Douwe Egberts coffee, Amstel and Grolsch beers, TomTom satellite navigation systems, Fokker aircraft, P&O ships, DAF trucks, TNT parcels. Many others were less recognised but still global leaders in their fields: Akzo Nobel chemical refining, Delta Lloyd container shipping, ING banking, KPN telecommunications, Aegon insurance, Endemol television, NXP semiconductors. Amsterdam's southern periphery bristled with modern corporate headquarters, while The Hague, a city roughly the size of Brighton, became a major hub for the banking, legal and energy industries. Some 200 years after the demise of the treasure-seeking VOC, one of Europe's smallest countries remained an improbable but welcoming destination for anyone seeking to make their fortune in business.

A Nation of Cyclists

In Rotterdam, a resurgent city soon adopted a new post-war motto: *Sterker Door Strijd*, or 'Stronger through Battle'. Sadly, in the rush to clean up, many of the historic canals and harbours that had survived the bombing were filled with rubble. The docks, however, were quickly restored to their former glory and became one of northern Europe's major gateways for trade – buoyed, ironically, by a rebounding German economy. When British dockworkers went on strike over the introduction of new standardised shipping containers, Rotterdam invested heavily in the new technology, and prospered as a result. In keeping with the pro-American principles of the Marshall Plan, much of the city was redeveloped in typical American style, with grid-like streets and one of the world's first dedicated shopping centres.

Another major legacy of post-war reconstruction was visible on the riverbanks close to the Erasmusbrug: the scores of cyclists crowding the narrow streets. In Britain, cycling remained largely a sport, practised by dedicated enthusiasts with expensive bikes and special clothing. In the Netherlands, though, cycling was simply another routine mode of transport, like the bus or tube, used to travel to weddings and airports and hospital appointments. I saw smart businessmen on their way to meetings, delivery men riding overloaded cargo bicycles, young women with one child attached to the handlebars and another strapped behind, and even a man whose dog running alongside him was tethered to a spring-loaded arm sticking sideways off the saddle. To the Dutch, bicycles themselves weren't specialist pieces of sports equipment to be carefully maintained and polished, but unglamorous tools that people treated much like an umbrella or a spoon. In Amsterdam alone, local government crews collected more than 50,000 lost or discarded bicycles every single year.

Even before the war, bicycles were hugely popular in the Netherlands. When novelist Virginia Woolf visited Amsterdam in 1935 she wrote in her diary of 'cyclists [who] go in flocks like starlings'. This love of bicycles was partly for geographical reasons. The flat landscape made travelling by bicycle relatively effortless, and the small size of the country meant that cycling from point to point rarely took long. Narrow streets also resulted in driving in cities being bothersome, while the general lack of space led to frequent difficulty in finding a parking place. Economics played a role too – Dutch fuel taxes were high, while because of the lack of major national car manufacturers, cars had to be imported and so were very expensive.

During the war, the theft of bicycles by Nazi soldiers and the destruction of bicycle factories dealt a major blow to the bicycling tradition. After the war, however, those reconstructing the country were determined to put cycling back at its heart. When cities like Rotterdam were rebuilt, care was taken to plan not only new roads and train lines but also miles of new cycle lanes, complete with clear signposting and dedicated bicycle-only bridges, tunnels and traffic lights. Cyclists were given automatic priority at roundabouts, and thousands of bicycle parking spaces were provided at train stations. Many areas were designated as *woonerven*, 'living streets' in which cars were forbidden to move faster than walking speed. As commuters in other countries began using new motorway systems to commute from their suburban homes to their workplaces or shopping centres, the Dutch became increasingly accustomed to cycling everywhere. The fact that cyclists had no legal obligation to wear a helmet meant the fashion-conscious were not deterred from cycling, while strict legal liability laws meant that if an accident occurred, car drivers almost always took the blame.

In the 1960s and 1970s Dutch bicycle use dipped somewhat, but it then recovered. By the time I moved to the Netherlands, more than a third of all short journeys in the country were made by bicycle. From my own house I could easily cycle thirty or forty miles without ever having to share space with cars, sticking to the red *fietssnelweg* (cycle highway) connecting Rotterdam with other cities. According to the Dutch government, by 2009 the Netherlands was the only European nation with more bicycles than people.

Recovery and Recrimination

The Dutch people themselves bounced back quickly after the war, including those who had survived the Hunger Winter, who formed a valuable research group for doctors. The 'Dutch Famine Birth Cohort' was one of the first studies to prove that malnutrition during pregnancy could be seriously harmful to babies. In other pioneering research, a doctor in Den Haag, Willem-Karel Dicke, noticed that children on his wards who were suffering from coeliac disease appeared to have recovered more quickly during the wartime shortage of bread and cereals. Dicke wrote his findings in a series of influential academic papers, and the gluten-free diet was born. Elsewhere in the country, a doctor called Willem Kolff tried to get around shortages of medical equipment and save the lives of his patients by experimenting with two new tools he had invented: the blood bank and the blood-filtering dialysis machine. The first fifteen patients to use the equipment died, perhaps because it was made from sausage skins and old washing machine parts. But the sixteenth, a woman in her sixties who had fallen into a coma after suffering kidney failure, lived – the first person ever saved by a dialysis machine. Her first words on waking up were: 'I'm going to divorce my husband.'

The Netherlands' post-war recovery was reinforced – and perhaps partly enabled – by a widespread belief that although the war had been physically devastating, it represented a moral triumph for the country. In 1944, the American anthropologist Ruth Benedict was sent by the US government to write a report on the behaviour of the Dutch people, for American soldiers to read before being deployed there. Her main conclusion was that the Dutch were almost uniquely convinced of being in the right. 'No country in Europe is so jealous of its moral rightness as Holland,' she wrote. In one example quoted in her report, a German officer complained that the Dutch behaved as if *they* had won the war. In the Dutch perception, theirs was a country that had heroically resisted totalitarianism, been persecuted as a result, and then somehow come back brighter. As the Dutch writer Ian Buruma put it, to grow up in the post-war Netherlands, surrounded by elders who had suffered at the hands of totalitarianism, was 'to know that one was on the side of the angels'.

This tendency to glorify the country's wartime experiences unfortunately included a propensity to whitewash some of the more shameful episodes. The Dutch rightly lionised the heroes of the military and the anti-Nazi resistance, but in doing so did not always acknowledge that evil had also been done at Dutch hands. Anne Frank, for example, became a national and international symbol of bravery in the face of cruelty, her house in Amsterdam reminding the world of how the plucky Dutch had bravely hidden her from the Nazis, only for the evil Germans to capture her anyway. Less remarked on was the fact that the Franks were actually arrested by three Dutch policemen, at least one of whom continued serving in the Amsterdam police force until 1980.

Although many Dutch had resisted the Nazis, many had loyally served the occupying regime, and others had simply looked the other way while atrocities were taking place. Dutch government officials approved official declarations of Aryan origin, and Dutch policemen arrested Jews and escorted them to Westerbork. In 1942, the head of the Netherlands' security forces wrote in a secret letter to Heinrich Himmler: 'The new... Dutch police do an excellent job in the Jewish question and arrest the Jews by the hundreds day and night.' Himmler scrawled 'Very good' across the top of the report. As Hannah Arendt noted in her book *Eichmann in Jerusalem*, relatively low levels of anti-Semitism among the Dutch were firmly counterbalanced by a strong pro-Nazi movement that could be trusted to do the Nazis' bidding.

When I happened to pay a visit to Denmark, I couldn't help but notice that a comparison of the two countries' wartime records did not present the Dutch in a favourable light. Danish authorities largely cooperated with the Nazis – but only on the condition that Jews in the country were not treated too harshly. In one famous incident, the King of Denmark told his prime minister that if the Nazis made Jews wear yellow stars then he would wear one too, forcing the occupiers to scrap the plan. The Danish police refused to assist in rounding up Jews and when the Nazis announced plans for mass deportations, the entire Danish government resigned. Partly as a result of such actions, around 1 per cent of Jews in Denmark fell victim to the Nazis, compared to around 75 per cent in the Netherlands.

After the war, some Dutch collaborators were punished severely. Anton Mussert, the collaborationist leader of the Dutch fascist party, was convicted of treason and executed. Nazi sympathisers and Germans left behind in the Netherlands were taken to Camp Westerbork. Also punished were the Dutch women, sometimes called *Moffenmeiden*, or

'kraut-girls', who were believed to have had sexual relationships with occupying German soldiers. Scores of them were
literally tarred and feathered, their heads shaved before they
were paraded through the streets to catcalls and abuse. Yet
in the rush to rebuild the country, some of the guiltiest went
unpunished. As the Dutch writer Harry Mulisch once joked,
many Dutch people were happy to join the resistance once
the war was over.

Until relatively recently, it was rare for Dutch historians
to challenge the approved narrative of the Netherlands as a
country that heroically resisted the Nazis and was punished
for doing so. In 1993, for example, a historian who compared
the conduct of Dutch military forces in Indonesia after the
war to that of the occupying Nazis was prosecuted for slander.
More recently, however, there had been some steps towards a
proper accounting that would allow for not only heroes and
villains, but also shades of grey in between. The national railway company formally apologised for its role in transporting
Jews to concentration camps, and municipal authorities in
Amsterdam announced that they would *consider* refunding
the money paid by Jewish residents who had returned to the
city from concentration camps, only to be issued with ground
rent bills by the authorities. But there was still a way to go.
In 2012, for instance, Prime Minister Mark Rutte refused to
apologise for the Dutch government's policy towards Jews
during the war. Browsing a slick, government-funded website commemorating the Rotterdam air raids, I couldn't help
noticing that every section had been carefully translated into
English apart from one: 'Collaboration'.

The Germans

If the Dutch were sometimes unduly forgiving of fellow
nationals who had collaborated with the Germans, they were
decidedly less so of the Germans themselves. Growing up in
Britain, I had been accustomed to a degree of Jerry-baiting
tabloid jingoism. Popular culture served only to reinforce

longstanding stereotypes, whereby the Germans were all humourless automatons hell-bent on world domination or, failing that, securing the best sun-loungers before breakfast. In the Netherlands, the animosity went much further. As the US Council on Foreign Relations put it in 1947: 'Those who have lived for five years under German occupation have found in German pillage, imprisonments and executions plenty of reasons to hate the Germans.' Years later, the prevailing attitude was summarised well in a 1995 *New York Times* headline: 'For Dutch, It's OK to Despise Germans'. Referring to 'one of Western Europe's most enduring prejudices', the *Times* quoted the then Dutch ambassador to Germany, Peter van Walsum: 'we have been given a picture of Germany that has not changed since April 1945. As a result, tolerant Dutch citizens who would never discriminate against other foreigners see no deadly sin in behaving that way toward Germans.' A sixteen year-old student offered a more succinct analysis: 'They're fat, ugly and eat too much.'

Perhaps the most famous example of Dutch hostility to their eastern neighbours concerned the royal princesses' unfortunate habit of marrying Germans. Princess Juliana – the current King's grandmother – married the German Prince Bernhard in 1937, overlooking the fact that he had served in the SS. As Bernhard's official biography later put it, with some understatement: 'the news that Princess Juliana was going to marry a German prince was not received with unmitigated joy by the Dutch people.'

Three decades later, when Bernard and Juliana's daughter repeated the trick, the reaction was even less positive. Princess Beatrix (whom I later saw resign the throne in Dam Square) announced her engagement to the German Klaus van Amsberg in 1965. Tall and good-looking, Klaus was a scion of a noble family and not a bad catch for a young woman like Beatrix. Unfortunately, he had also been a member of the Hitler Youth and served in the German army during the latter stages of the war. Just twenty years after the Nazi occupation of their country had ended, this was a bit too much for even the tolerant Dutch to bear. Swastikas were daubed on government buildings and German cars smashed in the street. Several government ministers threatened to resign, but the Princess stuck to her guns and Parliament – which still had an effective veto over royal weddings – eventually voted to allow the union. On the day of the wedding, in 1966, thousands of soldiers lined the streets of Amsterdam, facing around two thousand protestors shouting *'Claus, 'raus!'* ('Claus, get out!') As the golden carriage carrying the happy couple passed by, youths threw bicycles into the street, followed by homemade smoke bombs. In the city where fleeing German soldiers had stolen thousands of bicycles, Beatrix's husband-to-be travelled to his wedding past banners and placards declaring *'Mijn fiets terug!'*, 'Give me back my bike!' In time, the Dutch view of Claus/Klaus mellowed. However, a popular joke suggested he was never fully embraced: a man parked his bike in front of the Royal Palace and a guard told him, 'Sir, you can't park here; the Prince is coming!' 'It's alright,' the man replied. 'I locked it.'

Dutch teutonophobia had weakened over time, thanks partly to younger generations' lack of direct experience of the conflict. Ambitious, worldly young Dutch people were as likely to be impressed by Berlin's nightlife as repelled by the Germans' war record. European integration meant the Dutch–German border was practically invisible, and as the largest buyer of Dutch exports Germany was admired for its powerhouse economy. Nevertheless, traces of the old enmity endured, and outright hostility was not uncommon. Close to the German border it was still possible to see old wartime bunkers adorned with graffiti aimed at visiting Germans: *'Zimmer frei!'*, 'Room available!' Sports events were common flashpoints. Commentating on a strong German performance at a winter Olympics biathlon event, a Dutch television commentator famously said: 'Shooting and running through the forest – that's a sport Germans are good at!' Residents of Dutch seaside towns inundated with German tourists could sometimes be heard complaining that the Germans celebrated the wartime invasion of the Netherlands by doing it again every summer. On the very day I visited Westerbork, I flipped on the television to be greeted by a Dutch sitcom character discussing, against a backdrop of riotous canned laughter, his reasons for buying a new truck. 'No, grandpa, it's not so I can gather up all the Germans in our country and take them away!' 'The best kind of recycling?' an old Dutchman once asked me on a train to Dusseldorf. 'A German eating pork!'

Legacies of War

In cities like Rotterdam, the physical legacy of the war was clearly evident in the modernist skyline, the soulless city centre and the endless modern cycle lanes. In Amsterdam and other cities, emergency air-raid sirens were still tested every month, causing endless confusion among tourists fearing a zombie invasion. Other legacies were less obvious: the echoes of war detectable in the country's culture, habits and outlook. I was wary of seeing causes and effects where none existed, but it seemed fairly certain that Dutch people's belief in equality and minority rights was linked to their direct experiences of living under a brutal dictatorship, and their shame at having failed to adequately resist it.

Less tangibly, as I watched street sweepers scrubbing already clean pavements, I sometimes wondered if their diligence was linked to the fact that those same streets had been littered with rubble a few decades before. I also harboured suspicions that the wartime experience of hardship and destruction might have encouraged Dutch habits of thrift and frugality. It was not for nothing that the practice of splitting restaurant bills down to the last penny was known internationally as 'going Dutch'. Amsterdam had its snappy dressers, for sure, but overall the Dutch had a strong inclination to frown on conspicuous consumption. Tipping in restaurants was viewed as unspeakably decadent; there were strict limits on daily withdrawals from cash machines; and the Dutch word for 'debt' (*schuld*) was the same as the word for 'guilt'. The Netherlands was even the proud birthplace of the 'bottlescraper', a long-handled plastic spatula designed specifically to remove the last traces of mustard or mayonnaise from the bottom of the jar. 'Do you know how copper wire was invented?' an old geezer at a supermarket counter once asked me as we watched a customer at a neighbouring checkout argue about his change. 'Two Dutchmen were fighting over a penny!' Dutch thrift had deep roots in the Protestant work ethic, but it was easy to believe that it had been strengthened by wartime exposure to hardship. In a country where thousands had lost their homes in living memory, was it any surprise that people were obsessive about saving for the future, and in the habit of buying insurance policies to safeguard against the risk of everything from accidentally breaking a friend's television to getting divorced?

Another possible legacy was the Dutch attitude to food. Their cuisine consisted largely of simple, earthy, calorific stodge: potatoes and cabbage and heavily processed meat that looked like pink toothpaste. Despite being one of Europe's smallest countries, the Netherlands was (according to the national statistics agency) responsible for nearly a third of the continent's total production of French fries. The contrast with the more delicate cuisines enjoyed elsewhere in Europe was stark, as any tourist unfortunate enough to have been treated to a *frikandel* fried meat-stick could testify. Bread and cheese was viewed by many Dutch people as a fine meal; cheap processed sausage a real treat. Perhaps most damning of all were the *Smullers* automated vending machines found in many city centres, selling pre-heated junk food that managed to be burnt and soggy at the same time.

In Dutch homes, the kitchen was usually a small corner of the living room rather than the focal point of family life, while in restaurants simple food was served slowly and eaten quickly. Even slightly exotic cooking ingredients – lemongrass, say, or fresh ginger – were difficult to get hold of outside Amsterdam, with many small supermarkets adopting the Henry Ford approach: you can buy any vegetable you

want as long as it's a potato. Tellingly, when the former Dutch
national football coach Louis van Gaal took over as manager
of Manchester United, one of his very first decisions was to
add chips to the menu in the players' canteen.

As with thrift (with which it was surely linked), the Dutch
attitude to food had deep historical roots. But again, it was
easy to think that previous habits had been exacerbated by
wartime experiences. In a country where many people had
lived through a serious famine, was it surprising that a tuna
salad would be considered a reckless extravagance, and a
cheese sandwich a delicious meal worth savouring?

The Fire Boundary

Back in Rotterdam, I left the river and retraced my steps
to the Sint Laurenskerk. In front of the church entrance, a
young man in a leather jacket was performing the most common of Dutch chores: searching for his bike in a long rack of
near-identical machines. In the vast, vaguely Stalinist plaza
behind, bars were overflowing with people meeting for after-
work *borrels*, or networking drinks, bragging noisily on the
darkening pavement.

I walked in circles for a while, battling to hold a map open
in the wind, before finally finding what I was looking for
right beneath my feet. Set in the surface of the pavement,
easily missed among the manhole covers and litter, were a
series of round lamps the size of coffee cups. Each was dimly
backlit with a faint red bulb and emblazoned on top with a
flame symbol that resembled a bad tattoo. Spaced at intervals of a few metres, the lamps ran down the pavement, stopping and then resuming where roads and tram tracks crossed
their path, before disappearing round a corner. Together, they
formed the *brandgrens* – the 'fire boundary' marking the edge
of the area destroyed by the wartime bombing raids and subsequent fires. An upward glance confirmed the difference
between the two sides. To the left were the remnants of the
old city: tall townhouses of red brick, with sloping roofs and

pulleys poised to hoist furniture up five skinny floors. To the right were grey modern blocks with flat tops and concrete façades and bicycles hanging off the sides of cramped balconies; the unattractive evidence of a city reborn. Where the weak bulbs now blushed in the pavement, there had once been a searing wall of flame. A plane flew low overhead on its way to the nearby airport, and I flinched.

Five

Total Football

Feyenoord, Ajax and the Pride of a Nation

I had always hated football. As a child in southeast England, I dreaded Wednesday afternoons when teachers forced me to don a thin Umbro football kit and stand in the freezing rain, waiting what seemed like hours for the opportunity to get stamped on by a sharp-toothed boot, or slapped painfully by an icy ball on a skinny thigh. As I grew a little older I became slightly more enthusiastic, because playing football provided an opportunity to stare at girls playing netball on a neighbouring patch of tarmac, but I still rarely touched the ball, and switched to basketball as soon as the portly PE teacher allowed it. When my cheering classmates greeted the England football manager Graham Taylor on a visit to my school in the early 1990s, I had no idea who he was.

As an adult, my playing days behind me, I came to dread the awkward Monday-morning banter about the weekend's results, and the awkward silences that inevitably followed the question 'Who do you support?' Major cultural landmarks like Gazza's tears or Beckham's red card went unnoticed, and I learned simply to smile and nod while colleagues bonded over discussion of the FA Cup tie or what Rooney had done on Saturday. Football, that great leveller and lingua franca of British men, was to me a vaguely menacing mystery; a sport of thrown chairs and punched police horses. It was a universal language that I didn't speak. No, I did not like football.

In the country I'd moved to, however, football was practically a national religion. The Dutch – not just men, but plenty of women too – were completely in love with the beautiful game. In a country half the size of Scotland, the national football association claimed to have over a million members and to oversee more than 30,000 games every week. Nationwide, there were over 3000 football associations and more than 40 stadiums. Every evening, hours of television time were allocated to grizzled ex-players discussing prospects and tactics. There were smaller amateur football pitches everywhere, and many Dutch seemed to take their role as secretary or treasurer of a local amateur team more seriously than their actual day job. Sons would play for the same local sides as their fathers and grandfathers had, the whole family cheering from the sidelines. At weekends, train stations across the country were flooded with fans and police. A few hours later, you could usually tell how the local team had done just from the sound – either car horns honking happily in the distance, or police sirens wailing their way towards a skirmish between unhappy fans.

When the *Wereldkampioenschap*, or World Cup, came around the whole country ground to a halt, offices emptying and bars filling as everyone donned their best orange clothing and went crazy. Even the women's World Cup, which passed almost unnoticed in England, was followed closely. In an otherwise straightforward, sensible country, football was – like Carnival and King's Day – a way for people to let off steam, cheering and shouting in a way they never would on a boozy night out. In a country where unity and community were everything, football was a glue that helped bind people together.

On the international stage, the Dutch were the Brazilians of Europe – both technically skilled and entertainingly flamboyant. The list of world-famous Dutchmen was a short one, but included several footballers: Ruud Gullit, Dennis Bergkamp, Robin van Persie, Ruud van Nistelrooy, Marco van Basten. The tiny nation had produced one of the world's best footballers of the last fifty years, Johan Cruijff, and one of the best managers, Louis van Gaal. Perhaps more importantly, the Dutch had pioneered a new style of football that transformed the way the game was played around the world.

A Late Entry

For a long time I resisted Dutch football's siren call. As far as I was concerned, football was a waste of time, and Ajax was something you used to clean the kitchen sink. But then, in 2014, my resolve cracked. The World Cup was under-way in Brazil, and the Dutch were to play the first game of the tournament finals against one of their oldest enemies, the Spanish. I went with a few Dutch friends to watch the game on a large television screen in Rotterdam city centre. Seemingly the whole city had gathered in a narrow street to drink beer and cheer for their country, dressed from head to toe in orange. The Dutch had lost 1–0 to the Spanish in an ill-tempered World Cup final four years previously, and many now feared a repeat of that performance.

These fears were realised when the Spanish were awarded an undeserved penalty after less than half an hour, and scored. But then came a breathtaking fightback from the Dutch: a superman-style header from Rotterdam boy Robin van Persie, followed by no fewer than four more Dutch goals. Team Orange ran like clockwork and the crowd in Rotterdam became frenzied with excitement. When the whistle blew and the final score appeared on the screen – NED 5, ESP 1 – the sensible, sober Dutch went almost insane, cheering and jumping and sending plastic cups of beer soaring high across the crowd. I went to take a sip of my beer and found, to my surprise, that I too had thrown my cup skyward in delight.

Dutch hopes of winning the World Cup died a few weeks later, but my curiosity had been piqued. A few months after that, at the ripe old age of thirty-two, I did what I had always sworn I never would and made a late entry into the game. I went to a football match.

Feyenoord, known to locals as *De club aan de Maas* ('The Club on the Maas'), is Rotterdam's most popular side, one of a triumvirate of teams, including Ajax and PSV Eindhoven, that dominate the top of the *Eredivisie*, or Dutch premier-ship. Feyenoord draws enormous support from among

Rotterdam's working classes and is as intricately linked to the city and its no-nonsense working-class culture as Liverpool or Manchester's clubs are to theirs. In Rotterdam, as in so many other cities around the world, football isn't simply a matter of life and death. It is far more important than that.

On a chilly winter Sunday, I was going to watch Feyenoord play at home against SC Cambuur, a smaller club from the northern Dutch market town of Leeuwarden. After a long and glorious history including 14 *Eredivisie* titles and a European Cup, Feyenoord's performance had dipped somewhat in recent years. Beset by financial troubles, the club had lost several star players to English clubs and suffered some embarrassing defeats, like a 10–0 drubbing in 2010 by rivals PSV Eindhoven. Things had improved a bit since then, but sitting third in the *Eredivisie* behind Ajax and PSV, Feyenoord could do with a win. Cambuur, in ninth position, looked likely to provide it with a comfortable victory. In the teams' previous meeting nearly a year before, Feyenoord had romped home 5–1, and pundits were now predicting another comfortable victory.

My companion for the day certainly hoped so. My girlfriend's brother was a twenty-four-year-old Feyenoord fan so devout that he refused even to set foot in the city of Amsterdam lest he be tainted by association with the rival team based there, Ajax. Today, wearing a red-and-white Feyenoord shirt and matching hat, he assured me that I'd love the match. Like a first-time father worried he wouldn't like his own newborn baby, I wasn't so sure.

The game was taking place in Rotterdam's main football stadium, De Kuip or 'The Tub', a 60,000-seater arena that looked as if it had descended from outer space to land just south of the river Maas, not far from where I'd arrived by ferry on a previous journey. As I filed through the turnstiles with hundreds of excitable fans, I couldn't help but feel I was undergoing a rite of passage, albeit belatedly and not very enthusiastically. Inside the stadium, the noise was deafening. I had arrived late, of course, and tens of thousands of people had already taken their seats in the bathtub-shaped arena – more people than I had ever seen in one location before. De Kuip consisted of three tiers of seats: a flat area for die-hard fans close to the pitch, and then two levels of banked seats stretching upwards above them, shielded by an oval-shaped metal roof that resembled the banked track of a velodrome. The pitch itself was open to the sky, and even on a bright winter's day was illuminated by dazzling spotlights. It all felt strangely like a film set: the pitch looked very close, but also very far away. To my great disappointment, the bar we passed on the way in had turned out to be alcohol-free. Even worse, I learned that there wouldn't be any cheerleaders at half time.

We ascended the stairs and my companion steered us expertly to our allocated seats, high up in the third tier, behind the home side's goal. A stiff wind was sweeping in off the Maas and it was bitterly cold, but no one appeared to mind. Bundled up in thick coats and woolly hats, the Feyenoord fans around me were already munching happily on *stroopwafel* caramel wafers and mayonnaise-soaked French fries. I was one of the few present who didn't have a Feyenoord logo displayed somewhere about my person.

Well armed with prejudices about football fans, I was surprised by the diversity of the crowd. There were a lot of buzzcut young men who wouldn't have been out of place on an army parade ground, but also well-off-looking couples, old geezers being taught how to use their grandsons' digital cameras, grey-haired women peering at the pitch through spectacles, and a few young mothers with children. To my right, I could even see a group of schoolchildren on a field trip, running their young teacher ragged with repeated attempts to escape the stands. Sitting next to me was a fat man of about fifty wearing, for some reason, a smart Manchester United tracksuit. Looking around, I realised that we were very close to the section allocated to visiting Cambuur fans, isolated behind a row of security guards, a high glass screen topped with fierce spikes and a net to catch any thrown debris. High

up above the real fans, with the security guards and the kids
and the old people, seemed the ideal place for a cowardly first-
timer like me.

Having booked a cheap ticket at the last minute, I was also
surprised to find I had an excellent view of the pitch, through
the back of the home team's goal net and down the stripes
mown into the pitch like lanes in a motorway. On the upper
tier of seating, a series of signs recalled some of Feyenoord's
past glories: *'Winnaar UEFA Cup 1974, Winnaar UEFA Cup
2002, Winnaar Europa Cup 1'*. Above them all was the no-
nonsense Feyenoord motto: *'Club van iedereen, voor iedereen'*, 'Club from everyone, for everyone'. Ironically, in this
city whose identity was still strongly linked to its wartime
experiences, one of the main match sponsors was a German
carmaker, Opel.

A vast, parachute-like Feyenoord logo was removed from
the centre of the pitch and the home team jogged into view,
in their harlequin-style half-red half-white kit, greeted by a
deafening roar from the stadium. Then their rivals appeared,
looking strangely Oompa-Loompaish in bright yellow shirts
and blue shorts. The heavily outnumbered away fans made
their own impressive racket on the other side of the glass
screen. In the stands below us, Feyenoord fans began working themselves up for kick-off, waving red-and-white scarves
in the air. The man next to me finished his *stroopwaffel* and
joined in a lusty rendition of Queen's 'We Will Rock You' with
adapted Dutch lyrics that I couldn't decipher over the din of
the crowd. When the referee blew his whistle, I almost didn't
notice the game begin.

The Dutch Revolution

For Rotterdammers with a chip on their shoulder about
their much-disputed status as the Netherlands' second city,
De Kuip was the centre of the footballing universe. To the
outside world, however, the epicentre of Dutch football lay
not in Rotterdam, but some fifty miles further north, at

Amsterdam's Olympic Stadium, historic home of the club that a few decades previously had transformed the way the game was played forever.

Although football was always popular in the Netherlands, for many years the Dutch exhibited no particular skill at or passion for the game. In a waterlogged country, sports like swimming, rowing and ice skating often garnered equal attention and won the Dutch more acclaim on the international stage. As late as the 1960s, most Dutch football teams played in a style that outsiders thought of as relatively simple and straightforward; fitting, perhaps, for a sensible, slightly dreary country still recovering from a devastating war. As David Winner explained in his book *Brilliant Orange*, Dutch players were for many years banned from turning professional, and even top scorers might earn their living selling magazines or working in warehouses rather than on the pitch. The Dutch national side's performance was generally pretty poor. According to Jonathan Wilson's history of football, *Inverting the Pyramid*, of the twenty-seven international games the Dutch played between 1949 and 1955, they won just two. Between the 1930s and the 1970s they didn't qualify for the World Cup once.

In the 1960s there was a revolution. Freed from the shackles of war, the Dutch economy was booming, and when the rigid system of religious 'pillars' crumbled a new generation began to embrace new freedoms. As Amsterdam gradually became a more playful, creative, cosmopolitan place, its main local team – Ajax – followed suit. Starchy, disappointing football was replaced by something altogether more exciting.

The man most responsible for the change, Rinus Michels, had grown up close to the Ajax stadium in Amsterdam. He was given a football kit for his ninth birthday; his skills soon caught the eye of the local club's scouts, and he signed for the junior team. His early playing career was interrupted by the war and the 1944 'Hunger Winter', but Michels later became a sturdy, hard-working regular on the club's first team. He played in hundreds of Dutch league games and a handful of international matches before retiring in the late 1950s, suffering from a back injury. After a spell working as a gymnastics teacher at a local school, he was appointed to the top coaching job at Ajax in 1965. He quickly implemented sweeping changes, seeking to professionalise what had up to then been a rather ramshackle operation. Talented young players were hired and trained intensively, and paid proper wages that enabled them to drop their second jobs. David Winner explains that Michels introduced aggressive new training programmes, studied the performance of other teams carefully, and ordered the construction of professional medical facilities to treat players' injuries. He was ruthless in sidelining players who underperformed. Off the pitch, players were banned from partying ahead of important matches; Michels even chose the films they could watch on their nights off. Grumbling young players quickly came up with an appropriate nickname for their boss: 'The General'.

The most revolutionary change, though, was in tactics. Determined to increase the fluidity of play, Michels introduced 'position switching', which allowed players to swap places on the pitch at will during the course of a game. An Ajax player usually stuck in defence (for example) could surge forward and attack if he saw the chance, while frontline strikers fell back to defend the goal. Michels encouraged his players to break formation and use every inch of the pitch, including the air above it. In a tactic known as 'pressing', defenders were also encouraged to range much further upfield than normal, luring opponents into the so-called offside trap if they ventured behind the Ajax lines. For coaches and analysts usually obsessed with debating the merits of different fixed formations, the Michels approach represented a sea change, opening up new possibilities for players to move diagonally across the pitch and chase the ball through gaps in the defence like water trickling through the streams of a polder. To Ajax's opponents, the new style was fast, fluid and impossible to predict. The club quickly became famous for its players' flamboyance on the pitch, and for their determination not simply to win, but to play well. To Michels, the beautiful game really should be beautiful.

Proof of the effectiveness of the new approach came in 1966, when Ajax faced Bill Shankly's mighty Liverpool in a European Cup game at Amsterdam's Olympic Stadium. It was just a few months since England's victory in the World Cup, and Liverpool was considered one of the best teams in the world. The Dutch won 5–1. Shortly after that, the two teams met again at Anfield. Ajax faced down a hostile home crowd to score a 2–2 draw. The Dutch team went on to lose the Cup, but Michels' new approach had been vindicated. A previously struggling side had beaten one of the world's greatest teams.

In order to take full advantage of the new approach, Rinus Michels needed not just new tactics, but also a skilled partner on the pitch. Luckily for Ajax, he had one. Johan Cruijff was born in 1947 and brought up, like Michels, almost in the shadow of the Ajax stadium, where his mother had a job as a cleaner. From a very young age Cruijff (sometimes spelled Cruyff in English) had only one ambition: to become a professional footballer. His father died from a heart attack when Cruijff was twelve and – to his mother's dismay – the boy soon dropped out of school to pursue his dream. Slight and skinny, with a big nose and floppy brown hair, he lacked the physical strength for long rough games, but he was quick on his feet and technically skilled. Early footage showed him seeming to dance around the ball, dribbling balletically and unleashing sudden bursts of speed. Talent-spotted by Michels, Cruijff made it into Ajax's first team at the age of only seventeen.

If Michels was the mastermind of the position-switching style, Cruijff quickly proved to be its on-pitch conductor, constantly pointing teammates to new positions like a traffic policeman directing cars. Nominally allocated to a centre-forward position, Cruijff himself would range all over the pitch, surprising his opponents with deep defensive runs and wide swings along the left or right wing. His ball skills were also dazzling. Particularly challenging for opponents was a feint that became known as the 'Cruijff Turn', in which he would appear ready to pass the ball, but then suddenly use one foot to drag it behind the other, before spinning 180 degrees and speeding away.

Cruijff was also a revolutionary player off the pitch. In an era when many players had still come up through the staid old semi-professional system, he made waves by demanding a top salary, plus insurance, and by refusing to wear officially approved clothing provided by team sponsors. His clashes with the Dutch footballing authorities embodied the late-1960s rebellion of the young post-war generation against the rules and hierarchies of their parents. Cruijff's willingness to challenge the established order set the tone for a future in which players were superstars, and expected to be treated as such. His attitude won him many admirers, but also enemies. He could be something of a know-it-all, reportedly even advising a surgeon who later operated on his heart on the best way to go about it. You could either choose his way of doing things or you could choose the wrong way.

With Cruijff on the pitch and Michels directing from the sidelines, Ajax went from strength to strength. The team won the Dutch national championship three years in a row, in 1966, 1967 and 1968, and made the final of the European Cup in 1969. In 1971, it won the European Cup at Wembley; it won again the next year, and again the year after that. In the space of a few years, Ajax had gone from a team of middling semi-professionals to one of the best clubs in the world, and the agile new style it had pioneered began to be adopted by other teams. Ironically, a country known for its good sense and unflashy dependability had started to become famous worldwide for its flair and creativity on the pitch. By the mid-1970s, the new style had acquired a new name: '*Totaalvoetbal*', or 'Total Football'.

The Beautiful Game?

At the Feyenoord–Cambuur game, I couldn't see much evidence of the graceful, fluid style the Dutch were famous for. The very few occasions I'd watched football before had always been on television, so I was used to a fairly sanitised version of the game, all slow-motion replays and sweeping aerial views. In real life it looked much scrappier, with bits of mud and turf flying as the players scrambled for control of the ball. Even sitting high in the stands, I could see the floodlit players swearing and spitting and shouting to one another. There were a few moments where they impressed with their skill and speed, but the game also often looked more like rugby, players floundering on the floor desperately trying to seize possession of the ball.

Without the assistance of televised commentary or replays, I struggled to understand a lot of what was happening. Feyenoord had won the coin toss, but to my untrained eye it looked like Cambuur had the upper hand. The visitors made an early break behind Feyenoord lines for a half-hearted shot at the goal, saved easily by the Feyenoord keeper, followed by a similar skirmish at the opposite end of the pitch. The noise from the crowd made it clear that some manoeuvres were considered masterful and others embarrassing, but I could hardly tell the difference. At a point when I thought Feyenoord were doing rather well, the man in the Manchester United tracksuit sitting next to me answered his phone and announced loudly that the game was going 'f**king terribly', and that Feyenoord were 'playing like a bunch of f**king retards'. Eavesdropping on those around me, I quickly learned a lot of new vocabulary, including the Dutch for hand ball and yellow card, and for several other things not in my English–Dutch dictionary. I was also reminded of the curious Dutch habit of using medical terms as swear words, whereby '*kanker!*' ('cancer!') and '*tyfus!*' ('typhus!') were common responses to a fluffed goal or clumsy foul.

With the home team underperforming, the crowd was growing listless. Then, after fifteen minutes of play, a Feyenoord striker suddenly made a long run down the pitch. Weaving between Cambuur's defenders, he looked set to score but was brought down by a clumsy tackle just outside the box. The referee reached into his pocket for a yellow card to wave at the guilty Cambuur player and the crowd around me came to life, singing and shouting and holding both arms aloft as if they were about to do the YMCA. A Feyenoorder stepped up to take a free kick and the whole stadium began clapping rhythmically, a metronomic thump echoing through the stadium like a heartbeat, building to a crescendo until the ball bounced harmlessly off a defending wall of yellow. The Cambuur fans on the other side of the glass screen began to jump up and down, and my seat shook as if I were riding a horse in an earthquake.

Total Football Goes Global

Within a few years of Ajax's turnaround, the new Total Football also proved its worth at international level. After failing to qualify for the World Cup for nearly four decades, the Dutch tore their way through qualifying and finals in 1974. A team dominated by Ajax players scored solid victories against giants like Brazil, Argentina and East Germany. They came unstuck in the final, but repeated the trick at the 1978 tournament, beating Austria 5–1 and Italy 2–1 before going down in the final against the hosts Argentina. After years of disappointment, the Dutch had come second at two World Cups in a row.

Observing the turnaround in Dutch footballing fortunes, other national teams tried in vain to emulate Total Football. Usually they failed. To the Dutch, the fluid, position-switching style may have been obvious – for those used to living squeezed on top of one another, shuffling past other people up narrow stairwells and cramming things into every corner of their tiny apartments, using every inch of the pitch made perfect sense. But to others it proved hard to master. In 1977, for example, England's Football Association organised sessions where it tried to get players to mimic the Dutch approach, but soon gave up. English players spent hours trying to replicate the pirouetting 'Cruijff Turn' in training, but could never quite perfect it. Even gifted players like Trevor Brooking struggled to match the Dutch team's skill in making forty-yard passes along the length of the pitch. A few weeks later, the English had a chance to try out their version of Total Football against the Dutch in a friendly at Wembley. England had beaten the Dutch five times before, had a solid team that included Kevin Keegan, and were optimistic they could outfox the position-switching Dutchmen. Nevertheless, the English were completely outclassed, and Johan Cruijff ran rings round his opponents. By one count Cruijff touched the ball nearly three times more often than one of England's star strikers, Trevor Francis. The Dutch beat England 2–0.

For a generation of football fans, the Dutch exemplified an exciting new way of playing the game. The international media also grew to love Dutch players, who not only performed on the pitch but could explain their performance afterwards in intelligent terms, speaking near-flawless English. Johan Cruijff in particular became known for his enigmatic pronouncements, which were – depending on who you asked – either deeply insightful or completely ridiculous. 'The game always begins afterwards,' he would declare with all the authority of a High Court judge. 'Every disadvantage has its advantage.'

As Total Football proved its effectiveness, and as the sport became increasingly globalised, Dutch influence rippled outwards. Players and coaches left the Netherlands for lucrative contracts elsewhere. Cruijff was, as always, the trailblazer. In 1973, at the peak of his powers, he shocked Ajax by leaving to join Barcelona for a record-breaking $1 million transfer fee. Political as well as financial considerations played a role in the move: the dictator Franco was still in charge in Spain, and the political climate in the capital of separatist Catalonia was tense. Even before his arrival, Cruijff had endeared himself to Catalonians by announcing that he could never play for rivals Real Madrid, as it was a club 'associated with Franco'. The authorities had forbidden Spaniards from christening their sons with Catalan names. When Cruijff had a son in 1974, he chose a name, Jordi, that was not only Catalan but also the name of Catalonia's patron saint. The love of the locals assured, Cruijff ended up spending half his life in Barcelona, racing around the city in a silver Maserati and speaking Catalan with a thick Amsterdam accent. His first spell there lasted five years, during which he helped Barcelona win both the Spanish championship and the Spanish cup.

Cruijff announced his retirement in 1978, but he didn't stay away from football for long. Three years later, he delighted the Dutch (or at least, those who supported Ajax) by returning to his old club in Amsterdam. This marked the beginning of a period known to sports reporters as Cruijff's 'Indian Summer', a glorious winning streak in which he, by now well into his thirties, helped Ajax win the double of the Dutch league and cup titles. In 1983, though, he broke Ajax hearts for a second time by committing the ultimate heresy of transferring to Feyenoord, where the Indian Summer continued with another double of league and cup titles. In 1984 he hung up his boots once and for all, joining the Ajax coaching team the following year. Within a few years, the club had won the UEFA Cup Winners' Cup.

In the late 1980s Cruijff returned to Barcelona, where he was almost as successful as a manager as he had been as a player, taking a struggling club to victories in four Spanish championships in a row, as well as the 1992 European Cup. He also created much of the programme at the famous Barcelona youth academy, later emulated by many clubs seeking to ensure a steady supply of fresh talent. Suffering from heart problems, Cruijff left Barcelona in 1996, and was most recently seen managing Catalonia and commentating on Dutch television. His legacy was assured: the greatest Dutch football player of all time, and almost certainly the most famous Dutchman alive.

Half-Time Heroes

At De Kuip, with the end of the first half approaching, Feyenoord made a series of scrappy attempts to cut through the throng of Cambuur defenders. To me the game looked energetic, but not particularly beautiful; the fans around me seemed to agree. My Dutch vocabulary continued to expand. Somewhere behind me, a spectator began tearing pages from the match programme and making paper planes, which drifted over the crowd before becoming entangled in the netting protecting the away fans. A flock of seagulls swooped low over the stands and someone cheered loudly, in English, 'Yeeeeeaaah, birds!', prompting lusty laughter from the crowd. With the temperature dropping and both sides yet to score, everyone was growing restless.

Just as I was thinking of taking a nap, in a scrappy moment of play the Cambuur keeper fumbled the ball, and Feyenoord's Dutch-Moroccan midfielder Karim El Ahmadi charged through a gap in the defence to hammer the ball past the prostrate goalie's outstretched fingers and into the net. The digital display around the edge of the pitch turned orange, a scrolling digital script chasing the celebrating players along the sidelines with 'OH OH OH OH OH OH OH OH!' Thousands of Rotterdammers sprang to their feet, cheering and shouting and waving scarves and throwing shredded programmes in the air like confetti. Too self-conscious to whoop or sing, I nevertheless found myself thrusting my fists in the air like a champion prizefighter. On the other side of the glass screen, the Cambuur fans sat in deathly silence.

Almost immediately after the goal, the whistle blew for half time. Unable to feel my hands and feet, I joined the crowd descending the steel staircases in search of something warm to eat or drink. In the belly of the stadium, under the sloping stands, devoted Feyenoord supporters were still celebrating, including one group of burly fans singing, rather improbably, a Dutch footballing variation of Gloria Gaynor's 'I Will Survive'. As I navigated the crowds of eaters and drinkers and smokers and queuers, I was pleasantly surprised by how friendly everyone was; another challenge to my snooty prejudices about football fans. 'No, please, after you,' a heavily tattooed man with a shaved head said, patting me on the back as he let me edge ahead of him in the coffee queue.

Immersed in the good-natured crowd, I began to understand some of the clichés about football clubs being rooted in community. Lots of fans knew one another, and if they didn't, merely wearing a shirt or scarf of the right colour was enough to win new friends immediately. Particularly in a country where people love being close to one another, and doing things together, and feeling part of a close-knit community, it was easy to see the appeal. I could also see how love of the game could become self-sustaining: if you cared about the club, you'd make friends and buy a season ticket and follow every game closely, making you care about the result even more. For people who perhaps didn't have much money or status at work, and for young men eager to emphasise their masculinity, passionate support for a club could even offer a shortcut to a kind of elevated social status. You might get shouted at by your boss all week and by your wife and kids in the evening, but here, proving your passion in the stadium and in the bar afterwards, you could be a lion.

The queue to buy coffee, in the half-light directly under the first tier of seating, was long. I had just been handed a steaming cup when there was a sudden explosion of noise overhead, as thousands of people jumped to their feet cheering. The second half had begun and Feyenoord had already scored again.

I returned to my seat to find the atmosphere transformed. *'Twee–nul!'* my neighbour told me jubilantly, two–nil! After two previous shots had bounced off the bar and off the keeper, the British-born, Turkish international player Colin Kazim-Richards had apparently found his target with a curving rocket into the left corner of the goal. With Feyenoord now firmly in the lead, the crowd was energised. Down near the pitch, fans started singing, in English, 'Always Look on the Bright Side of Life', followed by what my companion said was the official Feyenoord club song, 'Hand in Hand'. *'Rotterdam zijn we d'r klaar voor? Feyenoord wordt kampioen! Waar zijn die handen?'* they sang. 'Rotterdam, are we ready? Feyenoord are becoming champions! Where are your hands?' I later read that the song was written by a German.

God's Father, Louis van Gaal

With such frenzied activity on the pitch, I had expected to see the Feyenoord and Cambuur managers on the sidelines living up to long-held stereotypes, red-faced and bawling in gold sunglasses and long camel coats. However, I didn't see either manager during the whole game, as they remained sitting quietly in their respective dugouts. I mentioned this to my companion and learned that this was another of the stereotypical features of Total Football. While in British teams it was the manager who did all the talking, shouting from the sidelines and heckling underperforming players at half time, in Dutch teams it was the players who wouldn't shut up, endlessly discussing tactics and making suggestions to the manager. 'They all think they know best, and the manager lets them think that,' my friend said. In football, as in life, the Dutch loved to talk things through.

There was at least one notable exception to this rule – a man who was known for his bluntness and who, along with Cruijff, had played a huge role in turning the world of international football orange, in the process making himself another of the most famous Dutchmen alive.

Aloysius Paulus Maria van Gaal, better known as Louis van Gaal, was born in Amsterdam in 1951. The youngest child in a sprawling Catholic family of nine, he (like Cruijff) signed for Ajax while still a teenager. Van Gaal was a skilful player, his long neck and upright posture rendering him particularly adept at headers, and his bent nose telling of countless mid-air collisions with opponents' heads and elbows. With his hawkish features and regal stance, he was a charismatic figure both on and off the pitch. He was, however, a terribly slow runner and dribbler, and as such played in the Ajax first eleven only once, in a friendly when Cruijff was unavailable. The disappointed young player soon found himself loaned to Antwerp, and later to North Holland's SC Telstar, before winding up at Rotterdam's Sparta, a small club often overshadowed by its near neighbours Feyenoord.

It was at Sparta that van Gaal began to make a name for himself, playing dependably good football and serving as a mentor to younger players. Sparta was a relative minnow compared to the likes of Ajax and Feyenoord, but van Gaal exhibited a self-confidence that would later become legendary, telling reporters: 'I am a very gifted footballer.' Like Cruijff, he also acquired a reputation as a bit of a troublemaker. He fell out with Sparta's manager and openly advised the club's board to sell one of his teammates. Haughty and imperious, he was teased for his habit of speaking about himself in the third person.

In the mid-1980s, van Gaal moved from Sparta to AZ '67, a middle-ranking Dutch club from the northern cheese-making town of Alkmaar. After a brief spell on the pitch he ascended to the management team, becoming the side's assistant manager. He again proved excellent at coaching younger players, but also cocky, authoritarian and liable to rub people up the wrong way. Sacked from AZ, he was lucky to find a job back at Ajax, as head of the club's junior programme. In 1991, when his boss left for Madrid, he unexpectedly landed one of the top jobs in Dutch football: manager of Ajax.

Van Gaal promoted his own version of Total Football, encouraging his players to pass constantly and attack relentlessly, always searching for gaps in their opponents' defence to slip through. Like his legendary predecessor Rinus Michels, van Gaal was a strict disciplinarian. Having once worked as a gymnastics teacher, he was unafraid to treat superstar players like naughty schoolchildren, and became known for his prickly, confrontational attitude to members of the press. 'Are you so dumb or am I so clever?' he famously asked one inquisitive reporter. The German player/manager Uli Hoeness was once asked by *De Telegraaf* whether van Gaal acted like God. No, he replied, van Gaal acted like he was God's father.

Critics of van Gaal's managerial style were quietened by his team's performances. During his roughly six years in charge at Ajax, the club won the Dutch *Eredivisie* three times, as well as the UEFA Cup, the Intercontinental Cup and the Champions League. In 1997, after completing his contract at Ajax and picking up a Dutch knighthood, van Gaal followed in Cruijff's footsteps by moving to Barcelona, where he took over as manager from Bobby Robson. The Spanish team won two league titles under his leadership but he struggled to fit in at the club, falling out with star player Rivaldo after insisting that the Brazilian forget about dribbling and focus on passing. Barcelona legend Cruijff didn't help matters, sticking the boot in with allegations that van Gaal was ruining his old side. Typically, van Gaal blamed his problems on hostile media coverage, famously announcing his departure from Barcelona with the words: '*Amigos de la prensa, yo me voy. Felicidades*' ('Friends of the press. I am leaving. Congratulations').

His reputation was still high in his home country and he was appointed manager of the Dutch national team in 2000. However, his first spell as national manager was an abject failure, since the Dutch failed to qualify for the 2002 World Cup. Van Gaal soon returned to manage Barcelona, but again he disappointed. In half a season, he took the Catalans to within a few points of being relegated from the Spanish *Liga* before being fired.

Back in the Netherlands, van Gaal managed a remarkable turnaround. Returning to AZ as manager, he quickly led the low-profile club to victory in the *Eredivisie*. By Dutch standards this was a staggering achievement – the first time in decades the national title had been won by anyone other than the

'Big Three' of Ajax, Feyenoord and PSV Eindhoven. His career miraculously resurrected, van Gaal would perhaps have been happy to stay in the Netherlands, but after reportedly losing millions to the swindler Bernie Madoff, he found himself in urgent need of another big-money job. One presented itself in Germany, and he was soon leading Bayern Munich to both the German title and the Champions League final within a single season. However, his prickly style again caused problems – he was alleged to have had a major falling-out with Bayern striker Luca Toni after van Gaal, irritated with the way the player was slouching during a team lunch, pulled the Italian's ear to make him sit up straight. Van Gaal was a 'tracksuit dictator', one magazine said.

One of van Gaal's more notable enemies was Johan Cruijff. There were several parallels between the two famous Dutchmen: they both had fathers who died young, they had both played for Ajax early in their careers, and they had both developed strong links with Barcelona. They also both had prickly personalities that put them on a collision course. It was often said that the rivalry was rooted in their overlapping tenures in Amsterdam, when a vain van Gaal had resented the attention given to Cruijff while he could only watch from the reserves. In some ways the two men represented competing views of how football should be played – van Gaal thought that teams should be run with military discipline, while Cruijff believed that individuality was key. The quarrel peaked in 2011, during a backroom power struggle at Ajax rather melodramatically known as the Velvet Revolution. After his spell in Munich, van Gaal had been invited to return to Ajax as technical director, at a time when Cruijff was serving on the club's board. Other board members reportedly appointed van Gaal to the coaching staff without letting Cruijff know. Cruijff was enraged, and even went so far as to file a lawsuit blocking van Gaal from taking the new job, leading a group of other board members who supported van Gaal to resign in protest. With two of the giants of Dutch football at war, the club that had launched both their careers faced being torn apart. Ajax eventually recovered from its near meltdown, but several years later the two men reportedly were still not talking to one another.

Despite the unseemly squabble with Cruijff, van Gaal's rehabilitation continued in 2012 when he was appointed Dutch national coach for a second time, charged with delivering the 2014 World Cup. Although the tournament ended in disappointment for the Netherlands, van Gaal became an iconic figure, immediately recognisable for his smart suits and vaguely Elvis-like quiff, stalking the sidelines like a general surveying a battlefield. Then, in May 2014, he was named manager of one of Europe's biggest clubs, Manchester United, with Ryan Giggs as his assistant manager. Van Gaal soon ruffled feathers by declaring he had inherited a 'broken' squad from his predecessor, David Moyes, and the club made its worst start to the season in more than twenty years. He was, however, typically bullish about the future. 'This club has big ambitions. I too have big ambitions,' he said. 'Together I'm sure we will make history.'

At the time of my visit to the Feyenoord–Cambuur game, it seemed as if van Gaal's approach might be working. After spending a reported £100 million or so on new signings during his first summer in charge, the Dutchman had delivered some stronger results and won the support of his most famous predecessor, Alex Ferguson. He also appeared to be losing some of his previous chilly demeanour, sharing wine with journalists and even smiling during press conferences. Whatever the future held, van Gaal had guaranteed his place as one of the world's greatest football managers, and one of the best-known Dutchmen of modern times. He had also, for the Dutch, come to embody some of the values and contradictions at their heart of their country: hard-working and plain speaking, sometimes offensive, but always motivated by a basic underlying decency. He was a strict disciplinarian who cried when introduced to a terminally ill child on live television, nearly quit football when his wife died of cancer, and wrote heartfelt poems to read out at press conferences. He was, like the anarchic Dutch themselves, brilliant and slightly crazy at the same time.

Blood Feuds

Within a couple of minutes Feyenoord had nearly scored again, a swift shot saved by a desperate dive by the Cambuur keeper. On the back foot, the Cambuur fans grew even louder, making an impressive racket for such a small group of people. My neighbour told me they were probably from the 'M-I Side', a hardcore Cambuur fanclub known for its bitter rivalry with other clubs from the Frisian north of the Netherlands. 'They deserve to lose,' he said. 'Cocky bastards.'

The Feyenoord fans on the lower terraces clearly agreed, turning away from the game to taunt their rivals, waving goodbye and holding up red cards. In front of the dividing glass screens, a line of security guards in yellow jackets scanned the crowd tensely. Down below, a handful of policeman in riot gear were also watching the Cambuur supporters. Looking beyond the terraces, I was surprised to notice a deep concrete trench separating the fans from the pitch, like a medieval moat holding back an invading army.

As a novice, it struck me as utterly bizarre that such fortifications would be necessary. Men of the same nationality, who lived and worked alongside one another quite happily the rest of the week, had to be kept caged and fenced on weekends in order to stop them tearing one another apart. My thoughts inevitably turned to the TV images of my childhood: riots, street fights, Hillsborough. My companion, however, had assured me that the game between Feyenoord and Cambuur would be a peaceful one – 'boring' was the word he used. The stakes for this match were relatively low, the teams had no particular hatred of one another, and neither side was performing well enough to cause the others' fans to lash out in shame.

Dutch football was not always so peaceful. As elsewhere in Europe, many games in the 1970s, 1980s and beyond had been marred by serious violence. Most notoriously, matches between Feyenoord and Ajax had often ended in bloodshed, thanks to a bitter rivalry between the two clubs resembling Britain's 'Old Firm' rivalry between Celtic and Rangers. The first *Klassieker* ('classic') match between the two sides was held in 1921, ending in a 2–2 draw. Since then they had played more than 130 times, with Ajax winning roughly 60 per cent of the time. The rivalry really took off in the 1970s, when the two teams were among the best in the world, vying for dominance of the *Eredivisie* and of European tournaments. In Rotterdam, people still spoke proudly of famous victories over Ajax, such as the 9–4 drubbing handed out in 1964, or the 7–3 hammering in 1956. Recent years had seen a run of disappointing results for Feyenoord when it played Ajax, to the disgust of its supporters.

Commentators often noted the contrast between Ajax's flamboyant, free-wheeling Total Football and Feyenoord's more utilitarian, practical approach. The rivalry between the two clubs was nevertheless less about footballing styles and more an extension of the rivalry between their respective home cities. This was an example of another of the many things I found surprising about the Netherlands: the large number of distinct regional identities in such a small country, and the strength of the feeling these differences inspired. In a country where most large towns were practically within cycling distance of one another, it was relatively common to hear people dismissing those from other areas with crude stereotypes, or mocking them for their stupid accents.

The Netherlands consists of seventeen different provinces (roughly akin to British counties) and if my Dutch friends were to be believed, the people living in each one were entirely different from those from elsewhere. Southern 'Brabanders' were (I was told) all straight-talking beer drinkers, while people from eastern Twente were yokels and farmers. The Hague's 'Den Haagenaars', meanwhile, were a mixture of hooligans and smooth-talking diplomats. In Friesland, the northern home province of SC Cambuur, there was even a separatist movement, which followed closely the antics of Alex Salmond's Scottish National Party in hopes of one day emulating the Scots' efforts to break free.

Such rivalries were perhaps exacerbated by the fact that although many Dutch travelled widely, they often were not particularly mobile within their own country. People who lived in Amsterdam, in particular, rarely left the confines of the city. In Britain, it was common to be born in one city, go to university in another, and then live in a few more before finally settling down. In the Netherlands, many people seemed to have grown up, studied, found work and then had a family, all in the same place. The strong resulting loyalties were perhaps one reason why such a small country had such rich, competitive football.

The rivalry between Feyenoord and Ajax was an instructive example: an enmity rooted in Amsterdammers' and Rotterdammers' shared belief that the other came from a strange and distant place. Rotterdam's snootier residents sometimes claimed that their city was 'the Dutch New York'. Thanks to the docks, a better analogy would be Detroit or Pittsburgh: Rotterdam was a grimy, sprawling city of doers, not thinkers, salt-of-the-earth types who rolled up their sleeves and relished hard work. Rotterdammers were predictably scathing about those living in other, more refined cities, viewing people from Den Haag as slick, insincere beancounters who spent the day counting problems rather than solving them. Amsterdammers were even worse: effete, shallow, bohemian and celebrity-obsessed; ineffectual posers more concerned with their haircuts than with hard work. As a truck driver in a bar once told me: 'In Rotterdam we earn the money, in Den Haag they count it, and in Amsterdam they spend it.' The rivalry cut both ways: Amsterdammers looked down on their southern rivals as unsophisticated and uncultured; inhabitants of a sprawling, dirty city with unfashionable bars, lame restaurants and outmoded shops.

Predictably, others' disdain for their city only strengthened Rotterdammers' pride in it, their telephone area code

– 010 – becoming a proud battle cry to be shouted whenever its dignity was impugned: '*NUL-TIEN!*' In Amsterdam the only people wearing clothes printed with the city's name were tourists, but in Rotterdam most men under thirty seemed to own a 'ROTTERDAM ALL DAY' hoody or a '0-1-0 ISN'T JUST A CODE' T-shirt. It was, as the words of a popular Feyenoord football song put it, a city of 'No words but deeds'. To its supporters, Feyenoord was the epitome of Rotterdam's hard-working ethos and blue-collar values, even playing in a stadium that had supposedly been constructed by its own supporters as part of a government programme for out-of-work dockers in the 1930s. Although it had grown into a corporate behemoth worth millions, the club's own website still described it as a 'simple people's club from a poorer area in Rotterdam Zuid'.

The Ajax–Feyenoord rivalry was also complicated by the Jewish question. The city of Amsterdam had a rich Jewish heritage, thanks partly to its role as a haven for Jews expelled from Spain and Portugal before the Golden Age. As a result, Ajax had long had many Jewish players and supporters. The club paid a heavy price for these links in the Second World War: Ajax player Eddie Hamel was murdered in Auschwitz, and manager Jack Reynolds was held in a Nazi prisoner-of-war camp. After the war Ajax retained its reputation as a 'Jewish club', with numerous prominent Jewish players and officials, fans using Jewish slang in the stands, and friendly links with football clubs in Israel. Members of its 'F-side' supporters' club were even known for wearing clothes decorated with the Star of David, waving Israeli flags during games and singing songs about how proud they were to be 'Super Jews'. As a result of this history, the rivalry between Ajax and Feyenoord had often been tainted by anti-Semitism. During *Klassieker* matches, Feyenoord supporters would sing songs about the Holocaust and even wave Hamas flags; 'Hamas, Hamas, Jews to the gas' went one chant. Such abuse served only to strengthen the Jewish identity at Ajax, with non-Jewish supporters embracing Jewish symbols and getting tattoos of the six-pointed 'Ajax star' on their shoulders. Ajax supporters had also been known to display banners celebrating the wartime bombing of Rotterdam. Feyenoord fans were quick to reject allegations of anti-Semitism, pointing out how badly their own city had suffered at the hands of the Nazis, but with De Kuip echoing to the sound of hissing, in imitation of the gas being fed into ovens at Auschwitz, it was sometimes hard to hear them.

As someone who was not a football fan, I was astonished by the depth of the hatred between some supporters of the two clubs, and by the appalling violence that had sometimes broken out between them. In the early 1990s, for example, Feyenoord fans had thrown a home-made bomb into the Ajax section of the crowd during a match at Amsterdam's De Meer stadium, injuring eighteen fans. In 2004, Feyenoord player Jorge Acuna was hospitalised after he and teammate Robin van Persie were attacked by Ajax fans who invaded the pitch during a reserve team game. The players escaped only after being rescued from the mob by Ajax players and staff. When Greek striker Angelos Charisteas signed with Feyenoord rather than Ajax, he reportedly needed bodyguards at training sessions to protect him from irate supporters of the latter.

The most notorious instance of violence occurred in 1997, at what later became known as the 'Battle of Beverwijk'. On a day when the two teams were not even scheduled to play one another, rival supporters met in fields next to a stretch of motorway west of Amsterdam. The meeting was not spontaneous but arranged carefully in advance, following an earlier occasion at which Ajax fans had protested that Feyenoord fans had 'broken the rules' by arriving for an arranged fight with more people than expected. On this occasion, hundreds of men turned up and embarked on an open-air, Braveheart-style melee armed with knives, iron bars, baseball bats and hammers. Only a few police made it to the scene, and as Feyenoord supporters gained the upper hand, the outnumbered Ajax fans were forced to flee. During the retreat, one Ajax fan, Carlo Picornie, was beaten to death with a claw hammer. Another fan who tried to help him was stabbed but survived. It was later alleged that Picornie had been singled out as one of the established leaders of the Ajax hooligans, a figurehead whom Feyenoord-supporting hooligans wanted to bring down. The Feyenoord supporter who dealt the fatal blow was later arrested and sentenced to five years in prison. One group of Feyenoord fans paid for a newspaper advert expressing sympathy over the killing, but at the next game between the two clubs, other Feyenoorders allegedly taunted their rivals by holding up inflatable hammers.

In a country where violent crime was still rare, Picornie's death represented a turning point. Attempting to reclaim the game from hooligans, the police and the Dutch football association, the KNVB, introduced strict restrictions that would apply whenever *Klassieker* matches were held. These included banning alcohol from games, tracking known hooligans, installing security cameras in stadiums and handing out lengthy bans to anyone who misbehaved. Fans travelling to games did so in specially allocated trains, which – irritated away fans claimed – drove slowly with the heating turned up higher than normal in the hope of making passengers sleepy. Referees were given the power to halt games if they heard anti-Semitic songs. Keeping rival fans apart was an enormous security operation, and away fans were frequently banned from attending *Klassiekers* altogether.

Even at the low-key Feyenoord–Cambuur game, I was searched for weapons and fireworks on the way into the stadium and watched over by an astonishing number of security guards, policemen and CCTV cameras – another example, perhaps, of how a tolerant country had been forced to take a more restrictive line. According to my Feyenoord-supporting friends, many of the most hardcore supporters now had to stay away, watching games from bars rather than inside the stadium.

Nevertheless, violence between Ajax and Feyenoord fans remained a recurring problem, and plenty of Rotterdammers were still happy to describe themselves as 'hooligans' if asked.

When I tried to question one acquaintance about the rivalry between the two clubs, he wouldn't even accept the premise: 'Someone you look down on can't be a rival,' he said. Although extreme violence had become less common, there was no doubting the passion of Feyenoord's fans. 'There are three things in life that are important to me,' another acquaintance once told me, echoing the sentiments of many fans world-wide. 'Feyenoord, my son and my wife. In that order.'

Defeat and Disappointment

At the match against Cambuur, the shadow of a tall lighting tower swung slowly across the pitch as if the whole stadium was a sundial. After the initial excitement my attention had waned a little, and I was finding it increasingly difficult to stay focused. Thankfully, a little girl sitting two rows behind me, clearly also attending her first football match, provided some entertainment by interrogating her father with endless questions that I was too ashamed to ask. Who was the player with the black skin and the beard? Why did the man at the side of the pitch hold up a flag? Why did the man over there say he wanted the one who got the goal to be dead?

In the sixty-first minute, Cambuur made two substitutions, including a tall young man – Martijn Barto – who touched the pitch with his fingertips and then crossed himself as he ran on. The ritual clearly worked: within a minute he had scored, a low, speedy shot that slipped under the falling body of the Feyenoord keeper. The away fans behind the glass screen jumped and cheered at the sudden change in their fortunes: 2–1 down with half an hour to play, Cambuur had a fighting chance. A sweet-looking boy in a Feyenoord scarf sitting a few seats over from me stared coldly at the adjacent Cambuur fans as if they had just killed his family.

Having stood still for the best part of an hour I was chilled to the bone, and spent much of the next thirty min-utes concentrating not on the game but on an oval patch of sunlight slowly creeping its way around the stadium, hoping it would soon reach me and thaw out my face. Around me, the Feyenoord fans were clearly frustrated with their team's performance, although the home side looked likely to hold on to its lead. Red-and-white-shirted players made frequent sallies into the Cambuur box, and several tidy shots on target were saved only by the athleticism of the away side's keeper. As the digital clock at the far end of the stadium ticked towards ninety minutes, a sort of ease settled over the home crowd, as it became clear that Feyenoord would very likely win the match, or at worst score a feisty draw. Hopes of a decisive victory were briefly reawakened three minutes into extra time, when Feyenoord's number 29 bought the stadium to its feet with a shot that looked like it was on target. The angle proved deceptive, however, and the ball bounced harmlessly off the outside of the net. Thirty seconds later another stealth shot was blocked by the Cambuur keeper's warm embrace.

And then, surprisingly quickly, the game was over. The final whistle blew and the crowd applauded perfunctorily and stood to leave. I'd assumed the home crowd would be elated at the win, but apparently the final score mattered less than the feeling that their team had underperformed. Feyenoord fans looked simultaneously relieved and disappointed, like people who'd just learned that their cars would need expensive repairs, but that the cost wouldn't be quite as high as they'd originally feared. 'Well that was shit,' my companion said. 'I'm sorry, I wanted you to write about a better game.'

For Dutch football fans, disappointments of this kind were not unusual. One of the great ironies of football in the Netherlands was that despite having a deep and abiding love of the game, and despite having sparked a revolution in football tactics, the Dutch usually failed to meet expectations at the international level. After coming close to winning two successive World Cups in the 1970s, they spent much of the 1980s in the footballing wilderness. Their team dropped out of the Euro '80 tournament at the group stage, and then failed to qualify for the 1982 World Cup, Euro '84 and the 1986

World Cup. Things started to improve when Rinus Michels returned to lead the national side to victory in Euro '88, but this proved a temporary respite. With Michels gone again, the Dutch put in a lacklustre performance at the 1990 World Cup in Italy, and lost to Brazil in the quarter-finals of USA 1994. They finished fourth at France '98, but then failed to qualify again in 2002. The 2014 World Cup performance was an improvement, but followed a trajectory that was by then fairly typical: breathtaking dominance of early games that fizzled out into a good-but-not-spectacular third-place finish. The Dutch team, pundits often said, was the best never to win a World Cup.

As people who relished discussing and analysing problems, the Dutch naturally devoted hours to figuring out why their national side underperformed so consistently. One common theory was that its failures were rooted in the country's age-old approach to problem-solving, whereby every difficulty had to be discussed at length until a consensus was reached. As the football writer David Winner explained, this democratic approach was one reason why Total Football was so effective – position switching depended on players being treated equally and communicating effectively.

However, the system of collective responsibility also had its disadvantages. According to its critics, in the disappointing years following its 1970s glory days Ajax was run more like a trade union than a top football club, with players sometimes pooling their salaries and even electing their own captain. Such practices could (several fans told me) lead to a hopeless lack of leadership. Dutch national teams were said to have a tendency to waste hours arguing over tactics. Coaches lacked authority, and players were inclined to behave like prima donnas, with star players sometimes refusing to participate in international tournaments. As salaries rose and players became increasingly spoiled and distracted, the problems only got worse. At the Euro '96 tournament, for example, the Dutch team started as the favourite but was soon stricken by petty squabbles and infighting, eventually losing 4–1 to

England at Wembley before crashing out of the tournament on penalties to France.

Strangely, the Dutch belief in the importance of beautiful play was sometimes claimed to be self-defeating. They would, critics said, rather play stylishly and lose than play scrappily but win. Deeply patriotic and used to disappointments on the pitch, the Dutch also had a tendency to rejoice in failure, celebrating when they came third or fourth in a tournament, when other national teams in the same position might have been obsessing about why they hadn't done better. It was, I thought, perhaps also significant that the Dutch national side was famously bad at penalty shoot-outs: an individualistic, black-and-white, take-no-prisoners pursuit that was anathema to the Dutch preference for carefully thought-out, consensual outcomes.

The most notorious Dutch footballing failure occurred in 1974, when the national side narrowly missed out on winning the World Cup by losing in the final to a great historical rival, West Germany. More than four decades later, the 'Lost Final' was still seared on the national consciousness, brought up in any bar-room conversation about football, including by many who weren't even born when it was played.

Dutch hopes for the match had been high. The World Cup team that year was coached by the same Rinus Michels who had led Ajax to glory and included Johan Cruijff, visiting from Barcelona, along with Feyenoord legends Wim Jansen and Wim van Hanegem. The team had made a strong start in the tournament, thrashing Bulgaria, Argentina and East Germany in quick succession and putting in an impressive performance against reigning world champions Brazil. The West Germans, meanwhile, had generally failed to impress on their way to the final. There seemed a good chance that the 1974 World Cup would be Total Football's crowning glory. With the Nazi invasion of the Netherlands still well within living memory, the match was heavy with historical symbolism. Dutch player Wim van Hanegem was quick to point out that his father and two brothers had been killed by the Nazis. West Germany's star player, Gerd Muller, even went by the unfortunate nick-name 'The Bomber'. Rinus Michels once said that football was war; for many Dutch, this match would be a replay.

West Germany was the host of the tournament that year, and thousands of orange-clad fans had driven from the Netherlands to watch the game live in a Munich stadium seat-ing nearly 80,000 people. It was the first World Cup final to be televised in the Netherlands, and many Dutch families had bought their first colour television especially to watch their team thrash their long-time rivals. The Dutch had a dream start to the game. Less than two minutes after kick-off they were awarded a penalty – the first ever in a World Cup final. Johan Neeskens dispatched the ball cleanly into the left of the goal. The Dutch went 1–0 up before the Germans had even had a chance to touch the ball. However, they then failed to press home their advantage, demonstrating some impressive ball skills but not increasing the goal count. Late in the first half, a dive by a German player was rewarded with a penalty against the Dutch. Paul Bretner blasted the ball into the right corner of the net, and the Dutch suddenly found themselves facing a 1–1 draw. Scrambling to recover, they attacked relent-lessly, but couldn't find the back of the net. Near the end of the first half 'The Bomber' took a deft, twisting shot at the Dutch goal. The keeper could only watch as it sailed past him, and Germany was 2–1 up.

In the second half, the Dutch spiritedly tried to turn things around, but to no avail. The Germans blocked their attempts to score, and Muller scored another goal, although it was dis-allowed by the referee. When the final whistle sounded, a nor-mally sensible nation was utterly distraught. Every fan knew the infamous line uttered by a Dutch commentator, soaked in the history of conflict: *'Zijn we er toch nog ingetuind!'* 'They tricked us again!' The German-born Dutch Prince Bernhard reportedly put it rather more diplomatically, telling Johan Cruijff: 'The best team didn't win.' Recriminations began almost immediately, focusing on lurid tabloid allegations that Cruijff had been seen frolicking with German girls in a hotel swimming pool at the height of the tournament. Cruijff, still only in his twenties, denied the charges, but announced he would not play in the next World Cup. Decades later, the 1974 loss was often grouped together with the 1940 Nazi invasion and 1953 flood as the three great tragedies to have befallen the Netherlands in the twentieth century.

The Dutch had to wait nearly a decade and a half to get their revenge. In 1988, a national team coached by Rinus Michels found itself playing the West Germans again in the semi-final of the European Championships. Fittingly, the German team was coached by Franz Beckenbauer, one of the stars of the infamous 1974 match. Thousands of Dutch fans travelled to the stadium in Hamburg, singing anti-German slogans and waving banners asking for the return of their stolen bicycles. The game started badly for the Dutch, with the Germans scoring a penalty, before another penalty (probably given to the Dutch in a refereeing error) made them 1–1. Then in the second half, with just three minutes left on the clock, Marco van Basten scored a tidy goal to put the Dutch 2–1 up. When the final whistle blew, Dutch players danced a conga and the fans in the stadium went insane. In the Netherlands, a reported nine million people – roughly two-thirds of the population – went out on the streets to celebrate. In Munich, Prince Johan Friso joined in singing drinking songs about the Germans, while Ruud Gullit was heard complaining it was impossible to have a good party in Germany.

The Dutch went on to win the tournament, but that hardly mattered compared to the joy of having finally scored a victory over their old foe. A famous Dutch newspaper headline the day after the semi-final said it all: 'REVENGE!' Another newspaper remarked it was a pity they couldn't play against the Japanese too.

For the Love of Orange

For me, the strength of feeling displayed when the Dutch played internationally was a rather curious phenomenon

– not simply because I wasn't a football fan, but because of how Dutch patriotism exceeded anything I'd ever seen in my home country.

In England, plenty of people like football and will gather to watch the national side play in major tournaments. Pubs will certainly be overflowing with happy people if England win an important match, and the 1966 World Cup victory is brought up far more often than it should be. Real football fandom is, however, still largely the preserve of men, and doesn't extend far over the wider population. I couldn't imagine a whole city being filled with celebrating people – men, women and children – if the English won (say) a quarter-final match in the World Cup. In the Netherlands, though, love of football is far more universal. When the Dutch slumped out of the 2014 World Cup, I assumed that coming fourth after such a strong start to the tournament would be a major disappointment. However, the whole of Rotterdam nearly lost their minds with excitement: dancing, singing, waving flags and setting off fireworks in the street. For a country that usually excelled at sports (like ice skating) the rest of the world didn't much care for, doing pretty well at the world's most popular sport was a major cause for celebration. Traffic on the main roads ground to a halt as orange-clad revellers danced in the streets, in numbers that could have rivalled Carnival or King's Day. Through the haze of firework smoke, I caught a glimpse of one friend – not normally a football fan – jumping in front of moving cars and banging on their windscreens, shouting at drivers to beep their horns. Nearly all of them obliged. The Dutch celebrated as if they had not only won the tournament, but a clutch of Olympic medals and a world war to boot.

These varying reactions to football are perhaps rooted in the different strains of patriotism in the two countries. In Britain, patriotism is sadly rather tainted by association with a kind of small-mindedness and xenophobia. Symbols such as flags have been appropriated by far-right groups, so someone wearing a T-shirt with the flag of St George on it is likely to be sneered at and dismissed as a racist or a hooligan. Anyone who declares their love of their country too vigorously runs the risk of being branded a narrow-minded Little Englander, or worse. In the Netherlands, patriotism is less complicated. The Dutch love their country and are happy to show it whenever the opportunity arises. International football matches are a welcome opportunity to display this pride, not just for tattooed men in pubs but for young women, old couples and middle-aged parents too. You are as likely to see a national flag flying from a successful businessman's BMW as from a builder's white van. For the Dutch, used to being a small country on the margins of world politics, football offers a rare chance to play in the big league, to be treated as an equal by far larger and wealthier nations.

While Brits adhere to a long tradition of grumbling about their homeland, the Dutch can be almost American in their belief that they live in the greatest country on earth. Laid back about almost everything else, they are surprisingly easily offended if an outsider points out any flaws in the way they do things. It didn't go down too well when, a few days after arriving in the Netherlands, I asked a passing stranger why there were tricolor French flags on display everywhere. 'They're not French flags,' he harrumphed. 'They're Dutch. The French stole our flag and turned it sideways.' When Brits return home from holidays abroad they immediately start grumbling about how terrible it is to be back in the cold and rain. The Dutch, meanwhile, walk through the arrivals hall at Schiphol airport with huge grins on their faces, delighted to be back in their perfect little country.

Game Over

Dutch pride in their football teams may have been in ample supply, but whether they would ever triumph on the world stage remained to be seen. For a small country, successive top-four finishes at the World Cup were an impressive achievement, but the glory days when Dutch mastery of

Totaalvoetbal practically guaranteed a place in international finals were over. Ironically, the problem may have been that in their efforts to transform the game, and to export their expertise, the Dutch had been rather too successful. Dutch players like Cruijff or managers like van Gaal were now more likely to spend their careers in Manchester or Milan than in Amsterdam or Rotterdam. Many teams around the world played variations of the Total Football style, requiring players to act as passers, dribblers, defenders or scorers, depending on what the situation required. Fast, fluid, position-switching play was no longer a Dutch secret weapon, but a standard part of the football playbook. What had once made Dutch football unique was now commonplace, and the Dutch had lost their advantage. Like a company whose innovative technology had been copied by rivals, Dutch footballers had won the battle but lost the war.

As the players loped off the pitch in De Kuip, I left my seat and descended to the exits. On the concrete outside, a vast crowd streamed towards the gates, looking like flat-capped workers leaving one of L.S. Lowry's factories. I tried to take my time but was swept along past the waiting ambulances and riot vans, the police horses and motorcycles, the hot-dog stands and the shivering souvenir sellers. Around a corner, behind a high steel fence, a squadron of police motorcycles was waiting to escort the Cambuur supporters' buses through a hostile city to safety. Feyenoord fans, meanwhile, were heading off to drink their blues away and discuss the prospects for the next game.

I stopped to buy a hot dog. A man in a red-and-white hat saw me shivering and asked if I'd like to buy one of the Feyenoord shirts available from his stall. '*Misschien,*' I said. 'Maybe.'

Six

Mosques on the Maas

Immigration, Islam and Murder

'Death to Jews!' the crowd chanted in unison. Dozens of young men crowded the narrow street, many of them with their faces covered by black-and-white scarves and dark sunglasses. The sky was filled with long black banners and flags decorated in white Arabic script: the flag of ISIS, the Islamic fundamentalist group fighting to establish a caliphate in Syria, Iraq and beyond. A young man with a long dark beard and Castro-style military cap began to speak, and the crowd formed a rough circle around him. 'We are all Moroccans!' he bellowed. 'We protest against the West, America and the Jews!' Another young man cut in – 'Whoever doesn't jump is a Jew!' – and the crowd began jumping together, cheering and waving flags like football fans at full time. 'Allahu Akbar! Allahu Akbar!' they chanted. Such views were, sadly, not uncommon in parts of the world – but these young men were not in Morocco, or in Syria, or anywhere else in the Arab world. They were in the Schilderswijk district of The Hague, about twenty minutes' walk from the Dutch Parliament building.

Some three months later, another group of protestors gathered about fifteen miles south of Schilderswijk, in a windswept square in central Rotterdam. At weekends the area hosted a sprawling fruit and vegetable market, but on a Thursday evening there were only yards of empty concrete and seagulls bickering amid crisp brown leaves. At one end of the square about fifty people were gathered in front of a cheap sushi restaurant, facing a small white van with a loudspeaker bolted to its roof. In front of the vehicle, two cheerful Dutchmen in anoraks held a long blue-and-white banner hand-painted with the legend '010 = 1', a reference to Rotterdam's area code and to the unity they hoped to promote.

Compared to the earlier protest in The Hague, this had drawn a more gentle and diverse crowd – there were not only young Muslim men, but also young women in tight jeans and colourful headscarves, middle-aged white couples and Orthodox Jews. A man in a bright orange fleece jacket and matching orange skullcap greeted me warmly as I arrived. *'Hallo, hallo! Welkom!'* he said, holding a mobile phone aloft to take a photo of the crowd.

Although the organisers had not said so directly, the second march had been arranged as a kind of rebuttal to the first: an attempt to demonstrate harmony in a community that many feared was beginning to fracture. Like many Dutch cities, Rotterdam had a large population of so-called *allochtonen*: foreigners, either born in another country themselves or the child of someone who was. For decades, the *allochtonen* had lived happily side by side with the *autochtonen*, or native Dutch; living proof of the country's famous tolerance and hospitality. In recent years, however, tensions had begun to rise. While the pro-ISIS demonstration in Schilderswijk was an extreme example, it was not an isolated one. Swastikas had been displayed at another march. Kurdish protestors had invaded the Dutch parliament, and authorities reported a steady stream of young Dutch Muslims travelling to fight in Syria. Terrorist attacks elsewhere in Europe had put the Dutch on edge, and right-wing politicians had sparked a furore with pledges to deport foreigners.

At the protest in Rotterdam the atmosphere was warm and welcoming, but I saw a large group of police officers trying to be inconspicuous in a corner of the car park over the road. With beetly black body armour and long truncheons, they looked as if they expected trouble. No one quite dared to say it, but many feared that the country was on the verge of returning to the period, roughly a decade previously, when two of the Dutch who spoke out most passionately against Islamic extremism were slain in broad daylight, and two others had been forced to flee for their lives.

Nul-tien is één

The march was due to start at five o'clock, but the deadline passed unnoticed. By a quarter past, the sun was beginning to sink behind the apartment buildings around the square, casting weak yellow beams through a hazy blue sky streaked with contrails. As shops and offices closed, the crowd swelled gradually to perhaps a hundred people. Curious commuters paused to read the '010 = 1' banner as they passed, and a pair of bored young waitresses came out of a pizza place to see what was going on. I loitered self-consciously at the back of the crowd, fiddling with my phone and trying to look like I belonged.

At half past five, a man with a shiny bald head and thick glasses climbed onto a wooden crate in front of the van. He tapped on a microphone and the crowd fell silent. 'We are gathered here,' he said in Dutch, 'because we want to live together, side by side. We are here as Rotterdammers, for Rotterdammers and with Rotterdammers.' We would, he explained, be marching through the city for about an hour, demonstrating to residents that despite differences of race and religion, '*nul-tien is één*', 'zero-ten is one'. The crowd applauded and he introduced the next speaker, a young Muslim woman in an olive-coloured headscarf, who clasped the microphone with the confidence of a talent show contestant. 'We choose to make connections with each other,' she said. 'We all stand together as one.'

Until relatively recently, such sentiments had hardly needed saying. The Netherlands had long been a country of immigrants, from the Protestants who fled there from Spanish rule, to the rebels and innovators who sought refuge and reward in the Golden Age. For centuries, visitors had marvelled at the diversity of races, languages and cuisines in the tiny country. In the nineteenth and twentieth centuries, many immigrants had arrived from places with which the Netherlands had colonial links: the East Indies and the islands of the Caribbean. These immigrants were of a different race and religion, but because they often spoke Dutch, and were familiar with Dutch culture and customs, they assimilated relatively easily.

A more profound shift came in the late 1960s and 1970s, when the Netherlands' post-war economic boom created a demand for labour that the local population could not meet. The Dutch government responded by encouraging the recruitment of so-called guest workers from lower-income countries on the fringes of Europe, particularly Morocco and Turkey. Thousands came to work in Dutch docks, factories and building sites. Living in cheap boarding houses, they worked hard, saved hard and made long car journeys to visit their home countries each summer.

The government assumed that the 'guest workers' would be exactly that: guests who came on a short-term basis. However, it soon became clear that this would not be the case. The new arrivals gradually moved from the boarding houses into more permanent homes. Many were joined by relatives from their home countries – elderly parents seeking a comfortable retirement, younger siblings wanting work or young women looking for husbands. As the immigrant population grew there were occasionally tensions, but overall the Dutch took a relaxed view. In the mid-1970s, for example, an amnesty legalised the presence of some 15,000 immigrants who had arrived in the country illegally. In 1961 there had been exactly three Moroccans living legally in the Netherlands, but within a few decades more than a quarter of a million Turks and Moroccans had made the Netherlands their home.

In the 1980s and 1990s, the migrant workers were joined by refugees from war-torn countries such as the former Yugoslavia, Iraq and Somalia. Then, from the mid-1990s onwards, the Schengen agreement enabled Europeans to live and work in the Netherlands without obtaining a visa. More by accident than by design, the Netherlands acquired one of the largest immigrant populations in Europe. When I moved to Rotterdam, an astonishing 46 per cent of residents were from an immigrant background. Ethnic minorities were on the verge of becoming a majority.

One area where change was most evident was, coincidentally, my own neighbourhood. Oude Noord, the 'Old North' of Rotterdam, lay just on the wrong side of the threshold between the grimy city centre and the gentrified suburbs. Historically it had been a pleasant enough residential area, filled with red-brick townhouses, including one where the artist Willem de Kooning had been born. In recent decades, however, as its original Dutch residents either died out or moved out, their tall townhouses had been subdivided into small apartments and leased to migrant workers or lower-income immigrant families. There were a few Poles and Hungarians, but the new arrivals were overwhelmingly Turkish and Moroccan. On the street where I lived, non-Muslims appeared to be a distinct minority.

The streets were filled with halal butchers, haberdasheries offering long *djeballah* shirts and headscarves, shops selling long-distance phone credit and travel agents touting tickets to Casablanca and Anatolia. Close to my house, the doorway of a female-only gym was permanently surrounded by young Muslim women adjusting sweaty headscarves after a workout. Mini-supermarkets sold no pork or shellfish, but offered an enormous range of olives, couscous, hummus, pitta breads and spicy sauces. Most common of all were the kebab shops – one on almost every corner, each with the same spinning stacks of meat and groups of young Moroccans eating *durum* wraps on their motor scooters outside. At weekends, I often shuffled, hungover, to buy a surfboard-shaped Turkish bread for breakfast from a small bakery around the corner. The headscarfed young woman behind the counter would sometimes offer a free sticker alongside the paper bag of breakfast: 'I LOVE ISLAM'.

Heads in the Sand?

In Oude Noord and elsewhere, the rapid growth of the immigrant population inevitably caused some tensions. This was partly because of a lack of space. Talk of the country being 'full' might be a racist cliché in some places, but in the Netherlands it had the ring of truth. There were also economic pressures. In a city like Rotterdam, where unemployment rates were typically around triple the national average, the presence of a large guest worker population riled locals struggling to find work. Immigrants themselves were caught in a curious bind – resented if they took 'Dutch jobs' away from locals, but demonised as lazy scroungers if they failed to find work.

The biggest tensions revolved around cultural differences. As a proud, patriotic people, some Dutch were unhappy with the thought that their local shop might stop selling traditional Dutch food and hire staff who couldn't speak the local language. The values the Dutch saw as the bedrock of their national identity – gay rights, gender equality – were unfortunately anathema to some of those who were now their neighbours. Many Muslims, for example, believed that women's hair should be covered in public, but lived in a country where prostitutes stood naked behind red-lit windows without attracting a second glance. Newspapers reported cases such as that of a boy taken from his Turkish family by the Dutch authorities and placed in the care of lesbian foster parents, prompting vociferous protests from some in the Turkish community.

The Dutch government's policies didn't seem to have helped matters. In fact, they might even have made things worse. Under the traditional system of *zuilen*, or pillars, the Netherlands had long been divided along religious lines, with denominations given government funding to support schools and other institutions tailored to their beliefs. When it became clear that the guest workers were sticking around, the authorities naturally hoped that a similar system might work for the new minority groups. Islamic schools were awarded state funding, government subsidies provided to mosques, and travel costs paid so that imams could immigrate to the Netherlands.

However, many believed that this approach had backfired. The system of pillars that once helped maintain the peace between warring Catholics and Protestants served only to keep the new minorities isolated from one another, and from the Dutch at large. Generously subsidised to maintain their traditional beliefs, immigrants had fewer incentives to assimilate. Some scholars claimed that because imams brought to the Netherlands were selected by the Dutch government on the basis of their piety, moderate imams were less likely to apply – so the policy ended up importing precisely the intolerant ideas that would have been better left outside.

Whatever the reasons, it became clear that immigrant communities – particularly Muslim ones – were not integrating as well as the authorities hoped. Statistics showed that Turks and Moroccans were less likely to do well at school, more likely to get into trouble with the police, and less likely to be employed than their Dutch-born counterparts. Perhaps more worryingly, these problems did not seem to be easing much over time, with second- and third-generation immigrants facing many of the same challenges their foreign-born parents and grandparents did. Even second-generation immigrants with Dutch citizenship were still sometimes treated as outsiders. One survey of young Turks and Moroccans in Rotterdam found that fewer than one in five felt that others saw them as 'Dutch'. Well over half said that they did not *want* to be seen as Dutch.

Such problems were not unique to the Netherlands. In Britain, I had myself helped for a short while with preparations for a television debate between mainstream political parties and the British National Party (BNP), and struggled to find ways to recognise legitimate concerns about immigration without legitimising racist ones. British commentators often resorted to talking about immigration in enigmatic terms: how 'population growth' was causing traffic jams and putting strain on public services. The problem was, in my opinion, exacerbated by the tone-deafness of a political class who lived in areas with few ethnic minorities, with immigrants more likely to give them a good price for retiling the bathroom than to take their job.

In the Netherlands, the challenges were even more vexing. Although the Dutch were famously outspoken about most things, the trauma of the Second World War had led to a strong taboo around discussing ethnicity and race. Among major political parties, there was an unwritten agreement that issues of race and multiculturalism should be kept off the agenda, for fear of reigniting the kind of prejudices that had sent thousands of Dutch Jews to Auschwitz. The national media, for example, long refused to report the ethnic identity of convicted criminals. For a politician to raise questions about the desirability of immigration was seen as beyond the pale. When the centre-right politician Frits Bolkestein warned in the early 1990s that intolerant beliefs were being allowed to flourish, he was roundly condemned for pandering to racism and extremism. Within a few years, many people had come to believe that he was right.

As in many other countries, matters came to a head in 2001. Although most Dutch Muslims were naturally horrified by the 9/11 attacks, television cameras caught a group of Moroccan teenagers in the eastern Dutch city of Ede celebrating wildly as the Twin Towers fell. The pictures were beamed around the world, a gift to right-wing activists and bloggers seeking to condemn the 'Islamisation' of Europe. Journalists quickly uncovered other examples of fundamentalist behaviour, which were also widely publicised. A young man in Ede was quoted as saying Osama Bin Laden was his hero, and an imam claimed that 9/11 was an inside job. One survey – the findings of which were hotly disputed but widely reported – even claimed that a *majority* of Dutch Muslims supported the terrorist attacks against the United States. News reports highlighted instances of bigamy and female genital mutilation in the Netherlands. One imam sparked a furore when he publicly argued that homosexuals were 'pigs' and 'a contagious disease'. In normal circumstances such incidents might have been dismissed as merely foolish, but with the dust clouds barely settled on New York and Washington, and Dutch troops about to join the invasion of Afghanistan, every Muslim crank was seized on as evidence of a nefarious fifth column. After years of deliberately avoiding speaking about race and religion, Dutch politicians could suddenly talk of little else.

The Moroccans

At the demonstration in Rotterdam, I was growing increasingly impatient to get going, stamping my feet to keep warm as the sun sank in the sky. A grey-haired man stepped up to the microphone, his red scarf flapping in the wind like a gymnast's ribbon, and introduced himself as the pastor of the Protestant church nearby. After a few words about the purpose of the march – unity, solidarity, respect – he introduced a series of community leaders, each of whom gave their own variation of the same speech. My rudimentary Dutch struggled to keep pace with the rapid flow of well-intentioned clichés: Rotterdam was, they said, a 'melting pot', a 'city of peace' and 'a city risen from the ashes'. 'The Erasmusbrug links two halves of the city,' a Jewish community leader intoned. 'We are all people on the way to somewhere, all travellers,' said a Muslim. All the speakers shared a common refrain: '*Nul-tien is één*', 010 is 1.

As I scribbled some notes, a woman in a jaunty black beret clutched my elbow and asked intently: '*Vind je het leuk?*' 'Are you finding it fun?' Yes, I replied in my tongue-tied Dutch, it's very nice. Playing reporter, I asked why she had come. Leaning close, she answered with the grave intensity of a doctor giving a terrible diagnosis: 'It's a question of what sort of city you want to live in. There is too much hatred in the world. We are all equal, and we mustn't forget that.'

To those in the Netherlands who opposed immigration, however, not all immigrants were created equal. According to many commentators – both bar-room and professional – the real problem lay not with immigrants in general, but with one group in particular: the Moroccans. The issue was not one of numbers; in Rotterdam, the nearly 40,000 Moroccan residents were outnumbered by both Surinamese and Turks. Culturally, though, Moroccans were widely believed to be less well integrated than other minorities, and to cause more problems as a result. Most Moroccans in the Netherlands came not from cities like Marrakesh but from smaller, more remote towns and villages in the Rif, a mountainous region bumping up against the border with Algeria. The thinking among many commentators was that these rough village types were more likely to hold conservative views about women's rights and arranged marriage. Unfavourable comparisons were often drawn between them and the more educated, secular, socially liberal Turks. Some of my white acquaintances in Rotterdam asserted confidently that the city's Turks were 'good guys' and 'very hardworking', while all the Moroccans were 'lazy' and 'criminal'.

Although I tried to be wary of indulging such stereotypes, the facts appeared to support the theory that Moroccan immigrants in the Netherlands were less well integrated than other ethnic groups. Compared to the country's Turks, Dutch Moroccans were less likely to be employed, less likely to be well-educated and more likely to be caught breaking the law. Compared to the white Dutch population, Dutch Moroccans were nearly four times more likely to be unemployed. There was also evidence that they were indeed very conservative: one survey claimed that 76 per cent of Moroccan Muslims living in the Netherlands agreed 'somewhat' or 'strongly' with the statement that 'Western European women have too many rights and liberties'. Fewer than 6 per cent strongly disagreed.

Intolerance also cut the other way: according to one survey, roughly 40 per cent of Dutch people believed that Moroccan immigrants were 'dishonest', 'not law abiding' and 'violent'. While 81 per cent of Dutch people would be happy to have a Surinamese neighbour, only 68 per cent would be comfortable if a Moroccan moved in next door. Just 39 per cent would be willing to consider a Moroccan as a romantic partner. The Dutch liked to think of themselves as an unusually tolerant people, but surveys showed that they were roughly as likely to express negative sentiments about immigrants as Italians were. I had myself seen young Turks and Moroccans being hassled by police for no good reason, and even as a white Englishman found that older shopkeepers in Rotterdam became ill-tempered and unhelpful if I failed to speak perfect Dutch. For an outsider the causes and effects of these prejudices were difficult to disentangle, but I was left with a growing sense that when it came to immigration and multiculturalism, the country had indeed taken a wrong turn.

Pim

At the demonstration, the bald man with glasses regained control of the microphone and announced the route the march would be taking: a wide loop through the city to the Stadhuis, or City Hall, where we would be greeted by the Mayor, 'if he is available'. A police motorbike growled to life behind us and the crowd snapped to attention, ready to begin moving at last. A man with a clipboard led the way, flanked by a pair of policemen and a slow-moving police van with a CCTV camera protruding from a hole in the roof. The crowd trailed behind in a rough teardrop shape, the sagging '010=1' banner swaying overhead. An elderly couple on electric mobility scooters served as outriders, and a policeman on a Segway brought up the rear.

In near silence the crowd shuffled slowly past gleaming bathroom shops and hair salons and trees stripped naked by winter. It had grown almost completely dark by now, and the Sint Laurenskerk was beautifully lit, its sturdy clock tower golden under a darkening navy sky. The bells tolled loudly as we went by. I saw a passing drunk amble over and address the front of the crowd, swaying gently as he announced: '*Ik ben een Rotterdammer en jij bent een Rotterdammer.*' Yes, a man with a Jewish skullcap assured him, we are all Rotterdammers. Nul-tien is one. A group of cheerful young women in head-scarves rushed ahead of the crowd and posed for a photo in front of it, taken by a young policeman who looked like he was enjoying the attention.

Passing the church, we reached the new Markthal, or indoor market, an enormous structure shaped like an inverted horseshoe, lined with permanent vegetable stalls and take-away food joints under a colourful painted ceiling. Hungry commuters bustled in and out of the high glass doors clutching Korean steamed buns and Turkish spinach pizzas. At some invisible signal, the marchers stopped for a group photo, smiling and waving against a backdrop of the historic church clock tower and the futuristic Markthal, twin temples of mammon and God. I shuffled discreetly out of shot and wrote in my notebook: 'They seem to be having fun.'

When the shuffling resumed I broke away from the crowd. While the official march looped through the central shopping district, I wanted to take a brief detour to visit something I had heard about from friends – a monument to a man who for many Dutch, and for Rotterdammers in particular, was the proverbial canary in the coalmine. He had, they said, been the first to sound the alarm on the country's failed multicultural experiment, and he had paid for his bravery with his life.

After a brief hunt I found my man, at the centre of a small square tucked away behind a row of shabby shops. The office buildings lining the square were being renovated and the location was not particularly scenic, with wheelbarrows and jumbles of electrical cables scattered across the floor. The statue was striking, though: a large bronze bust mounted on a high plinth of cracked green marble, depicting a youngish bald man with one arm outstretched in a half-salute, as if patting an invisible dog. I took a photo and a passer-by stopped to nod his approval. '*Onze Pimmetje,*' he said, gesturing to the statue with a half-smile, 'our little Pim.'

Pim Fortuyn was born in 1948 in Driehuis, a small town about fifteen miles west of Amsterdam. For a country known for its sensible, colourless politicians, he was an unlikely future leader: a Marxist academic who read Mao by day and fraternised gay bars at night. In the late 1980s Fortuyn (pronounced 'Four-town') moved to Rotterdam and began a second career as a political consultant and magazine columnist. As his profile rose, he invested in a decidedly un-Marxist Jaguar and a fancy town house that he christened the 'Palazzo di Pietro', where he lived with two small dogs and a butler called Herman. Slim and shaven-headed with piercing blue eyes and a penchant for designer suits, he was a captivating media presence, espousing increasingly controversial views.

In 1998, Fortuyn published a book whose title summarised the philosophy that would come to define his life: *Against the Islamization of Our Culture*. Picking up where Frits Bolkestein left off, Fortuyn argued that a politically correct left-wing establishment had prevented honest discussion about the effect of immigration on Dutch society, even as immigrants undermined the permissive beliefs on which the nation was founded. 'This is a full country,' he once said. 'I think 16 million Dutchmen are about enough.'

As anxiety about Islam increased after 9/11, Fortuyn deftly exploited fears that the Dutch had taken tolerance too far. Multiculturalism, he said, legitimised repressive practices associated with Islam, and sometimes even encouraged them. 'How can you respect a culture if the woman has to walk several steps behind her man?' he asked. As a gay man, Fortuyn reserved particular vitriol for the assault that he perceived Muslim immigrants were making on sexual liberty. If the Netherlands were to maintain its traditional freedoms, he said, it would have to address the hidden danger lurking in its midst.

Fortuyn formally entered politics in 2001, joining a small Rotterdam party called *Leefbaar Nederland*, or 'Liveable Netherlands'. The country was at that time governed by a 'purple coalition' of left- and right-wing parties. Over several years, the major Dutch parties had crept ever closer together on many policy issues. This made grand coalitions across the right/left divide possible, but also led many people to think that the large parties were essentially offering variations on the same theme. Come election time, the victors were usually dull technocrats who were adept at agreeing backroom deals to hold on to power, rather than bold leaders who pledged to change the country.

In that context, Fortuyn was a breath of fresh air, a flamboyant character willing to burn bridges and say the unsayable. He deftly used his underdog status to reinforce the perception that Dutch politics was a stitch-up that paid little attention to the wishes of the working man. 'He made politics simple,' one friend told me years later, unable to hide the warm glow of admiration in her voice. As Fortuyn denounced Islam in ever more strident terms, many Dutch were appalled, but many others were entranced. By one estimate, Fortuyn at one point garnered as much media coverage as the sitting prime minister, minister of justice and the leaders of the two largest opposition parties put together. Fortuyn's no-nonsense conservatism proved capable of uniting what the Dutch called *kerk en kroeg*: the people sitting in the country's churches and those propping up its bars. There was also something typically Dutch about Fortuyn's undisguised pride in his country and its culture. Wealthy, flashy and openly gay, he was an unlikely champion of the Dutch working classes, but epitomised a f**k-the-establishment attitude that endeared him to many in Rotterdam. '*Ik zeg wat ik denk en ik doe wat ik zeg!*' he declared. 'I say what I think and I do what I say!'

Even among the notoriously straight-talking Dutch, Fortuyn's views caused a storm. Within a few months he had been kicked out of his party and formed his own, named – with typical modesty – the *Lijst Pim Fortuyn*, or Pim Fortuyn List (LPF). As he stepped up his anti-immigration rhetoric, pies were thrown and violence threatened. Fortuyn, however, didn't take his critics too seriously. According to one report, when he was assigned a new group of bodyguards, he took them out drinking for the evening and ended up helping them home.

Fortuyn's critics often lumped him together with other far-right politicians such as Jean-Marie Le Pen, but Fortuyn himself strongly rejected the comparison. He held no truck with anti-Semitism and urged the Dutch to support 'enlightened' Israel over its fundamentalist enemies. His trick was to present intolerance of Muslims as a means of safeguarding Dutch tolerance. When a Dutch imam famously said that homosexuals were pigs, Fortuyn said that the imam had a right to voice that opinion – but that Fortuyn himself also had a right to say that the imam's religion was *achterlijk*, 'backward' or 'retarded'. Only by kicking out intolerant foreigners could the Netherlands preserve its peace and prosperity, he maintained. In his personal life Fortuyn behaved in ways unlikely to endear himself to the far right, giving interviews in which he discussed not only his hatred of radical Islam but also his opinions on what semen tasted like. 'I don't hate Arab men – I even sleep with them,' he said. A local legend in Rotterdam told of Fortuyn bumping into a colleague when visiting a gay bar, and spending the evening discussing local tax policy while completely naked except for a pair of shoes.

In March 2002 came the first clear sign that Fortuyn might be something more than simply an outlet for protest votes. In local elections in Rotterdam, his party received a stunning 35 per cent of the vote, beating the governing PvdA (Labour Party) that had run the city almost continuously since the 1930s. A few weeks later, an official report fiercely criticised the Dutch government for its actions in Srebrenica, where thousands of Muslims had been massacred by Serbian forces while supposedly under the protection of the Dutch army. Taking responsibility for the failure, Labour Party prime minister Wim Kok resigned, triggering national elections. Opinion polls showed that votes were likely to be split across many parties, but that the LPF was among the front-runners. With the Dutch government collapsing over its failure to protect Muslims, the country's most prominent critic of Islam was in pole position to become prime minister.

On 6 May 2002, a little over a week before the election, a national opinion poll confirmed that Fortuyn's party was likely to win the most votes, making him the favourite to lead a new coalition government. His critics were horrified. The editor of *NRC Handelsblad* wrote an article arguing that it would be a 'huge disgrace' if Fortuyn were to triumph, proving that the Dutch had failed to learn the lessons of the Second World War. Responding to the poll and to the article, Fortuyn agreed to be interviewed for a radio programme in Hilversum, a small town near Amsterdam. The interview complete, he left the building to travel to his next appointment. As he strode towards his Jaguar, a young man stepped forward and shot him six times. Fortuyn bled to death in the car park.

The Netherlands was plunged into crisis. Those who had supported Fortuyn felt they had lost a political prophet. 'It was almost like if Obama was shot on election day,' someone later told me. The killing was also a deep emotional shock in a country where violent crime was rare and prime ministers had long been able to ride a bicycle to work without worrying about their safety. Fortuyn was, newspapers said, the first Dutch politician to be assassinated since William of Orange had been shot more than three centuries previously. The killing was not merely a tragedy, but 'un-Dutch'.

To the relief of those hoping to dampen anti-immigrant rhetoric, the assassin – who had been chased by Fortuyn's chauffeur and captured – turned out to be not a Muslim, but a thirty-two-year-old animal rights activist who said he viewed Fortuyn's growing popularity as comparable to the rise of Nazism in the 1930s. However, the assassin's background only added to the sense of moral dislocation: a gay defender of the rights of Muslim women had been slaughtered by a left-wing vegan.

In the days following the assassination, journalists rushed to Amsterdam from London, Paris and Berlin, ready with opinion pieces about the 'end of innocence' and 'paradise lost'. In Rotterdam, tens of thousands of people filed through the Roman Catholic cathedral to view Fortuyn's body. Thousands more visited the 'Palazzo' where he had lived, leaving a sea of balloons, flowers and stuffed animals across the pavement. Within three months, an estimated 150,000 mourners had visited his grave. Some of his supporters even visited tattoo parlours to have 'At Your Service' inked across their shoulders. In a survey conducted after the funeral, Fortuyn was named the second greatest figure in Dutch history, after William of Orange.

A little more than a week after the assassination, the national election went ahead. With no time to alter the ballot papers, Fortuyn's name still appeared at the top of his party's candidate list. Despite (or perhaps because of) the loss of their leader, the LPF trounced the parties of the purple coalition, winning 26 seats out of a total of 150. Fortuyn's party was invited to join a coalition government headed by the Christian Democrat Harry Potter lookalike Jan Peter Balkenende and it secured several Cabinet positions – including one, in an ironic twist, that it chose to fill with the first ever foreign-born member of a Dutch cabinet, a Surinamese television presenter called Philomena Bijhout.

In the space of a few months, Fortuyn's acolytes had gone from relative obscurity to national power. Yet without its namesake at the helm, the LPF struggled to hold together. Some of its key players were almost as colourful as their late leader – a porn website operator, a former Miss Netherlands, some students – but none had the stature to assume his mantle. Philomena Bijhout was forced to resign after literally a few hours in office when it emerged that she had lied about her service in a militia in Suriname. The LPF's new leader was soon ousted and another of its MPs suspended from parliament. People who had seen Fortuyn as the vanguard of a new way of doing politics were disappointed to see his heirs propping up yet another technocratic coalition government.

'A f**king farce' was how one former supporter described it to me.

The coalition government collapsed after fewer than six months in office. In the ensuing election, support for the LPF collapsed, leaving it with only eight seats in parliament. Less than two years later, the party filed for bankruptcy. In government, Fortuyn's allies had been a transient presence. Politically, however, he remained an enduring force, having dragged the political centre of gravity rightwards and made it impossible for politicians to ignore issues like immigration. Dutch politics would never be the same again. Among the public, Fortuyn was still widely loved – and hated. In Rotterdam, I soon learned that every conceivable subject was up for discussion bar two: Zwarte Piet (see Chapter 7) and Pim Fortuyn. Even the gentlest questioning about whether Fortuyn's views were perhaps a tad extreme would often be met with an angry admonishment about how, as a foreigner, 'you just can't understand!' A tiny minority were perhaps more honest: 'everyone f**king hated him until he died,' one liberal friend confided to me, well out of earshot of her Dutch friends. Yet to all intents and purposes, more than a dozen years after his death Pim Fortuyn had become Rotterdam's Princess Diana; someone about whom it was almost impossible to say a bad word.

Theo

Turning my back on Fortuyn's statue, I left the square and dashed back through the shuttered shopping district, hoping to rejoin the march. The sun had set fully and the city had grown darker, emptier and colder. I was hungry and made a brief diversion to a kebab shop, one of the scores scattered throughout the city. I ordered a Turkish pizza: flakes of lamb on a plate-sized flatbread, rolled up like a carpet. 'Have you seen the march?' I asked the young Turk behind the counter as he drizzled creamy garlic sauce. 'The religious unity march, with the Muslims and the Jews together?' No, he

replied grumpily, handing me the rolled pizza and returning
his attention to the Galatasaray game on the television above
the counter. 'I don't like politics.'

After the murder of Pim Fortuyn and the political turmoil
that followed, many in the Netherlands hoped for a period of
stability. Nevertheless, a little over a year and a half later it
happened again: another prominent Dutch critic of Islam was
slain in broad daylight.

Theo van Gogh was well known in the Netherlands, both
as a descendant of the famous painter who shared his sur-
name and as a critic of Islam even more provocative than
Fortuyn. Chubby, blond and a little slobbish, van Gogh was
a caricature of a louche newspaper columnist: a womanising
filmmaker and intellectual with a penchant for late-night
dinner parties, rarely seen without a cigarette or glass of
red wine to hand. Like Fortuyn, van Gogh had been quick to
capitalise on rising concern about Islam, writing a string of
newspaper columns and a book, *Allah weet het beter* ('Allah
knows better'), railing against the failures of Dutch multiculturalism. His father had fought in the Dutch resistance
during the Second World War and he was quick to draw
parallels with the threat posed by Islamism. 'The jackboots
are on the march again,' he wrote, 'but this time they wear
kaftans.' Like Fortuyn – whom he took to calling 'the divine
baldy' – van Gogh believed the Dutch had made a huge error
in allowing an intolerant religion to flourish in their midst.
For supporters of woman's rights and sexual freedom to
'respect' Islam was, he thought, an act of extreme hypocrisy.
Muslims should not be treated with respect, but derided as
the 'goat-f**kers' they were. Many people found his views
abhorrent, but some felt he was saying things the Dutch
needed to hear, picking up the baton that Fortuyn had been
forced to lay down.

In summer 2004, van Gogh released a short film,
Submission, in which a female narrator listed hardships
endured by Muslim women in the name of their faith:
raped by uncles, whipped by fathers, forced into marriage.

Accompanying these stories were images of text from the Koran written on naked female bodies. The film was no great work of art, but predictably it offended many Muslims. Van Gogh received death threats, although he reportedly refused an offer of police protection. 'No one kills the village idiot,' he said.

A few months after the film's release, in November 2004, van Gogh was cycling through Amsterdam on his way to buy cigarettes one morning when he was accosted by a young man with a dark straggly beard and a long Islamic-style shirt. Mohammed Bouyeri was twenty-six years old and had been born in Amsterdam to Moroccan parents, with a father who washed dishes at Schiphol airport. As a teenager he had seemed ambitious and hardworking, but he became increasingly troubled following the death of his mother. While serving a short prison sentence Bouyeri developed an interest in Islam, and after his release began attending the El Tawheed mosque in Amsterdam, which previously had been visited by the leader of the 9/11 hijackers. Bouyeri became increasingly radicalised, giving up alcohol, refusing to shake hands with women, and spending happy evenings watching videos of al Qaeda hostages being beheaded. Bouyeri and his circle dreamed of going to fight in Iraq or Afghanistan, but soon realised they didn't have to. With his blasphemous movie, Theo van Gogh gave them an opportunity to wage *jihad* without ever leaving the Netherlands. Bouyeri got hold of an automatic pistol and wrote a farewell letter to his family. 'By the time you receive this,' he wrote, 'I will be a martyr.'

On 2 November, while Americans headed to the polls to re-elect George Bush, Bouyeri pulled up alongside van Gogh on his bicycle. Drawing the gun, he fired several times, hitting van Gogh in the stomach and clipping a couple of passers-by. Van Gogh fell from his bike, staggered across the road and collapsed in a cycle lane. Horrified bystanders pleaded with Bouyeri to stop, as van Gogh (in perhaps the most Dutch response to being murdered imaginable) cried out: 'Surely we can talk about this!' Ignoring his victim's pleas, Bouyeri shot him a couple more times before producing a knife and sawing at his throat until the filmmaker was nearly beheaded. Bouyeri pinned a note to van Gogh's stomach with a knife, kicked the body and walked calmly away.

When news of the murder spread, the atmosphere in the Netherlands was perhaps even worse than after the first assassination. Van Gogh was less liked by the general public than Fortuyn, so there was not such a sense of grief, but people were horrified that another public figure had been gunned down. If anything, the morality of the second death was even clearer: a critic of Islam had been murdered by a fundamentalist Muslim. Van Gogh had not merely been killed, but slaughtered in broad daylight. That Bouyeri had been captured after a brief gunfight in an Amsterdam park offered little in the way of consolation. Hundreds of bouquets and candles were left in the street near the spot where two bullet holes were visible in the asphalt. Addressing a crowd of thousands in Amsterdam's Dam Square, immigration minister Rita Verdonk portrayed the killing as a tipping point for Dutch society: 'We say: This far, and no further. Stop!' The crowd roared their approval as she shouted: 'We will not accept this!'

Tensions rose and van Gogh's friends responded in a typically provocative fashion: with a raucous party at which champagne was served from the top of a coffin, against a backdrop of stuffed goats. Other people responded with violence. A bomb exploded outside an Islamic school in Eindhoven, and nearly two dozen others were attacked by vandals. The Anne Frank Foundation, which had the unhappy job of monitoring such things, recorded more than 174 threats of racist violence in the month following the killing. In The Hague, when police raided the apartment of a suspected terrorist cell linked to Mohammed Bouyeri, they were attacked with guns and hand grenades. Things seemed to be spiralling out of control.

Ayaan

My mouth burning from the spicy pizza, I dashed out of the café, peering down side streets in search of the march. I finally caught up with the procession's tail as it passed over the trench-like Koopgroot ('shopping gutter'), a dismal row of subterranean chain stores passing under the city's main road and tramway. The marchers were still plodding along, perhaps a little fewer in number than before, but the atmosphere had improved: less funeral march, more chatting and laughing. I couldn't help noticing, however, that the various religious groups didn't mingle much but remained separate – a cluster of Muslim women gossiping here, a handful of Jewish men there – which seemed rather to defeat the point of the exercise. Loitering on the edges of the group I caught snatches of dozens of conversations, all unrelated to the march itself: Feyenoord's recent performance, what someone's sister's husband had done, what to do about the downstairs bathroom. Protestant or Catholic, Muslim or Jew, there was nothing the Dutch liked better than chatting with strangers.

As the Netherlands reeled from Theo van Gogh's murder, attention inevitably turned to the woman who had collaborated with him on *Submission,* and who had been named as a future target in the note left pinned to his body. Ayaan Hirsi Ali was born in Somalia in 1969 and raised in Kenya, Ethiopia and Saudi Arabia. Her upbringing was traditional for the place and the time: she suffered genital mutilation as a child, wore a hijab, and was beaten by a religious teacher for failing to study the Koran. In her early twenties, Hirsi Ali fled from an arranged marriage to the sanctuary of the Netherlands. Changing her name and inventing a new birth date, she was granted political asylum and found work as a translator at immigration centres. As a youngster she had been a devout Muslim, but in Europe she became increasingly disenchanted with Islam. She learned Dutch, studied political science at university, moved in with a Dutch boyfriend and found work first in the marketing department of a drug company, and then at the in-house thinktank of the centre-left PvdA, or Labour Party. Over time, what began as mild disenchantment with Islam evolved into something more like outright hostility.

A couple of months after 9/11, Hirsi Ali attended a public debate in Amsterdam. According to the journalist Deborah Scroggins, a succession of speakers denounced the West as imperialist and arrogant, and called for greater understanding of the Muslim world. Hirsi Ali stood up. In a room filled with the white Dutch chattering classes, she made an immediate impression: dark-skinned, confident and strikingly beautiful. In fluent Dutch, she announced that everyone was wrong, and that Muslims were still awaiting their version of Europe's Enlightenment. 'The West has had countless Voltaires,' she announced. 'Allow us just one, please.' The room fell silent as journalists scribbled quotes in their notebooks. A star was born.

Following her outspoken appearance at the event in Amsterdam, Hirsi Ali was inundated with offers to explain her views. At a time when everyone was suddenly interested in Islam, her experiences gave her a credibility that many other commentators lacked. She had even lived for a while in the town where young Dutch Muslims had been filmed celebrating the fall of the Twin Towers. With her faintly regal air, she challenged people's expectations about how an asylum-seeker should appear. To journalists desperate for a new angle on Islamic extremism, she made an irresistible figurehead: half Naomi Campbell, half Christopher Hitchens.

Like Fortuyn and van Gogh, Hirsi Ali argued that problems with Islam were not confined to a handful of extremists, but were systemic. Islam, she wrote in an early op-ed, was directly opposed to individual liberty and freedom. Just as Fortuyn's homosexuality had given him a certain licence to criticise other minority groups, Hirsi Ali's race and gender and personal experiences enabled her to say things a working-class white man might be vilified for. 'It's my religion too,' she once said of Islam, 'and if I want to call it backward then I will.' Hate mail soon arrived, but she made little effort to win allies, launching fierce attacks on the political establishment and drafting an article referring to the Jewish mayor of Amsterdam as 'Ayatollah Cohen'.

In 2002, shortly after the collapse of the post-Fortuyn coalition government, Hirsi Ali shocked the political world by announcing she would leave the centre-left Labour Party for which she worked to join the centre-right VVD. The Labour Party historically had enjoyed strong support from immigrant communities, and Hirsi Ali felt it was unwilling to criticise Islam as strongly as it should. In 2003 she was elected to Parliament as a VVD member. Given a new platform to promote her ideas, she won a host of international awards and was named 'Person of the Year' by a Dutch newspaper. Nevertheless, her views were still wildly controversial.

As the US and its allies prepared to invade Iraq, the Dutch government backed the invasion 'politically but not militarily'. Hirsi Ali argued in favour of all-out invasion, and reportedly argued for an assault on Iran too. Notoriously, in an interview with the newspaper *Trouw*, she claimed that by western standards the Prophet Muhammad should be considered a paedophile. In 2004 she collaborated with van Gogh on *Submission*, helping to write the script and recording a voiceover. More death threats arrived and the government assigned armed bodyguards to protect her. She was in parliament when van Gogh was murdered; rushed away by her bodyguards, she was flown in secrecy to the United States, a refugee from her adopted country.

Being forced into exile did little to temper Hirsi Ali's views. On a brief trip back to the Netherlands, she delivered an open letter to the leaders of her party, declaring that she planned to be even more combative than before. According to the journalist Christopher Caldwell, when she was approached by a young Dutch Muslim convert in a café in The Hague who said he hoped that someone killed her, she handed him a knife from the table and replied: 'Why don't you do it yourself?'

Some two months after her departure, Hirsi Ali returned to The Hague for good, greeted by a standing ovation in parliament and cheers in the street outside. She was even nominated for the Nobel Peace Prize. However, the tide of public opinion was about to turn. The Dutch admired Hirsi Ali for her outspokenness, but many felt that she had gone too far. To speak honestly was Dutch, but to deliberately provoke and upset others was not. Ironically, this staunch defender of Dutch civilisation found herself accused of behaving in a way that was 'un-Dutch'. Others said she was an 'enlightenment fundamentalist' willing to trample on basic human rights – proposing, for example, that Somali girls should undergo compulsory genital examinations to check they hadn't been mutilated. Unbowed, Hirsi Ali announced she was working on a sequel to the controversial movie: *Submission 2*.

In 2006, the backlash against Hirsi Ali reached its zenith. A judge ordered her to leave secure accommodation provided by the government after neighbours complained about the security risk she posed; a ruling seen by many as indicative of a reduced willingness to accommodate her views. A few weeks later, a bigger scandal erupted when journalists alleged that Hirsi Ali had lied on her original application for asylum in the Netherlands, claiming to be fleeing a war zone in Somalia when she had actually been living in a middle-class area of Nairobi. Hirsi Ali admitted falsifying her name and age but said this was common knowledge, as she had admitted it in books she wrote before being elected. 'Have they all gone mad?' she asked of her critics. At the time, it was hard to find an asylum-seeker who hadn't lied on their forms, but for Hirsi Ali's opponents her admission offered an open goal.

Matters reached a head when Rita Verdonk, the populist Immigration Minister known as 'Iron Rita', announced moves to strip Hirsi Ali of her Dutch citizenship. Parliament eventually overruled Verdonk, but a threshold had been crossed. Hirsi Ali resigned from parliament and moved to the United States, where she would eventually join a right-wing thinktank and marry the British historian Niall Ferguson. Even so, she continued to polarise opinions – while some MPs warned that if she came to harm the Dutch 'would have blood on their hands', a former leader of her own party said her departure was 'no loss for the VVD and also no loss for parliament'. Hirsi Ali herself remained typically defiant. 'The questions for our society remain,' she said at a farewell press conference. 'It is self-deceit to imagine these issues will disappear.'

Geert

In Rotterdam, the crowd shuffled past the unimpressive 'World Trade Centre'. I fell into conversation with a couple of about my parents' age walking alongside me. They had lived in the suburbs of Rotterdam for twenty years, the man explained in Dutch, and had 'seen a lot of changes', but were proud of their city's ability to mix people from 'different countries, different cultures, different religions'. The march offered an opportunity to celebrate and defend that diversity. I was interested to hear their views and steered the conversation carefully until it landed on the subject of the latest figure-head of Dutch anti-immigrationists, another populist whose strident criticism of Islam had earned him death threats of his own, along with the passionate support of a sizable slice of society. '*Nooooow,*' the man said, in the drawn-out way with which the Dutch would often exclaim, enlongating his vowels until the word sounded like a saw rasping through wood. 'It's true that there are some problems with the Moroccans, but he goes too far. Pim Fortuyn never hated people, he even slept with Muslims. But this one, he is much more nasty.' 'I think he's just awful,' his wife interjected. 'More like a Nazi.'

Geert Wilders was born to a Catholic family in the far south of the Netherlands, the son of a man who reportedly was so traumatised by his wartime experiences that he refused ever to set foot on German soil. After studying law and living briefly in Israel, Wilders took a job as a speechwriter for Frits Bolkestein, the same politician who had controversially warned of the perils of Dutch multiculturalism and mentored Hirsi Ali. In 1997, Wilders was elected to Utrecht city council, and year later to the Dutch national parliament as a member of Bolkestein's centre-right VVD. Aided by a memorable physical appearance – a wig-like breaking wave of bleached blond hair – Wilders quickly made a name for himself, joining those arguing that Dutch tolerance had gone too far. In 2003, as the Dutch-backed invasion of Iraq became increasingly chaotic, Wilders and Hirsi Ali penned a joint op-ed in the *NRC Handelsblad* titled 'It's Time for a Liberal Jihad'. Calling on the authorities to close fundamentalist schools and mosques, they denounced Dutch integrationists as cowardly and naïve. In order to defend the human rights the Netherlands held dear, they said, it would have to remove them from those who sought to undermine them.

Such views proved unpopular with the leaders of Wilders' party, and shortly before van Gogh's murder he was expelled from the VVD. Taking a leaf out of Fortuyn's book, he promptly formed his own political party, the modestly named *Groep Wilders*, soon to be rebadged the *Partij voor de Vrijheid* (Freedom Party, or PVV), based on a populist anti-immigration platform. Islam and democracy were, he said, 'fully incompatible', and the Koran should be banned 'like *Mein Kampf* is banned'.

Needless to say, Wilders' views earned him many enemies. When police searched the apartment of van Gogh's killer, they found an alleged 'death list' naming both Hirsi Ali and Wilders, who responded by warning darkly that the filmmaker's murder was 'only the beginning'. Many of his provocations seemed calculated to be self-fulfilling: he would make an inflammatory statement about Islam, some Muslims would protest angrily, and he would point to their behaviour as evidence of the religion's aggression. Other prophecies were perhaps closer than to the truth than he had expected. In speeches, Wilders quoted the example of 'Henk and Ingrid', a fictitious Mr and Mrs Average who were meant to represent the overlooked middle-class majority in the Netherlands. This seemed like a neat enough allegory until 2012, when a real-life couple called Henk and Ingrid were reported to be suspects in the alleged murder of their Turkish neighbour.

However, Wilders vigorously rejected the far-right label others sought to attach to him, pointing to his belief in women's rights, support for homosexuals and backing of Israel. Like Hirsi Ali, some of his biographical details made it tricky to depict him as a racist: he was partially of Indonesian descent, had travelled widely in the Middle East, and was married to a Hungarian. 'I don't hate Muslims,' he explained, 'I hate Islam.' Like his predecessors, Wilders framed his arguments as not oppressive but enlightened. 'We should learn to become intolerant of the intolerant,' he said. Such statements proved popular with a significant section of Dutch society who agreed not only with Wilders' hostility to Islam, but also with his claims that the Dutch political elite were still deaf to the needs of ordinary, hardworking people. In 2006, Wilders' party won nine parliamentary seats – an impressive achievement given it hadn't existed a few years previously.

In an effort to build credibility, Wilders sometimes tried to build relationships with like-minded politicians in other countries. One such alliance was with the UK Independence Party (UKIP). In 2008, Wilders released *Fitna*, a short film that juxtaposed images of 9/11 and other terrorist atrocities with images of the Koran. It didn't win him many friends, but UKIP's Lord Pearson was impressed enough to invite Wilders to show his film inside the Houses of Parliament. Banned from entering the UK by the authorities, Wilders flew over anyway, was detained at Heathrow and then put on the next flight home, protesting that then Prime Minister Gordon Brown was 'the biggest coward in Europe'. Wilders appealed against the travel ban and won, and went back to London in late 2009. As protestors clashed with police, he was welcomed by Lord Pearson, who called the visit 'a celebration of the victory of freedom of speech over those who would prevent it in this country, particularly the Islamists'. In his speech, Wilders called Islam 'retarded'. A few months later, UKIP invited him back for a second visit, during which he reportedly described the Prophet Mohammed as a 'barbarian, mass murderer and paedophile' and allegedly said that Turkey's Muslim Prime Minister was a 'total freak'. Challenged by a Muslim peer about his support for Wilders, Lord Pearson reportedly asked: 'Why do you take the Koran so seriously?'

Such international shenanigans did little to quell Wilders' popularity with some of the Dutch electorate. While many Dutch told me they hated what he stood for, others described him in Churchillian terms: the only man clear-sighted enough to save the country from a gathering storm. Whatever the truth, Wilders differed from most other populists in that he had continued to win large numbers of votes over several years. In the Dutch elections of 2010, his party won nearly sixteen per cent of the vote, making it the third largest in parliament. In the subsequent coalition negotiations, Wilders' PVV agreed to support the Cameronesque government of Prime Minister Mark Rutte, giving Wilders a significant say over government policy. Ultimately, the arrangement would not last – the coalition collapsed in 2012, forcing elections that returned Rutte to power but shut Wilders out.

Even so, Wilders had proved he had enough support to put his hands on the levers of power. More than ten years after van Gogh and Fortuyn's murders, he remained in parliament and was an almost daily presence in Dutch newspapers, particularly after forming an alliance with French National Front leader Marine Le Pen in mid-2015. To his supporters he was the last man standing, still saying the unsayable after others had been murdered or forced into exile. To his detractors, he symbolised everything that had gone wrong with the Netherlands in the last decade. '*Een echte slimme vent*', 'a really a smart guy', was how I heard two barflies in Rotterdam describe him. 'F**king Wilders' was the epithet preferred by several of my friends. As the man himself once said: 'half of Holland loves me and half of Holland hates me. There is no in-between.'

Going Native

The march idled towards a conclusion and I chatted with the participants, trying to make sense of my own views. Many of the Dutch I knew had settled on a consensus: Fortuyn had been a good guy, Hirsi Ali and van Gogh kind of had a point but had pushed their luck, and Wilders was hateful. Among the professional classes, views were even sharper: anyone who criticised immigration was a borderline racist. Myself, I wasn't so sure. Talking to the marchers, I realised my views about immigration had shifted in much the same way that the collective Dutch view had, from extreme tolerance to something verging on intolerance.

Before moving to Rotterdam, living in an area of London with a large ethnic minority population, I had never really understood why people got so worked up about immigration. Most immigrants seemed to be honest and hardworking, often labouring long hours in jobs that locals could not or did not want to do. Muslim immigrants seemed, if anything, less likely to cause trouble than 'native' Londoners: they often didn't drink alcohol, and their teenage children frequently conformed to the swotty stereotype. The economic case for free movement of labour was clear-cut, and the cultural benefits also obvious. Southwest London's blend of cultures and cuisines – its curry houses and sari shops and jerk chicken takeaways – added colour to what might otherwise have been a dreary part of town. The problems associated with immigration were, it seemed to me, largely exaggerated by the media and by politicians hunting for votes. Working in Westminster, I would often find myself arguing that promises of a clampdown on immigration were simply scaremongering and vote-chasing, not worth dignifying with serious debate.

After moving to Rotterdam, my views began to shift. In my first few months in the city, its diversity added to its appeal. As in London, imported cultures and cuisines helped add colour to a hard-scrabble city. Wandering Oude Noord's markets and ethnic groceries and takeaways, I could have a *broodje kaas* for breakfast, a Surinamese *roti* for lunch and a Moroccan *tagine* for dinner, perhaps with some delicious Turkish *baklava* for dessert. As an immigrant myself, I also appreciated how welcoming most Dutch were towards those who wanted to live and work in their country.

In time, though, I came to see things differently. The friendly owner of the local Moroccan restaurant was, I realised, the exception rather than the rule. Many immigrants were poorly integrated: fraternising only within their own communities, shopping in their own stores and apparently speaking little or no Dutch. The local Dutch, for their part, appeared to take little interest in the lives of their foreign neighbours, preferring to condemn them from the comfort of the local bar. What had initially looked like a proverbial melting pot turned out to be more like the *spekkoek* Indonesian cakes sold in the local corner shop: lots of colourful layers that sat neatly side by side but never mixed.

As time progressed, I was dismayed to find myself agreeing more often than I would care to admit with those in Oude Noord who blamed '*kut Marokkanen*' ('c**t Moroccans') for dragging the neighbourhood down. Many local Moroccans were kind and friendly, but I couldn't help noticing that the tearaway kids who repeatedly tried to steal my bike, the young men who deliberately bumped shoulders when they walked past, the teenagers who shouted through my open apartment window, were always of Moroccan descent. The playgrounds around my house were permanently populated by *hangjongeren* – young, predominantly Moroccan 'hang-around-boys', who spent much of the day and night perched on the vertical backrests of benches, spitting on the floor and reacting aggressively towards anyone who asked them to keep the noise down. The contrast with ever-polite Dutch teenagers was stark. It didn't help that parents sometimes made little effort to discipline their children – on one occasion, I saw a Moroccan boy of about twelve try to pull a passing blonde woman's hair for no reason. When she shouted at him the boy's father, who was standing nearby, told her angrily to leave his son alone. On another occasion, a Moroccan man nearly ran me over in his car as I cycled to the train station one morning. When I rang my bell at him he drove after me all the way across town, and then followed me through the station repeatedly challenging me to a fight. Making generalisations about ethnic groups was a dangerous habit to get into, but in the area where I lived, the young Moroccan men were considerably more confrontational and less friendly towards me than the Dutch were.

My views were also shaped by my own experience as an immigrant. Within a few weeks of arriving in the Netherlands, I had found work and begun attempting to learn the Dutch language. Admittedly, I enjoyed certain advantages as an immigrant, including a skin tone that made racial discrimination rare and a CV that made finding a job not particularly hard. However, having made an effort to integrate myself, I began to share the frustrations of those who felt that many others simply did not try. Why should I go to work at eight o'clock every morning and straight to Dutch lessons afterwards when my foreign-born neighbours sat outside gossiping in Berber all day?

I would never have voted for a far-right party, and I knew that a great many immigrants (Muslim and otherwise) led happy, productive, well-integrated lives. I also objected to the way critics conflated Islamic extremism with the religion at large, assuming that every Muslim was a woman-hating fundamentalist. The harsh rhetoric of people like Hirsi Ali was hardly likely to draw wavering Muslims away from extremism; but I also thought she had been brave and right to speak up for the Muslim women shuttered behind chintzy Dutch curtains. It seemed to me that many of those who defended immigration did so partly because they were never exposed to any of its disadvantages. Many well-off Amsterdammers who denounced Fortuyn's supporters as racist could probably go weeks without so much as seeing a Moroccan immigrant.

I also thought Fortuyn was probably right when he said Dutch tolerance had sometimes enabled intolerance. As with drugs and prostitution, the Dutch policy of allowing people to do almost anything caused serious problems when those people chose to behave badly, or believed that oppressing others was their right. I found it easy to believe Hirsi Ali when she said that if a white Dutchman hit his wife he would be denounced by his neighbours, but if a Muslim did the same he would be treated with sensitivity, for fear of offending his culture. I even considered Wilders to have a point when it came to the failure of political elites to tackle extremism, although I objected to his ultimate conclusions. Fundamentally, when it came to multiculturalism, I was inclined to agree that the Dutch had lost their way. Ironically, the experience of being an immigrant in the most tolerant country on earth had made me much less tolerant of immigrants. Perhaps G.K. Chesterton was right when he said that travel narrows the mind.

The Muslim Mayor

After what felt like hours of idle wandering, the march finally arrived at its destination: Rotterdam's Stadhuis, a fine beaux-arts building that had miraculously survived the wartime bombing. Twin statues of the legal scholars Hugo Grotius and Erasmus stood guard over a wide flight of steps leading up to the entrance. Inside, the council seat once filled by Pim Fortuyn apparently remained empty, forever dedicated to his memory.

Appropriately, my only previous visit to City Hall had been in my first few days in the Netherlands, as an immigrant registering with the local authorities. For a citizen of an EU country the procedure was straightforward: a kindly bureaucrat behind a glass window copied some details from my passport and welcomed me to Rotterdam. I left the building perhaps fifteen minutes after I arrived, carrying an armful of leaflets and an official welcome gift of a stuffed toy bird. Had I been born outside the EU I would not have had it quite so easy, facing not only a lengthy visa process but also compulsory language lessons and integration tests quizzing me on my knowledge of Dutch history.

It was clear the authorities had expected a far larger crowd of marchers. In addition to the Segways and vans accompanying the demonstration, dozens more police were awaiting our arrival. The busy main road in front of the Stadhuis had been closed to traffic, and metal fences and coloured plastic tape cordoned off a large area of pavement. While the dwindling band of marchers gathered on the steps, the police hurried to clear the fences away, enabling traffic to resume.

A door opened and a man stepped out to a brief crackle of applause: Ahmed Aboutaleb, the same mayor of Rotterdam whom I had seen speak at the wartime remembrance ceremony a few months previously. A former Cabinet minister from the Labour Party, Aboutaleb had been appointed as the first Muslim mayor of a major Dutch city about five years previously. He was born in Morocco and immigrated to the Netherlands at the age of fourteen, held joint Dutch and Moroccan nationality and was the son of an imam. Needless to say, this caused some controversy when his appointment was announced.

When I'd seen him speak before, the mayor had seemed like a gentle and rather mild-mannered man, with none of the bombast Londoners usually associate with mayors. I'd been surprised to read later that he was known for taking a hard line on immigration issues, saying things like: 'Whoever doesn't want to follow Dutch society and its achievements can pack their bags.' Soon after his appearance in front of City Hall, he hit headlines across Europe for declaring that Dutch nationals who wanted to travel to Syria to join Islamist militias should be allowed to do so, but then banned from returning to the Netherlands. 'If you think [Dutch] society is depraved, then go,' he said. 'But there is no way back. Hand over your passport and risk getting bombed.'

Thanks to such views, Aboutaleb had in the past travelled with armed bodyguards after receiving death threats. Today, his tone was more conciliatory. The crowd fell silent and a floodlit TV news camera thrust indecently close to his face as he began to speak. '*Nul-tien,*' he said, '*is één.*'

Rising Tensions

By the time I moved to the Netherlands, national concerns about the alleged 'Islamisation' of the country had eased. At the prodding of figures such as Amsterdam's Jewish mayor, Job Cohen, the Dutch authorities had made concerted efforts to reach out to alienated Muslims. One notable ambassador and role model was the rapper Ali B, a Dutch-Moroccan chart-topper who caused a sensation when he hugged the beautiful Queen Maxima. In Rotterdam, city authorities had proposed a code of conduct for residents that included recognising Dutch as the city's language. Authorities also encouraged the famous Muslim scholar Tariq Ramadan to relocate to the city, offering him a post as an official 'integration adviser' and a job at Erasmus University. In the area where I lived, local authorities and civic groups were forever arranging street-cleaning parties and ethnic food fairs aimed at bringing communities together. Such schemes were derided by critics as 'drinking tea in mosques', but seemed somewhat effective in helping combat extremism in the years following the assassinations.

In just the few years I had lived there, however, many of the old fears had been resurrected. In 2011, the government announced a new integration policy that was noticeably less accommodating than its predecessors. As a ministerial press release put it: 'With this change of course, the government is distancing itself from the relativism embedded in the model of the multicultural society... integration is not the responsibility of the public authorities but rather of those who decide to settle in the Netherlands.' Immigrants, the government said, had a responsibility to learn the Dutch language and to know about Dutch society. New rules banned forced marriage and restricted the right to hold dual citizenship. Tariq

Ramadan was unceremoniously sacked after taking a side job with Iranian state TV at a time when pro-democracy protests were being bloodily repressed in that country.

The months leading up to the 'o1o=1' march had been particularly fraught, thanks partly to the resurgence of a vicious sectarian war in Iraq and Syria. The Netherlands was revealed to be a major source for jihadist recruiters, with an estimated 200 Dutch Muslims travelling to the Middle East to fight, including a dozen who were killed. A propaganda video released on YouTube showed young jihadists boasting of their exploits in fluent Dutch, while a photo circulated on social media showing Dutch-language graffiti praising ISIS on a wall in Syria. Closer to home, a Muslim member of The Hague's city council sparked a furore when he posted on Facebook, in Dutch, 'Long live ISIS, and God willing on to Baghdad to clean up that scum'. A staffer at the Justice Ministry's own Cyber Security Centre was fired after tweeting that ISIS was a Zionist plot to 'blacken Islam's name'.

In 2014, Geert Wilders again managed to make himself the centre of attention, giving a speech in The Hague at which he asked a crowd of supporters: 'In this city and in the Netherlands, do you want more or fewer Moroccans?' '*Minder! Minder!*' the crowd replied. 'Fewer! Fewer!' 'Then we'll make that happen,' he replied. The crowd laughed, but in pledging to remove a specific ethnic group Wilders had crossed a line. Several politicians promptly resigned from his party, while the prime minister said the comments 'left a filthy taste in my mouth'. Over 50,000 people backed a campaign to press hate speech charges against Wilders, while young Dutch Moroccans launched a social media campaign under the hashtag '#BornHere', posting pictures of themselves holding their Dutch passports.

With impeccable timing, just as the Wilders furore was fading, the animal rights activist who had murdered Fortuyn was released from jail. He had served two-thirds of an eighteen-year sentence for murder. A court later ruled that forcing him to wear an electronic ankle tag after his release was 'unreasonable' and ordered that it be removed.

The months leading up to the unity march in Rotterdam had been marred by a series of other events. Swastikas were displayed at a march in The Hague, and fliers for pro-ISIS marches were pasted over Anne Frank's face on advertisements for a musical about her life. A Jewish woman who hung an Israeli flag from her balcony in Amsterdam was beaten up by three men 'wearing Palestinian-style scarves'. One survey of Dutch Turks aged 18 to 34 found that an astonishing 80 per cent thought there was nothing wrong with waging *jihad* against non-believers. The findings were disputed, but were worrying nonetheless. Then, as 2015 dawned, terrorists rampaged through the offices of *Charlie Hebdo* magazine in Paris. The Dutch were naturally horrified that such a thing could happen so close by, and feared they might be next. Rotterdam's Ahmed Aboutaleb condemned Islamic extremism so strongly and repeatedly that people began speculating whether he was positioning himself to become northern Europe's first Muslim prime minister one day. Soon after the rally on the Stadhuis steps, he even managed to wangle an invitation to the White House to meet Barack Obama.

The Limits of Tolerance

Like many countries, the Netherlands agonised over how best to prevent future atrocities. Part of the problem was that the discussion on how to tackle extremism forced the Dutch to reconcile two competing beliefs: that their country should be a beacon of freedom; and that discipline and order were needed to preserve the national fabric. In practice, this meant many Dutch people behaved just as inconsistently as the British did, claiming to be completely relaxed about immigration while getting quite annoyed with immigrants. Weighing the tradition of tolerance against the need to act decisively, the Dutch were never sure quite how far to go. In 2011, for example, Wilders was put on trial for hate speech after making inflammatory comments about immigrants, but then acquitted by a judge who said his comments were 'acceptable within the context of the public debate'. After the Paris massacre, some Dutch newspapers reprinted cartoons of Mohammed from *Charlie Hebdo*, but most did not. The black flag of ISIS was eventually banned from all public demonstrations in the Netherlands, and the mayor of The Hague banned all public demonstrations in the area where the 'Death to Jews' march had been held. After years of letting everyone say whatever they wanted, the limits of tolerance were being tested, and it looked possible the Netherlands would become a less permissive place in the future.

On the steps of the Stadhuis, the demonstration was drawing to a close. Overall, the event struck me as having been a charming and decent thing to do, but unlikely to affect those who disagreed with the principle of Dutch unity. The mayor finished speaking and the floodlights attached to the TV news camera went out, abruptly casting the steps into shadow. A final, rousing cheer went up – '*Nul-tien is één!*' – and the crowd dissolved into the darkness.

Seven

Anything Goes

Sex, Drugs and the Tradition of Tolerance

It was six weeks before Christmas and Sinterklaas was coming to town. He would arrive, as usual, by steamboat from his home in Spain, and a large crowd had gathered to welcome him in Rotterdam. Perhaps a thousand people were crowded into a triangular plaza on the banks of the river Maas, close to the deltoid Erasmusbrug, waiting in front of a stage decorated with banners saying 'Sinterklaas Fever!'

In the Netherlands, Sinterklaas (the original inspiration for Santa Claus) made his first appearance not in December but in November, his arrival marking the traditional kick-off of the Dutch festive season. Rather confusingly, he was a completely different character from the Kerstman (Father Christmas) who would also visit the country a few weeks later, but bore a striking resemblance to him, with red robes, a long white beard and a sackful of presents. Wearing a tall hat like a bishop's mitre, Sinterklaas would ride his white horse Amigo all around the country until 5 December, when he landed on top of the homes of well-behaved children to deliver their pre-Christmas gifts. For Dutch youngsters it was 5 December, not 25 December, that was circled in red ink on the family calendar.

The children of Rotterdam could hardly wait. It was a bitterly cold day and so misty that the new office blocks looming on the far side of the river, just a few hundred metres away, were all but invisible. The puddles of rainwater in the plaza were capped with thin sheets of ice, and my breath rose quickly through the air like smoke from a cigarette. Even wearing a thick coat, gloves and a woolly hat, I was very cold. The arctic conditions had, however, done little to detract from the enthusiasm of the crowd. Bundled up in puffy jackets (the adults) and brightly coloured costumes (the children), they fairly buzzed with excitement, constantly checking the time and asking one another whether Sinterklaas would be arriving soon. On the stage, a group of about half a dozen performers in sequinned outfits were dancing maniacally to booming festive music. Jester-like figures tottered on tall stilts through the crowd, handing out balloons and candy, and I counted no fewer than four face-painted clowns making balloon animals for shivering children.

All in all it was a charming family day out – with one exception. On the stage, the satin-suited dancers entertaining the crowd were dressed in blackface, with black afro wigs, thick chocolatey face paint, bright red lipstick and chunky gold earrings. Perhaps a third of the people in the crowd were similarly attired. Close to where I was standing, near the steps leading up to the Erasmusbrug, a cute young girl shared a bag of pink candy with her bobble-hatted younger brother, both of them wearing fuzzy black wigs and black makeup. Behind them, their sandy-haired mother clapped happily along to the music, a wide grin cracking her thick dark face paint. Everywhere I looked there were blackface characters in striped gold-and-purple uniforms: clowning for the children, handing out crunchy *pepernoten* cookies, riding unicycles and directing traffic in the car park. In a country known for its enlightened attitudes, a tradition that was banned in much of the western world – and outlawed in Germany by Adolf Hitler in the 1930s – was apparently still going strong.

As an outsider, I was shocked by the scene, but not entirely surprised. After a few years in the Netherlands I had become accustomed to the fact that some of the normal rules of polite behaviour didn't quite apply. The straight-talking Dutch generally did as they pleased, thought nothing of saying whatever was on their mind and cared little for the unnecessary rituals of courtesy. 'I don't like your shirt!' a Dutchman might cheerfully shout at a business acquaintance, messily eating a sandwich as he strolled in late for a meeting in his sandals. Political correctness was an alien concept, and people would talk openly in public about even the most delicate of subjects – their new boyfriend's sexual preferences, say, or their sister's embarrassing health problems. Under the national organising principle of 'anything goes', almost anything did – and that included dressing up in costumes that might get one arrested for racist behaviour on the streets of London.

A Land of Liberals?

Outside the Netherlands, the prevailing view of the country was that it was so liberal and easy-going as to be a kind of Woodstock writ large: a place where office workers smoked weed over their desks, visited prostitutes at lunchtime and euthanised their grandparents in the evening. When I told Brits I lived in the Netherlands, they invariably greeted the news with a sly smile that hinted at debaucheries best left unsaid. Dutch friends in turn often expressed annoyance at foreigners' assumptions that all Dutch men were always stoned and every Dutch woman was just waiting for the chance to jump in the sack. To many outsiders, the Netherlands was best known not as the homeland of Rembrandt and Vermeer, but as a nation of drug dealers, brothels and banana-themed sex shows. Amsterdam in particular loomed large in the popular imagination as 'the most liberal city on earth', worth visiting not for its Golden Age art and architecture but for its loose women and 'coffee shops' selling quarter-ounce bags of bliss. The Japanese, it was said, were even in the habit of referring to inflatable sex dolls as 'Dutch wives'.

When I moved to the Netherlands, initially I was pleased to have many of my prejudices about the country confirmed. Compared to stuffy and class-ridden Britain, it seemed at first to be a country without rules. During my very long lunch breaks at work, for example, I often delighted in watching the Dutch approach to raising children being acted out in the park near my office. Several times a week, a group of twenty-five children would arrive on foot from the nearby junior school for an afternoon session of physical activity. They frequently brought with them a cart filled with old wooden packing boxes, and the six- or seven-year-olds would spend a happy hour competing to see who could jump from the highest pile of boxes, or make a precarious treehouse from broken wood, or build a raft to float across a nearby lake. Meanwhile, the lone teacher accompanying them would snooze in the shade of a distant tree. For the Dutch, protective helmets were an unnecessary fad, and health and safety experts unheard of. Waiting at a suburban train station, I once heard a girl of fourteen or fifteen complaining noisily about the curfew her unbearably strict father had imposed: 'He said I had to be home by 4am!'

For a while I jotted down in a notebook examples of what I denoted 'Crazy Dutch Liberal Policies'. I soon gave up when I ran out of room. Cannabis was almost as easy to buy in the Netherlands as coffee, and nudist beaches as common as non-nudist ones. Terminally ill children could be euthanised; speeding moped riders need not bother wearing helmets; prostitutes were entitled to sick pay and pimps lobbied the government to cut payroll taxes. Gay couples had been able to marry and adopt for more than a decade, and 95 per cent of people said they would be comfortable having a gay prime minister. The whole country had roughly the same number of police officers as New York City, and in 2009 the Dutch justice ministry had announced plans to close several prisons because (despite offering to accommodate some of Belgium's prisoners too) there were simply not enough criminals to fill them. Dutch soldiers were able to join trade unions. The few prisoners who did remain in captivity reportedly were entitled to visits from clairvoyants to help them contact dead relatives. The list went on. I considered myself fairly liberal, but even I sometimes recoiled at news headlines that Dutch friends took in their stride, such as the thirty-five-year-old woman who was legally euthanized because she was depressed, or the political party for paedophiles that campaigned to reduce the age of consent to twelve.

As I travelled around the country, however, I came to realise that many of the rebellious behaviours that were – to foreign eyes – 'typically Dutch' were in the process of being discouraged or even outlawed. Ironically, just as other countries were increasingly following the Dutch lead in setting social policy – the legalisation of gay marriage in the UK, for example, and of cannabis in much of the US – the Netherlands was entering a less permissive age, introducing a raft of new regulations aimed at restricting things like prostitution and cannabis use. Many Dutch people believed this change of course was long overdue, but for others the prospect of tightening the rules raised serious questions about what the country stood for. For people who had often defined themselves in terms of what they allowed, the debate about what to ban had sparked something of an identity crisis. A headline published in a British newspaper a few weeks before the Sinterklaas event had summarised the tensions well, if rather dramatically: 'Fading Liberal Dream Tears Dutch Apart'.

The habit of dressing in blackface was one example. For much of the nineteenth and twentieth centuries, such characters were hugely popular across Europe, with 'golliwog' toys selling almost as well as teddy bears and blackface cartoons used to promote everything from jam to perfume and toothpaste. However, the characters often carried menacing undertones and were rooted in the assumption that black men were either happy-go-lucky simpletons or uncivilised savages. When Enid Blyton's Noddy had his car stolen in the forest, naturally it was by a dark-skinned 'golliwog' to whom he had kindly offered a lift. In later years, blackface characters came to be recognised for the crude racial tropes they were, and became increasingly unacceptable in much of the world. In the UK, the *Black and White Minstrel Show* was cancelled in 1978, and blackface characters on product packaging were replaced by less controversial alternatives such as pirates. By the time of my move to Rotterdam, even the most right-wing of British tabloids would react to news of someone dressing in blackface with condemnatory fury.

The Netherlands, though, was a special case. In one of the most liberal countries in Europe, the blackface tradition had not only survived, but thrived. Each November and December children and adults throughout the country relished dressing up as Sinterklaas's dark-skinned helper Zwarte Piet (Black Pete), who fulfilled a role similar to that played by Santa's elves in other countries. The Rotterdam welcoming party for Sinterklaas and Zwarte Piet was just one of scores taking place in Dutch towns each year, sometimes drawing crowds numbering in the tens of thousands. Major department stores would host acrobatic displays by costumed Piets in black-face, while supermarkets sold dark face paint, frizzy wigs and racially insensitive stuffed toys. Zwarte Piet had even appeared on the Dutch version of *Sesame Street*. The characters remained as integral to Dutch festive celebrations as elves and reindeer were to British ones: a beloved national tradition around which much of the country could unite.

There were signs of a shift, nevertheless. At the time of my visit to the Rotterdam event, a particularly intense debate about the future of Zwarte Piet was underway, with public figures arguing over whether blackface should be banned in light of the changing times. The debate had been sparked by the chair of a UN Working Group of Experts on People of African Descent, a Jamaican professor called Verene Shepherd, who dared to say that if she lived in the Netherlands she 'would object to' the ubiquity of Zwarte Piet. Perhaps, she suggested, it was time for the Dutch to lay the tradition to rest. To say that Shepherd's comments struck a raw nerve would be an understatement. Pro-blackface protests were held in several locations in the Netherlands, accompanied by widespread media coverage criticising the UN's insensitive meddling. Leading politicians rushed to support the right to dress as Zwarte Piet. Facebook groups backing the tradition proliferated, and a canny marketing firm launched a hugely popular pro-Piet petition – the 'Pietition' – while photoshopped pictures of a blacked-up 'Brad Piet' spread on social media like a seasonal flu. The mere suggestion that dressing in blackface might be a slightly outdated tradition had caused the normally laid-back Dutch to respond with outrage.

At the event in Rotterdam, the handful of black people in the crowd appeared to be nonplussed rather than offended by the presence of others in blackface. I couldn't help noticing, though, that almost everyone in attendance was white, despite the fact that roughly half of Rotterdam's population came from ethnic minorities. Presumably those who were most offended had stayed away. In search of a better view of the crowd, I climbed up the steps to the bridge over the Maas, where a few dozen people were standing along the railings. From above the event looked even more bizarre, with blackface characters on stilts tiptoeing through crowds of children like balletic giraffes. A family standing nearby gasped and raised their arms in unison, and I looked to see what had caught their attention. Down below us a small group of protestors – four young men and two women – were beginning an anti–Zwarte Piet protest. Standing with their arms linked, they shivered in T-shirts hand-painted with the slogan '*Zwarte Piet Is Racisme*'. A large empty space quickly formed in the crowd around them.

Predictably, international criticism of the Zwarte Piet tradition had served only to unite the Dutch around it. In a bold rebuttal to the UN's allegation that the practice threatened to violate equal rights protections, the Dutch pressed on with a bid to include Zwarte Piet on a UNESCO register of the world's most valuable 'intangible cultural heritage', alongside Buddhist chanting, Iranian carpet-weaving and Spanish flamenco dancing. The UN in turn said it was 'deeply troubled by the virulent intolerance' expressed by those who could not accept criticisms of Zwarte Piet. The right-wing politician Geert Wilders responded by calling for the entire UN to be abolished. Still the debate rumbled on, periodically rejuvenated by ill-advised comments from politicians, commentators and celebrities. Foreign news outlets expressed amazement at the latest example of crazy Dutch behaviour, while the Dutch media remained firmly in the pro-Piet camp.

Soon after the event in Rotterdam, the leading *Telegraaf* newspaper reported of recent events in South Africa: 'There have been reactions abroad and in the Netherlands to the death of Nelson Mandela, who died, of all times, on Sinterklaas evening, with Zwarte Piet.'

However, some of the more egregious features of the traditional celebrations had been ditched. In Amsterdam, the mayor refused to ban the annual Sinterklaas parade but conceded that change might be needed, emphasising (as any good Dutchman would) that 'the first matter of importance is gradualness'. Golden hoop earrings were apparently being phased out in many places, and comedy African accents discouraged. In Rotterdam I saw several children wearing full Zwarte Piet costumes but no black makeup, or just a token dark smudge on each cheek.

For many Dutch, nevertheless, even these modest changes represented a frontal assault on their cultural heritage. I soon learned that while Dutch friends would happily debate the rights and wrongs of issues like abortion or gay marriage, attempting a dinner-table discussion about Zwarte Piet was like marching into a minefield: bound to end in a horrible mess. Almost everyone I spoke to insisted that those who objected to the tradition were creating problems where none existed. 'It's not racist,' they would say. 'The children don't think of it that way.' 'The only ones who oppose it are foreigners who don't understand the joy it brings,' was another common refrain. If it made children happy, they said, then no one could possibly object. Other supporters sought to defend the tradition on a technicality, claiming that Piet was black simply because of the soot in the chimneys he climbed down, shiny clean clothes and afro wig notwithstanding. That such traditions had been abolished in other countries was, they said, merely proof of how important it was to maintain them in the Netherlands. Perhaps the most popular argument was that if Zwarte Piet costumes were not *intended* to be offensive, then no one had the right to be offended. People shouldn't have to moderate their behaviour to account for the feelings of others. For the Dutch, being tolerant included respecting the right to be intolerant.

The Tradition of Tolerance

The Dutch tradition of tolerance was rooted partly in the country's geography. Flat, open and without many obvious geographical borders, it had historically been impossible to fence off outsiders or hold new ideas in quarantine for long. 'Holland doesn't have mountains,' the great Dutch novelist Cees Nooteboom once wrote. 'Everything's out in the open. No mountains, no caves. Nothing to hide. No dark places in the soul.' As a local saying went, the Dutch always preferred to approach things *rechtdoorzee*, or 'straight on through the sea' – directly and honestly, with no room for face-saving or beating about the bush.

The constant need to defend against flooding had also reinforced the tolerant tradition. With one person's land likely to flood if another person failed to maintain their dikes, it was essential that decisions be made jointly. In the Dutch 'polder model' of government, minority groups like homosexuals were not repressed or ignored but given an equal voice. Another major influence was the country's religious and political history. Having been occupied at various times by the Spanish, French and Germans, the Dutch developed a tendency to rebel against excessive authority, together with a sentimental attachment to ideas of resistance and freedom. During the great Dutch struggle for independence from Spain, the country had remoulded itself into a refuge for Europe's repressed minorities. A willingness to accommodate dissidents like Locke, Voltaire and Galileo had helped make it a centre of enlightenment thinking. As commerce flourished during the Golden Age, the nation also became accustomed to hosting salesmen, merchants and sailors from around the world. For the trade-loving, international-ist Dutch, mercantile pragmatism beat moral conservatism almost every time.

Tolerance was also encouraged by the fact that the country was so crowded. With a population density roughly fourteen times that of the US, the Netherlands was absolutely crammed with people. Most people lived in small apartments with thin walls and narrow rooms, hemmed in by multiple neighbours. Everyone could hear their neighbours cooking, fighting and having sex. Large windows offered clear views into homes from the street, and those lucky enough to have back gardens would sit in them scrutinised by scores of neighbours from their balconies. Many people even installed angled mirrors – *spionnetjes* – on wall mounts next to their upstairs windows, so they could spy on the comings and goings below. It was perhaps not a coincidence that it was a Dutch television company that invented *Big Brother*.

Travelling around the country, I was surprised to discover that the Dutch didn't merely tolerate living in one of the most crowded places on earth, they relished it. Sharing a restaurant table with strangers or being squeezed into a train compartment with a chatty family were, to my Dutch friends, not annoying inconveniences but delightful opportunities to make new friends or share stories with strangers. Holidays were taken in groups, sports played only in teams, and birthdays celebrated not just with friends but friends of friends, and ideally their friends too. To the intensely sociable Dutch, a restaurant with small tables packed close together was preferable to an airy, spacious one, and an overcrowded café better than a half-empty one. Being close to others was always *gezellig* (cosy) and never annoying, while spending time alone was seen as a little odd. 'We're all crowded together, so we have to either be tolerant or go crazy,' as one Dutch friend explained to me.

Personally, I found this easy intimacy one of the most appealing things about Dutch culture: a central part of the welcoming outlook that had made the country so simple to move to. Yet it was also sometimes infuriating. To a stuffy Brit, Dutch people could seem remarkably insensitive, with their famous 'honesty' and 'openness' often coming across as downright rude. For many Dutch, 'good table manners' meant licking their fingers clean after they'd eaten with them. I never realised it was possible to talk with a mouthful of soup, but apparently it was if you tipped your head back far enough. In contrast to the Brits, the Dutch made very little effort to adjust their behaviour for the benefit of others. Even kind, caring people would think nothing of talking loudly outside someone's window in the small hours, or beeping their car horn repeatedly when picking up a friend at six o'clock in the morning. If you wanted to talk loudly with your friend on a train, then you had an absolute right to do so – even if it meant shouting across the stranger sitting in between. When queuing in Dutch supermarkets and train stations, one soon learned either to push or to be disappointed.

The Dutch also attached little value to privacy or solitude. It was, for example, almost impossible simply to enjoy one's own company in a public place. Seeking a quiet spot in a park to sit and read, I would almost always be joined within minutes by someone who would ignore the empty grass spreading into the distance and sit right next to me. Working on my laptop on the train to work, it was not unusual for a stranger to read openly over my shoulder and then loudly suggest improvements and corrections to whatever document I was working on. If you carried a sealed package on a train, people would tap you on the shoulder to ask what was in it. Designated quiet carriages, meanwhile, were viewed merely as ideal locations to hold loud conversations about embarrassing personal problems. One friend even told of how, walking down the street making wedding plans on her mobile phone, she had been stopped by someone who told her she was doing it wrong and should have different flowers from those she was in the process of ordering. There was, as far as I could tell, no such thing as a shy or introspective Dutchman. To the Dutch, there were no secrets. Even baked beans were sold not in metal cans but in transparent glass jars.

In the first half of the twentieth century, Dutch diversity had been regulated by the system of *zuilen*, or pillars, which effectively divided the population into distinct cultural groups. Although restrictive in many ways, this approach ensured that respect for minorities was hard-wired into the system. In the Netherlands everyone was equal: even the Queen had sometimes insisted on being called *Mevrouw* (Mrs) rather than *Majesteit* (Your Majesty). The experience of the Second World War also reinforced the habit of tolerance: after seeing minorities like Jews and homosexuals cruelly persecuted on their turf, the Dutch were determined to better protect the freedom of such groups in the future. After the war, the development of a generous welfare system also helped ensure that vulnerable minorities could thrive.

When the *zuilen* began to crumble in the 1960s and 1970s, a new generation rushed to reject the conservatism of their parents. Amsterdam became the *magisch centrum* ('magical centre') of Europe's hippy movement. The city's Dam Square and Vondelpark were turned into massive campsites, while John and Yoko enjoyed a 'bed-in' at the Hilton. The 1960s also saw the birth of the 'Provos', an anarchist group that took its name from the Dutch word *provoceren*, meaning 'to provoke'. The group became most famous for their 'White Bicycle Plan', a proposal to close the whole of central Amsterdam to motorised traffic and create a free bicycle-sharing scheme, using bicycles that had been painted white. In July 1965, a group of young Provos met at Amsterdam's Spui square, where a small crowd watched as they slopped white paint on three bicycles and announced they would be left on the streets for anyone to use. The Amsterdam police quickly seized the bicycles, a heavy-handed response that only drew more attention to them. The small ceremonies at which people would donate bikes to the scheme became more like political rallies, with Provos setting off fireworks, lighting bonfires, vandalising statues and brawling with the police.

The White Bicycle Plan soon captured the public imagination and received enormous press coverage worldwide. While holding their bed-in, John and Yoko were given a white bicycle as a wedding present. The police continued to confiscate white bicycles whenever they found them and the movement eventually fizzled out, but its symbolism endured. Some thirty years later, activists in Oregon who heard about the White Bicycles were inspired to start their own bike-sharing scheme in Portland. Their scheme in turn provided the inspiration for public bike-sharing programmes in major cities around the world. Years later, the Dutch White Bicycles' descendants could be borrowed from docking stations in London, Paris, Brussels and New York.

Money for Nothing

As a recent immigrant, to me one of the most striking con-sequences of the Dutch liberal approach was the generos-ity of the welfare and employment systems. Compared to the British, Dutch citizens seemed to get an excellent deal. It was customary, for example, for employers to pay the train fares for their employees' journeys to work. Homeowners received substantial tax relief on their mortgages and even relatively wealthy people lived in subsidised social housing. House prices were remarkably low – as little as €50,000 for a decent enough apartment on the fringes of a major city like Rotterdam – and it was common for those in their early twen-ties to own their own home. Even as a recent arrival, when I went to register my residency at Rotterdam City Hall I was assured by a kindly bureaucrat that if I lost my job or fathered a child, I would be entitled to a host of financial benefits. Those unfortunate enough to become unemployed could be consoled with the knowledge that they would receive special grants from the government to cover the cost of going on holiday, on top of generous out-of-work benefits. One Dutch friend was paid roughly three-quarters of her former salary when she found herself 'unemployed' for a month while on holiday in Indonesia, after quitting one job and waiting for the new one to start. In at least one case, it was reported that an out-of-work Dutchman had been given a government grant to cover the cost of his regular visits to a prostitute.

My friends who had jobs did not usually treat them with undue concern. On average, the Dutch work fewer than 27 hours per week – by far the lowest rate among all developed countries, and more than an hour a day less than the Brits. No fewer than half the adult population work part-time, and I knew several people who were paid a full salary for working a 32-hour week. Part-time work is in fact so common that people often expressed surprise when I told them I worked in an office five days a week. 'But when do you have time for your hobbies?' one part-time colleague asked me in amazement.

When I talked with Dutch friends about these quirks, I noticed that they often had radically different ideas about the role of the state compared to people in the UK. The Dutch invariably viewed their government not as authoritarian or incompetent, but as completely benign: like a kindly uncle who deposited regular cheques in the letterbox and helped out with the children. People expected a generous level of state support and were not shy about claiming it. In Britain, claiming unemployment benefits was tinged with stigma, but in the Netherlands there was no shame in doing so. At one dinner party I attended, a group of successful thirty-somethings expressed outrage that a mutual friend, unemployed after quitting a job he did not like, could no longer afford to have the first baby he and his wife had been planning. 'The government should give him more money so he can get a bigger house and have kids,' said one, to unanimous agreement.

Dutch people with children received a particularly good deal. Parents were accustomed to having their bank account topped up with generous *kinderbijslag* (child benefit) payments to cover the cost of childcare and schoolbooks, in addition to a healthy *zorgtoeslag* (care allowance) and *huurtoeslag* (housing allowance). Many parents opted to work part-time, enabling them to spend at least one weekday with their child. In the case of those with very young children, the system was even more generous. Visiting a friend who had recently had her first baby, and sitting down to eat the dry rusks with coloured sugar sprinkles that traditionally celebrate such occasions, I was startled to see a ruddy-cheeked, matronly stranger in a blue dress appear and start cleaning up the kitchen. 'Don't worry,' the new mother explained, 'that's just the government nurse', a sort of nanny/maid provided by the state to help bridge the difficult gap between excellent hospital care and heavily subsidised childcare. Perhaps as a result of all this attention, the Dutch children I met were invariably bright and charming, exuding the happiness and self-confidence one would expect from those who had always been treated like pint-sized royalty.

Of course, this generosity came at a price. After a month or two living and working in the Netherlands I was feeling fairly self-satisfied, until I happened to take a closer look at my pay slip for the first time. Studying the small print, I realised that almost exactly half my income was being taken in tax each month, and that health insurance would cost me another significant slice of what remained. After paying various taxes, insurances and fees, I was left with perhaps one third of my pay packet to live off. Given that I had never actually used the Dutch health, education or welfare systems, and had no children or car, this seemed a little harsh. My Dutch friends and colleagues, however, coughed up willingly. Tax rates were very high – 52 per cent on earnings higher than about €55,000 a year – but I never heard the kind of bloody-thieving-taxman grumbling that echoed around offices in Britain on payday. One well-paid friend's cheerful comment that 'the government takes a lot out of my bank account in taxes, but they put a lot back in there as well' was typical.

Perhaps the most surprising thing about the Dutch approach to government was that it actually appeared to work. Having spent several years working for conservative politicians who warned that socially liberal, fiscally generous policies would lead to *Mad Max*–style dystopia, I was surprised to find that extreme tolerance of sex, drugs and everything else didn't seem to have done the Dutch any harm at all. On almost every social measure, the Netherlands was outperforming many of its neighbours. Compared to most other countries in Europe, the Netherlands had (relative to its population) fewer murders, fewer divorces and fewer children born outside marriage. Compared to his British or German counterparts, the average Dutchman was wealthier, healthier and more likely to own his own home. He would also probably live longer and work less. In 2007, Unicef announced that of twenty-one countries in the developed world, the Netherlands was the best in which to be a child. Over the course of several years in the country, I don't think I ever saw a homeless person.

Less tangibly, the Netherlands also appeared to have little of the menace and petty aggression that plagued other countries. Living in various cities in Britain, I had become accustomed to a degree of petty crime and antisocial behaviour. Certain areas of many major cities were off-limits after dark, and wailing police sirens could be heard at all hours. Jogging home from work through London at night, I came to expect showers of abuse and hurled chips whenever I passed a group of teenagers. Dutch cities appeared to be everything British ones were not: safe, tolerant and rather quaint places where children could play in the street after dark, ride bicycles in the road, and take public transport to school on their own. In the Netherlands, bored teenagers were unfailingly polite and would never dream of wasting their chips by throwing them at strangers. There was no such thing as an area where it was foolish to walk alone at night, and the park near my house was filled with women jogging alone after dark. In several years of bar crawling, I never once saw a punch thrown. On occasions such as King's Day and Carnival Dutch revellers would consume ungodly amounts of Heineken, but there was rarely a policeman in sight – they simply weren't needed. Even in rougher parts of Rotterdam, retired couples would plant their small front yards with daffodils or tulips, knowing they would never be ripped up by a bored teenager or angry drunk. Serious crime was almost unheard of.

There were still problems, of course: bicycle theft was rife in the Netherlands, graffiti and litter common, and people were often inconsiderately noisy in the street at night. Amsterdam on a Friday night was certainly no Garden of Eden. Yet overall, the Dutch approach to rule-setting was quixotic but effective. The Netherlands was, according to the UN, the fourth happiest country in the world, and the tolerant, laidback culture appeared to have played an integral role in achieving that.

Grey Area

At the Sinterklaas party, the crowd was still waiting for the man himself to arrive. The mist had cleared a little by now, and the cluster of glassy towers on the opposite bank of the Maas had come into view, poking through the white clouds like toes in a foamy bathtub. Up on the bridge, I waited impatiently with a group of black-smudged children and their long-suffering parents. As the mist ascended the temperature had dropped further, and a biting North Sea wind was cutting up the river. I rested my forearms on the steel handrail of the bridge and recoiled immediately – even with a thick coat on, the polished metal was too cold to bear.

A motor scooter with an 'I LOVE IRAN' sticker on its windshield pulled up to the kerb behind me. Two teenage boys in black hoodies and baseball caps dismounted and joined the line of spectators at the railing; they clearly were old enough to drive a scooter, but not quite old enough to have fallen out of love with Sinterklaas. As the children around them sang songs, one of the boys reached into his pocket and removed a clear plastic bag of crushed green leaves. His friend produced a packet of cigarette papers and they squatted out of the breeze to roll a joint. The parents and children around them looked unconcerned. A policeman approached, tall and faintly menacing in a boxy black jacket, with a hexagonal black hat perched on his head and a squawking radio on his lapel. One hand resting on his pistol, he stopped abruptly and glared down at the boys, who were carefully twisting the ends of a large cone-shaped roll-up. *'Goeiemorgen, jongens,'* the police-man intoned, wishing them a good morning in a voice drip-ping with what sounded to me like sarcasm. *'Goeiemorgen, meneer,'* they replied. 'Good morning, sir.' I braced myself for an arrest, an argument, or perhaps an exciting chase over the bridge. But the policeman was already gone, marching away in search of a real crime to prevent. Rolling a joint in public, even at a family event, was barely worth noticing.

Of all the liberal policies in the Netherlands, the per-missive approach to drug use is probably the most famous. Foreign perceptions of the Dutch are inextricably linked with their assumed addiction to cannabis, and thousands of visi-tors travel to the Netherlands each year in search of a legal high. Most of these visitors would be surprised to learn that they are toking under a misapprehension. Drugs including cannabis are not legal in the Netherlands, but *gedoogd* – ille-gal, but with the ban so lightly enforced as to be meaningless. Those enjoying a joint in one of Amsterdam's many coffee shops are merely exploiting a loophole in the law, epitomised by the name of one establishment I passed on my walk to work each morning: 'Grey Area'.

The Netherlands has a long history of tolerance of drug use. In the seventeenth century, the opium trade played a not insignificant role in ensuring the profitability of Dutch colo-nies overseas. In later years, the Dutch government enforced a highly profitable monopoly on the production and trade in opium, which ended only with the Japanese invasion of the East Indies during the Second World War. In the early 1900s the authorities opened an official cocaine factory in Amsterdam, which did a roaring trade in drugs for medical use until 1963. I'd heard it claimed that the stunned looks on the faces of people in some seventeenth-century Dutch paint-ings was due to the fact that they'd been smoking something stronger than ordinary tobacco. Even the word 'drug' was thought to be derived from the old Dutch term *droge waere*, or 'dry goods'. While other countries battled to prohibit mind-altering substances, the Dutch had, for much of their history, viewed them as simply another good to be traded.

Within Dutch society drug consumption was generally low, and authorities were determined to keep it that way. Cannabis use was outlawed in 1953 and the police cracked down hard on anyone tempted to dabble. In the 1960s and 1970s views began to shift when a series of influential reports emphasised the difference between drugs that caused serious harm and those that did not, and poured cold water on the idea that cannabis could be a 'gateway drug' between the two categories.

A defining moment came in 1976, when revisions to the Opium Act made the distinction between harmful and less harmful drugs official. 'List I' hard drugs, such as heroin, were defined as those that posed an unacceptable risk to personal health. The risks of 'List II' softer drugs, such as cannabis, were more acceptable. Possession of the latter would not be a serious crime but a petty offence or misdemeanour, roughly as serious as a parking fine or speeding ticket. When small-scale dealers of cannabis were identified, mayors, police and public prosecutors would jointly decide whether or not to prosecute them, under what became known as the 'expediency principle'. Given that decisions to prosecute were rare, the small-scale distribution of cannabis was effectively legalised. Drug-vending 'coffee shops' were free to go about their business as long as they abided by guidelines prohibiting them from advertising drugs, selling to minors, selling large quantities or dealing in harder drugs. In the case of harder drugs like heroin, the emphasis was on harm reduction, with methadone and needle-exchange programmes made readily available. For the Dutch, the decision whether or not to use drugs was a personal one, and not something for governments to get involved in. The authorities' overall approach was one of tolerance and discretion, aimed at reducing the harm caused by drug abuse rather than eliminating drug use altogether.

For many years this approach worked well. Easy access to cannabis did not seem to promote excessive use. The proportion of fifteen- and sixteen-year-olds who smoked it was generally lower than in countries with more punitive drug laws, like the US or the UK. The clear distinction in the eyes of the law between cannabis and harder drugs such as cocaine also helped shield casual weed smokers from exposure to more dangerous substances. According to one study, Amsterdam cannabis smokers were less likely to use cocaine than were cannabis smokers in the US, where penalties for hard drug use were much more severe. The tolerant approach meant that Dutch prison populations remained small, and drug use had few of the negative social connotations common in other countries.

Among my friends and colleagues, cannabis use was viewed somewhat like how driving too fast or drinking too much was viewed in other countries – a bit cheeky and unprofessional, but nothing to be particularly ashamed of. When a thumb-sized package of weed was found in a bathroom at my work, my co-workers reacted as if they had found a misplaced briefcase or umbrella: 'Oh dear, someone's lost their drugs. Shall we give them to the security guard to put in lost property?'

A Nation of Rules

After nearly an hour of waiting in Rotterdam, Sinterklaas still hadn't arrived, so the cheerful master of ceremonies did exactly what one would usually do in such a situation: he called him on the phone. The great gift-giver answered on the first ring, his disembodied voice rumbling from the onstage speakers and echoing across the river. 'Sorry, kids!' Sinterklaas chuckled. 'I am running late because I have forgotten my sports shoes!' *'Ik ben er zo,'* he promised. 'I'll be there soon.' Most of the children in the crowd accepted this excuse without question, although a small girl standing near me burst into tears when her mother explained she would have to wait a little longer.

On stage, a black man and a white woman in matching green tracksuits did their best to work the crowd into a frenzy with promises that Sinterklaas was nearly here. The audience happily obliged. The compère left the stage and half a dozen dancers in shiny blue suits appeared, all wearing black afro wigs, dark brown face paint and thick red lipstick. The crowd cheered as if seeing a retired boyband launch a comeback tour. Wigs bouncing as they jumped around, the band launched into an interminable series of covers of seventies disco songs, including an execrable rendition of SI-IN-TER-KLAAS sung to the tune of 'Y-M-C-A'.

A horn sounded, the singing stopped and the compère directed the crowd's attention to an even more impressive distraction: two Zwarte Piets standing on the roof of a tall apartment block. They were almost entirely obscured by the mist, but I could just make out their silhouetted afros and puffed sleeves, and could see that one of them was waving a Dutch flag. To the delight of the crowd, the two Piets launched themselves off the side of the building. Abseiling speedily down the front face of the tower, they tumbled and turned like marionettes. Children clapped and people inside the apartment building leaned out from their balconies to photograph the passing Piets. Everyone was impressed but for one small group: the six anti-Piet protestors shivering in their homemade T-shirts. Most people were still making a point of ignoring them, but I noticed four burly policemen hovering nearby in case things turned ugly. As the abseilers reached the ground, a man of about forty with a shaved head braved the exclusion zone around the protestors to accost them. Standing almost nose to nose with a curly-haired young man in an anti-Piet T-shirt, he jabbed a finger against the protestor's chest. 'It's a racist tradition!' shouted the young man. 'No, it's a *Dutch* tradition!' bellowed his opponent. The policemen dutifully looked the other way, one taking a photo of the blackface performers on stage with his iPhone.

Elsewhere in the country such protests had not always gone so smoothly. In the north of the Netherlands, one group of parents who proposed the modest compromise of painting their children with rainbow-coloured rather than black face paint gave up the idea after reportedly being threatened with violence. In The Hague, a black woman had to be rescued by police from an ugly stand-off with pro-Piet protesters. It could have been worse. In 2009, when a black poet called Quinsy Gario wore a *'Zwarte Piet Is Raciste'* T-shirt to a Sinterklaas parade in Dordrecht, he was pepper-sprayed by police and arrested. A few weeks before the Rotterdam event, Gario had lodged an official complaint to try to prevent a Zwarte Piet parade in Amsterdam from taking place. 'After that,' he told reporters, 'it's been one death threat after another.'

Although the intensity of the debate about Zwarte Piet was difficult to understand, it was indicative of something I found fascinating about the Netherlands – the fact that despite the country's liberal reputation, it could in some ways be an old-fashioned and even intolerant place. In my home country, people's behaviour was still dictated largely by the need to maintain a stiff upper lip, act appropriately and mind what the neighbours say. Strict rules about things like drug use and prostitution went hand in hand with disapproval of any kind of licentious behaviour or sexual adventurousness. In Britain, to dress scruffily, eat messily or arrive late for a meeting was not simply unappealing but downright rude. However, these fustier attitudes were tempered by a pervasive disrespect for authority. Things like speed limits, red lights and pedestrian crossings were all strictly advisory. The British viewed ostensible authority figures like policemen, government ministers and civil servants as kindly meddlers at best, or devious cheats at worst. The rules were often strict, but people prided themselves on ignoring them.

In the Netherlands, the situation appeared to be the opposite. People had absolute freedom to do whatever they liked in their private lives, but minor rules and regulations were sacrosanct. Speed limits and red lights were obeyed, policemen rather feared and the government respected. I gradually realised that the country's thick liberal veneer was buttressed by a hidden web of *regels* (rules) that might astonish people from other, ostensibly less permissive societies. Euthanasia was legal in the Netherlands, but saying mean things about the King could land you in jail. Prostitutes could sell sex in Amsterdam, but residents of the same city needed permits to park their cars in their own garages. Anyone calling in sick to work could expect a swift visit from an official inspector to check they were actually as ill as they claimed. Roadside herring sellers – a common sight in Dutch towns – could be fined for peddling fish before the official herring season had started. Military service remained compulsory until the mid-1990s. Dogs needed a ticket to ride on a train. The list continued. To an outsider, the sheer range of petty rules to follow could be bewildering, and many expats found themselves hit with heavy fines for minor bureaucratic offences. I was always forgetting to carry my ID card, which by law I was supposed to keep on my person at all times.

Although they loved to boast of how laid-back and free they were, many Dutch were actually quite conservative, conformist people. Modest of dress and suspicious of wealth, they tended to frown on anything that might mark one out as 'flashy' – the slogan for the national lottery offered gamblers the chance to become 'Un-Dutch Rich'. '*Hoge bomen vangen veel wind*', the Dutch would mutter disapprovingly of anyone they saw as too obviously successful, 'high trees catch a lot of wind'. Agendas were sacrosanct, and in the workplace it was impossible to order so much as a new box of paperclips without first holding several meetings to debate the merits of doing so. (I once asked a senior oil company executive who had moved from Houston to The Hague what the main difference between the two working cultures was. 'In the Netherlands we have a lot more meetings,' she said. 'A lot more.') While many licentious behaviours would go unchallenged, anyone inadvertently breaching accepted social codes would soon know about it. In Amsterdam, I once saw a sixty-something prostitute in a gold bikini come out from behind her window to berate a man smoking in the street. 'You are not making the neighbourhood look so nice!'

she hollered angrily, to a chorus of approval from her scantily clad colleagues.

The juxtaposition of liberal and illiberal could create bizarre double standards. On one occasion, I went to the annual Gay Pride parade in Amsterdam and spent a pleasant enough afternoon watching men in pink leather chaps spank each other on passing canal barges. I then returned home for dinner, only to be shouted at by no fewer than three angry neighbours for having left a neatly sealed bag of rubbish on the ground next to an overflowing dustbin. If I did it again, my neighbours warned me, they would report me to the authorities, who would despatch a special bin-inspecting team to analyse the contents of the bag and issue a fixed penalty. To flaunt one's exposed buttocks at a carnival was apparently fine, but to stretch municipal bylaws was a grave breach of acceptable behaviour.

Another time I was walking through Rotterdam on my way to work, dressed in a dark suit and behaving – I thought – like the paragon of a respectable young man going about his business. As I approached the central train station, a large white police van roared up next to me, wheels mounting the pavement as it screeched to a halt. Two policemen jumped out, each with a pistol mounted on one hip. Instinctively I stepped back and looked around for the armed bank robber hiding behind me. But it was me they were looking for. 'Didn't you see the light?' one shouted at me, jabbing towards me with an outstretched finger. 'What light?' I asked politely, in my best Dutch. 'The traffic light! It hadn't turned green yet, but you walked across the road anyway!' Wracking my brain, I remembered that a minute or so previously I had waited at a crossing for perhaps thirty seconds before the lights turned red and the few cars on the road came to a halt. I then walked over the road, the illuminated man turning from red to green when I was about two-thirds of the way across. 'When the light is red, you wait,' said the other cop accusingly. 'You didn't wait, so you must pay a fine.' 'Give me your ID,' his colleague interjected. 'You must come with us to the police station.' Hurriedly switching to English, I played the dumb-tourist trump card and claimed I hadn't understood what the rules were. I said I was very, very sorry, and called a policeman 'Sir' for the first time in my life. The officers were unsympathetic, but I was saved by a chirping radio inside the police van, calling them to attend a more serious crime scene – someone dropping litter in the street, maybe, or wearing the wrong colour trousers. 'Don't do it again, or we'll be back!' one officer shouted as the van charged away. Left indignant on the pavement, I was consoled by a passer-by who had seen the whole incident. 'Don't worry about it,' she reassured me. 'After legalising drugs and hookers, they had to outlaw something.'

Over time I developed the theory that the contradiction between indulgence and restriction was rooted in the delicate equilibrium between two competing forces in Dutch culture. On the one hand, the Netherlands had a long tradition of providing refuge to religious, political and scientific heretics. The Dutch therefore placed a high priority on protecting individuals' rights to behave however they pleased, regardless of what others thought. On the other hand, theirs was also a country forged in conflict with nature, facing a constant existential threat from flooding. Good order, cooperation and discipline were essential in order to ensure the country remained dry, and hence the Dutch had developed a strong attachment to these traits. Tolerance of personal quirks was therefore balanced by intolerance of anything that suggested disorder or a lack of caution. For an outsider, the hidden undercarriage of restrictive regulation could be both confusing and annoying. I started to understand the sentiment once expressed by the Sex Pistols' manager Malcolm McLaren. 'We hate the bores, Jesus Christ and the Dutch,' he said. 'Especially the Dutch.'

The Death of Dutch Liberalism

For much of the twentieth century, the battle between the competing forces of laid-back liberalism and orderly conservatism had a clear winner. In the post-war era, as conservative institutions like the Catholic Church retreated from public life, liberal policies were ascendant. With the organising 'pillars' collapsing, political leaders were keen to embrace policies that appealed to more secular voters. A national pension scheme was introduced in 1947, followed by child support allowances in 1963 and social security in 1965. Cannabis was effectively decriminalised in the 1970s, euthanasia and prostitution at the turn of the century. One Dutch MEP even once proposed that the government introduce a ban on banning things.

In recent years, though, the scales had begun to tip in favour of more conservative outcomes. Immigration, urbanisation and globalisation had changed the country, and there was increasing concern about the excesses that liberal policies might encourage. The meteoric rise of right-wing populists such as Pim Fortuyn encouraged mainstream political parties to adopt more hardline positions on social issues. Another major shift was economic. Financed in part by the huge gas reserves of the northern Netherlands, social security spending had ballooned from roughly a tenth of national income in the 1940s to a quarter in the 1970s. When traditional industries such as agriculture and shipbuilding went into gradual decline, reliance on the welfare state began to increase. By 2014, the Netherlands was one of only a handful of countries worldwide where government spending represented more than half of GDP. When the country fell on harder times, such largesse began to look like an unaffordable luxury.

The global economic crisis of 2008 hit the Netherlands hard. The flagship Dutch bank ABN Amro was sometimes even blamed for having helped trigger the global meltdown, after overreaching with an ambitious expansion plan and forcing the near-collapse of its owner, the Royal Bank of Scotland

Group. A bailout of failing financial institutions cost the Dutch taxpayer an amount equivalent to almost a third of GDP. Dutch exports to neighbouring countries slumped and by 2012 the unemployment rate had spiked to roughly double what it had been a decade previously. As jobs dried up, house prices fell by more than a fifth. With the Dutch budget deficit straying beyond the threshold set by EU authorities, the government announced that public-sector salaries would be cut, foreign aid slashed and complex benefits merged into a single universal credit. In the coming years, the government said, there would be further cuts, layoffs and tax increases. Politicians even proposed introducing a new 'Dagobert Duck Tax', or 'Scrooge McDuck Tax', aimed at those who had swimming pools full of gold coins to rival Disney's miserly bird. After years of state profligacy, the good times were over.

Deepening economic gloom was accompanied by increasing concern about social issues. By the time I visited the Sinterklaas event, the Netherlands had one of the higher overall crime rates in Europe. Statistics showed that the proportion of people who said they felt unsafe was growing. Pim Fortuyn had been assassinated in 2002, followed by Theo van Gogh in 2004. In 2009, there had even been a terrorist attack on the Dutch royal family, during which a man rammed the royal convoy in his car, killing several bystanders. In 2012, European authorities reported that Amsterdam, ostensibly the most liberal city in Europe, was the continent's fourth most murderous metropolis, thanks partly to violence between foreign criminal gangs. In 2015, the city saw six gangland assassinations in the space of just two months. Less dramatically, the growing influx of stag parties and drunken tourists in search of a night they'd never remember had caused problems with petty crime and alcohol-related violence. In parts of the country there were also tensions with immigrant communities, particularly the large Turkish and Moroccan Muslim community. Tolerance, it seemed, had not insulated the country from change but merely delayed it, and made it all the more jarring.

Perhaps the clearest example of this was the reversal of the previous tolerant approach to drug use. For many years the Dutch were confident that their laissez-faire experiment had paid off handsomely, with a lack of penalties for drug use leading only to lower drug use. However, by the time I arrived in the country, some challenges had emerged from the smoke. In a continent where crossing from one country to another had become as easy as driving between two British counties, lax Dutch drug laws inevitably attracted large numbers of 'drug tourists' in search of easy highs not available at home. In the southern city of Maastricht, hundreds of cannabis tourists arriving by car often brought traffic to a standstill, despite a drive-through service aimed at saving customers time. In Amsterdam, budget airlines brought thousands of tracksuited young Brits on pilgrimages to the city's coffee shops. According to some reports, more than a third of the roughly five million tourists who travelled to Amsterdam each year would visit a coffee shop at some point during their stay. This was not necessarily a problem in itself, but locals were increasingly concerned about the side-effects of growing drug tourism: antisocial behaviour, noise, drunkenness and petty crime. More than half a century after Albert Camus wrote that Amsterdam's concentric canals resembled the circles of hell, parts of the historic canal district had become a dingy warren of brothels, kebab shops for the suddenly hungry, and tacky souvenir emporiums selling 'Stoner Simpson' T-shirts and bongs. As a friend who lived in the city centre once texted me: 'Amsterdam on Friday night is hell. Nothing but drugged-up Englishmen and Italians looking for the nearest dealer or whore.'

Another problem was the illegal export of drugs. The value of the black market was hard to calculate, but one Dutch MP claimed that exports of illegal drugs from the Netherlands had overtaken those of flowers. According to the CIA, the country was a major European producer of synthetic drugs including ecstasy and cannabis, and an important gateway for heroin and cocaine entering Europe. At one point, US authorities claimed that 80 per cent of all the world's ecstasy supply was manufactured in the Netherlands. Ironically, the huge number of drug-vending coffee shops in operation meant that harder drugs had become easier to find: as competition increased, cannabis profit margins plunged, encouraging dealers to sell harder, more profitable drugs on the side. Criminal gangs began to assume control of what had once been a largely peaceful, hippyish trade.

The Dutch responded by taking steps to reverse their previous tolerance. City mayors were given the power to close coffee shops on public order or public health grounds, and some more harmful drugs were outlawed. Strong 'skunk' cannabis was reclassified as a hard drug amid concerns about its psychotic effects, and hallucinogenic 'magic mushrooms' were banned after the death of a young French woman on holiday in Amsterdam. More recently, police started working with electricity companies to identify the high power bills that were a tell-tale sign of warming lamps being used to grow cannabis. One study reported that some 6000 Dutch cannabis-growing sites were identified and closed in two years alone.

In Amsterdam, the authorities started to enforce more strictly some of the rules that traditionally had been ignored. Coffee shops were prohibited from advertising to customers or from selling more than five grams of cannabis to a customer in a single day. If a coffee shop failed to comply with the rules, it was forced to close. As a result, the number of coffee shops in Amsterdam fell steadily, from roughly 1200 in 1995 to around half that number by 2009.

In the southern provinces most seriously affected by cannabis tourism, in 2012 the government introduced the 'Weed Pass', a sort of membership card ensuring that only local residents could be served in coffee shops. Many shops were fitted with glass security gates that would only open if swiped with a registered card, effectively turning them into private members' clubs. The new system was due to

be rolled out nationwide the following year, but swiftly
backfired. Discouraged from using gated coffee shops, both
tourists and local residents turned increasingly to the illegal street trade, and street peddlers reportedly became more
aggressive in their sales tactics. In the south of the country, the Weed Pass scheme was beset by boycotts and legal
challenges, including from coffee shop owners who argued
the passes were illegal because they discriminated between
EU citizens depending on where they lived. Fearing negative effects on the lucrative tourism industry, the mayors of
the country's four biggest cities – Amsterdam, Rotterdam,
Utrecht and The Hague – spoke out against the scheme. In
Amsterdam, cannabis supporters even managed to drag
themselves off the couch for long enough to march in
opposition to the changes. When a new government was
elected late in 2012, it promptly announced a softening of
the reform plans. Most of the country's large cities opted
to ditch the passes, but some in the south decided to keep
them, including Maastricht. In mid-2013, three coffee shop
owners there were hit with heavy fines after selling cannabis to foreigners – an ironic twist, given the city's status as
the birthplace of the European Union that had collapsed the
continent's borders.

At the time of my tour, the Netherlands had settled on
a new status quo of stricter rules in the southern border
regions most accessible to drug-hunting road-trippers, and
looser ones in the urban centres of the north. However, pro-
posals to tighten the rules further continued to spark debate.
In 2015, authorities in Amsterdam installed a new electronic
display outside the front doors of the central station, warning
arriving tourists of 'DANGEROUS COCAINE SOLD IN THIS
AREA'. The sign immediately became a tourist attraction in
its own right, with crowds of young Englishmen posing for
photos around it, giving thumbs up as they headed towards
the nearest coffee shop.

Free Love

Another, more successful attempt to tighten liberal rules concerned prostitution. As with the permissive drug rules, a laissez-faire attitude to sex-for-sale, provided it was voluntary and no children were involved, had long been one of the defining features of the tolerant Dutch state. And like cannabis, the effects of this approach were most evident in Amsterdam – including on my walk to work. Living in Rotterdam, I would take the train to the Dutch capital each morning, and then walk for about twenty minutes to my office in the canal district, passing through alleyways with high black-painted walls that zig-zagged like a river canyon. About halfway to work, deep in the canyon, I would pass by a row of windows used by prostitutes. Squeezed in between a small butcher's shop and a youth hostel, the half dozen windows were decorated with a single red lamp outside and red velvet curtains on the inside, usually pulled back to reveal the plastic-covered beds awaiting within. The women themselves (and they were always women) would sit on high stools between the curtains, pouting at passers-by or fiddling with their mobile phones. Childishly scrawled signs in the windows gave the women's names together with some of the services they offered: 'TANYA – MASSAGE', 'ANNA: SPEAKS ENGLISH', 'EVELYN: S&M, ANAL'.

In the evenings, I noticed, the women present were young and attractive, with figures that wouldn't have looked out of place in a lingerie catalogue. In the mornings, however, when there were fewer customers around, the windows were filled instead with sturdy Dutch housewives aged fifty or more. Heavily made up and wearing provocative nurses' uniforms or French maids' outfits, they would wave a scolding finger at me as I passed, like neighbourhood matriarchs reprimanding young boys for playing football on their lawns. The first few times, I wasn't sure where to look. Was it rude to glance at the breasts they pressed against the glass, or rude not to? In time, though, I came to recognise those who worked the morning shift, and they me. They quickly guessed that I wasn't likely to become a customer, and we began to greet one another with friendly smiles and waves each morning, like commuters who regularly shared a train.

Magda, a woman of about sixty with fishnet tights, a high blonde beehive and a fearsome leather whip, was a particularly cheery presence. As I hurried past each morning I would receive a shouted *'Goeiemorgen!'* through the glass, a friendly wave, and perhaps even a flirty blown kiss. The only problem came on the occasions when I found myself walking along the same streets with a colleague, and had to engineer a swift detour to avoid passing the windows. I wasn't sure how he would react if he saw Magda and I waving to one another like old friends, or how I'd convince him that our relationship was purely platonic.

As early as 1413, city authorities in Amsterdam decreed that 'whores are necessary in big cities and especially in cities of commerce such as ours' and for that reason 'the court and the sheriff of Amsterdam shall not entirely forbid the keeping of brothels'. For centuries thereafter, laws banning prostitution were lax, and enforced only occasionally. As the number of international visitors to the city soared, scores of brothels opened for business, catering to both local customers and horny tourists keen to visit the famous Red Light District.

In 2000, the ineffectual ban on prostitution was scrapped altogether. Dutch brothels were allowed to operate openly provided the correct licences were obtained from local authorities, sex workers were over the age of consent and voluntarily employed, and the brothels were equipped with a ready supply of condoms, panic buttons and cleaning facilities. As the Dutch government said in a factsheet for foreign tourists, with perhaps a hint of pride: 'The Netherlands [was] one of the first countries in the world to recognise voluntary adult prostitution as a normal occupation.' Dutch sex workers had most of the same rights as any other employee, and their employers had to comply with labour laws, offer sickness benefits and pay taxes just like anyone else. An official lobby group for brothel owners acted as a kind of pimps' union, campaigning for lower taxes and fewer regulations.

In some larger cities, authorities designated areas where sex workers could ply their trade, equipped with not only adequate car parking but lounges where women could take breaks, shower and make coffee. By the early twenty-first century, Amsterdam was home to an estimated 25,000 prostitutes – roughly as many as the whole of France. There were even persistent rumours that government job centres encouraged unemployed women to enter the sex trade. A city once synonymous with free love had become synonymous with paid-for sex.

However, as with the drugs trade, recent years had brought increasing concern about the practical implications of such a tolerant approach. In the late 1980s, the collapse of the Berlin Wall had sent a wave of young women from Eastern Europe to Amsterdam. In the 1990s, the Schengen agreement meant a citizen of any EU country could set up (or be set up) as a sex worker, without needing a work permit or visa. By 1999, just a third of Amsterdam's prostitutes were Dutch, with the rest coming from Eastern Europe, Latin America and the Caribbean. Inevitably, not all these women had joined the sex trade of their own free will. One UN study found that the Netherlands had become one of the world's top destinations for trafficked women; another investigation identified 'serious abuses such as trafficking in women, prostitution involving girls under the age of consent and forced prostitution'.

Within the Netherlands, sensational newspaper stories described the phenomenon of 'loverboys', the middle-class father's nightmare of young men who posed as loving boyfriends before coercing girls as young as nine into becoming prostitutes. Brothels, once run by retired older prostitutes, were increasingly controlled by male pimps from foreign gangs. One Dutch brothel owner told the *New York Times*: 'In the old days, pimps mostly stuck to the rules, and police would warn people, like, "Hey Jan, you're crossing the line."

There was a kind of balance. But the local sex bosses are too old or dead or in prison, and the market has opened up.' According to one report, a police list of eighty violent pimps included only three who were born in the Netherlands. In one case in 2009, two Nigerian men were convicted of trafficking 140 women into the country, removing them from asylum centres and then convincing them they had been placed under voodoo curses that could only be lifted by having sex with around 3000 men.

Growing concern about the women involved in sex work was matched by concern about the effect the sex trade was having on local communities. Walking around Amsterdam's Red Light District, it was hard to ignore the sense that copious brothels, together with coffee shops, were lowering the tone of the once-stately city – not just by their presence, but because they encouraged the proliferation of peep shows, sex shops, cheap hotels and bars. It was, as I overheard one American tourist say to her husband, 'easier to buy a dildo in Amsterdam than a postcard'.

In 2007, the Amsterdam city council decided that enough was enough and voted to clean up the Red Light District. Legalising the sex trade 'hasn't worked', said the city's mayor at the time, the left-wing stalwart Job Cohen. 'We've realised this is no longer about small-scale entrepreneurs, but that big crime organisations are involved here in trafficking women, drugs, killings and other criminal activities,' he said. Armed with strict new zoning rules and powers to revoke brothel licences, authorities began buying up brothels and converting them to other uses. Within a year, roughly a third of the city's 150 or so brothels had closed. In one deal, the city council reportedly paid €18 million to acquire eighteen large-windowed shopfronts from a brothel landlord known as the 'Emperor of Sex'. Some of the former knocking shops were subsequently rented, at subsidised rates, to budding young designers, live women in the windows replaced by plastic mannequins modelling expensive trenchcoats and handbags.

As with other policy changes, the new restrictions were not without their opponents. In Amsterdam, some people feared that clamping down on prostitution would – as with reducing drug use – undermine the tourism industry. Other, tenderer hearts feared that the clampdown risked driving sex workers underground, where they would be more vulnerable to exploitation by violent pimps and gangs. A few liberals also expressed discomfort at the idea of restricting women's rights. 'It's up to them what they do with their bodies, not the government,' one left-leaning friend argued to me. Sex workers, hit hard by an economic crisis that had reportedly cut the price of a good time from fifty euros to thirty, lobbied vociferously against efforts to curb their trade.

Yet efforts to limit prostitution continued unabated. In early 2013, Amsterdam's city council announced fresh plans to raise the minimum age for sex workers to 21 in an effort to protect younger women from exploitation. Brothel owners would be required to produce written business plans explaining how they would protect the health and safety of their employees, and forced to close their doors during the lightly policed early hours of the morning. At the national level, the Dutch parliament debated legislation that would require all sex workers to register with the government, and anyone visiting one to check their registration before paying for their services. The left-wing Labour Party, a member of the governing coalition, even announced an investigation into the possibility of criminalising visits to prostitutes – something that would have been unthinkable a decade or two previously. At the time of writing it remained unclear how far the changes would go, but I wondered whether Magda would continue smiling and waving on my way to work for much longer.

The Right to Die

A third area where Dutch tolerance was in retreat concerned the right to legal euthanasia. The Dutch parliament had decriminalised so-called assisted suicide in 2001, amending the national Criminal Code to include an exemption for doctors acting to end 'unbearable suffering' for patients who could be offered 'no other reasonable solution'. According to the national statistics agency, in 2013 nearly 5000 people died after doctors either directly assisted their suicide or deliberately withdrew treatment that was keeping them alive. The majority of the deaths involved someone suffering from cancer.

According to the government, 'termination of life on request could represent a dignified conclusion to good palliative care'. That may well have been true, but the difficulty of judging whether someone's suffering was truly 'unbearable' meant that much rested on the discretion of the doctors involved. As euthanasia became increasingly common, there was growing unease at some of the ends to which the law was being put, such as the case of a physically healthy sixty-three-year-old man who was euthanised after becoming distressed at the prospect of retiring from his long career as a civil servant. Faced with intense media coverage of such cases, even some supporters of the law became uneasy about its implications. Were all of the hundred-odd people killed every week really suffering unbearably? There were still many voices supporting the permissive approach – one group of pensioners lobbied the government to introduce a right to request euthanasia for anyone aged over seventy, regardless of their physical condition – but others were no longer sure. Boudewijn Chabot, a psychiatrist who became famous after a 1991 conviction for helping a patient end her life, told journalists in 2014, 'In the last two years, things have started happening that make me feel uncomfortable', claiming that the law he had helped champion had now 'gone off the rails'.

An Uncertain Future

At the time of writing, the debate over how to resolve these tensions continued unresolved. Unlike with drugs and prostitution, no significant rolling back of the existing liberal laws on euthanasia looked likely. However, the fact that the issue was even up for discussion indicated how far the political landscape had shifted. Almost every week, Dutch newspapers included more minor examples of the great liberal society in retreat: immigration laws tightened, retirement ages raised, the legal age for drinking alcohol increased.

In the economic sphere, a sluggish recovery spurred efforts to roll back the generous welfare state. When the Netherlands was stripped of its prized triple A credit rating, ministers accelerated efforts to cut costs. The government proposed requiring people who did not speak Dutch to learn the language in order to receive welfare payments, and that the elderly and disabled people should carry out voluntary work in return for free social care. A landmark moment came in late 2013 when, a few months after taking the throne, King Willem-Alexander used his first annual appearance before parliament to make a speech – written for him by the government – that was widely interpreted as confirming the demise of the generous Dutch welfare state. 'Due to social developments such as globalisation and an ageing population, our labour market and public services are no longer suited to the demands of the times,' the King said. The classic welfare state was 'unsustainable', he added, and would have to be replaced by a 'participation society' in which 'citizens will be expected to take care of themselves'. Coming less than six months after his joyous inauguration in Dam Square, the King's downbeat message was a shock. Dutch austerity, it seemed, would not be a case of temporary belt-tightening but something more permanent, shifting the country away from the Scandinavian model towards something rather more British or American.

It was difficult to see where it would all end. Authorities often sought to portray changes as reinforcing, rather than reversing, the liberal tradition. Regardless of the rationale, there was little doubt which way the wind was blowing. 'The nation's ideals are being tested by the reality they brought,' the Dutch sociologist Dick Houtman told the *Daily Telegraph*.

'The Netherlands went further in allowing all sorts of liberties than many other countries. The test is severe. There is a
feeling that our tolerance is the principal cause of many of
the problems we experience now. The debate is about where
liberty and tolerance should end and where order should
begin.'

To me, it seemed fairly certain that future generations of
Dutch would enjoy fewer freedoms and fewer subsidies than
their parents. However, the political fortunes of the conservative right waned as often as they waxed, and the tradition
of tolerance was so deeply embedded in the national identity
that a complete reversal was highly unlikely. For every liberal
policy scrapped or tightened, another remained intact. Even
if some freedoms were curtailed, the Netherlands was likely
to remain one of the world's most liberal countries for a long
time to come, with all the fun that entailed.

In the case of the Zwarte Piet tradition, significant change
looked very unlikely. Most Dutch remained defiantly proud
of their love of blackface, and were sticking to the 'We don't
think it's racist, so it can't be racist' line. Newspapers reported
that 'secret negotiations' were underway between anti-Piet
campaigners and political leaders, but when asked about possible changes even the reformist prime minister Mark Rutte
could only say: 'My friends in the [Caribbean] Antilles are
very happy when it is Sinterklaas because they don't have
to paint their faces.' 'When I play Zwarte Piet I am for days
trying to get the stuff off my face', he said.

At the Sinterklaas festival there were few signs of change.
Just as I was getting ready to leave for somewhere warmer,
the man himself finally arrived. A small flotilla of boats
appeared through the mist on the Maas: first a speedboat
filled with waving Zwarte Piets, then two old tugboats puff-
ing like pipe smokers, and then Sinterklaas's own larger ship.
A stately white steamboat with a single smoking funnel, it
looked more Aristotle Onassis than old St Nick. As a crowd of
excited children surged towards the waterfront, a Praetorian
guard of Zwarte Piets rushed from the stage to the jetty on

the riverbank. The large vessel docked and Sinterklaas disembarked to a huge cheer. The Piets formed two lines through the crowd and Sinterklaas passed between them, a glossy white beard tumbling down his chest like a waterfall. Surrounded by sycophants and wearing red robes, he looked like a Pope arriving to give Mass. The crowd kept cheering wildly, and parents held their children aloft to catch a glimpse of their hero.

As the masses parted to let him pass, the six young protestors shouted something about racism and turned their backs on him. A chorus of boos and jeers erupted, quickly drowned out by the pounding festive music and cheering children. A tall young man standing next to me picked up his curly-haired daughter and gestured gleefully towards the face-painted Zwarte Piets in the distance. 'Look at the stupid black men!' he said. The Dutch, as always, were determined to keep having a good time.

Epilogue

Going Dutch

After nearly five years in the Netherlands, it was time to return to Britain. It would be a short visit: my passport was about to expire and replacing it would require a long day trip to the passport agency offices in London. I had been back a few times before but always very briefly, rushing to attend weddings and business meetings with not a second to lose. This would be the first time in years I'd been in Britain with time to spare, even if only for a day.

Unable to face the orange-tinged purgatory of easyJet, I chose to travel the slow way, by train. The high-speed service to Brussels headed south from Rotterdam, passing a graffitied wall proclaiming in large letters: 'It Was All a Dream'. The train slid smoothly through the industrial suburbs of Rotterdam, behind the Feyenoord football stadium, over the river Maas in Dordrecht, past crumbling Nazi gun emplacements, and down through carnival country to the Belgian border. It had snowed the previous night and the journey south was unexpectedly beautiful, the usual boggy farmland transformed into a lacy blanket of snow and ice.

After a quick stop in Brussels for a Belgian beer and a croissant, I boarded the Eurostar to London. The train was very crowded and in a spectacular piece of bad luck, I had been allocated a seat next to a man with a broken elbow in a plaster cast that stuck out sideways like a bird's wing. After ten minutes of being jabbed in the ribs, I gave up and went to the dining car. The slender carriage swayed violently as it cruised into France at 180 miles an hour, adding to the balance problems of the three English people drinking beer for breakfast – reassuring proof that moderate alcoholism was still endemic in the country of my birth. At ten in the morning I wasn't quite ready to join them, but – in an effort to speed my reintegration – I ordered a cup of milky tea rather than a coffee, and a flapjack rather than a cheese sandwich. A few British newspapers on the counter offered a crash course in current affairs: 'OLD PEOPLE AUCTIONED OFF TO CARE HOMES ON INTERNET', the *Daily Mail* said. Inside, the pages were dominated by fears and grumbles about Europe, a place most Brits clearly still considered corrupt and work-shy and generally best avoided.

Despite the busy train and efficient multilingual staff, the Eurostar felt strangely like entering Britain through the back door. One minute we were in France, and then after what seemed like a few minutes in a dark tunnel, we were in England. As if to welcome returning exiles, the weather was far better than on the continent, with a clear blue sky and fluffy popcorn clouds.

The flat farmland of Kent was at first strangely reminiscent of the Netherlands, with its miles of level fields, foggy greenhouses and towering electricity pylons. There were even modern windmills idling on the horizon, many more than I remembered from the last time I passed through here. Once part of the same land mass, southeastern England and the Netherlands were in some ways still not very far apart.

As we travelled further from the Channel, however, the landscape quickly became more English: an anarchic, rolling patchwork of grassy fields, rough hedgerows and spidery oaks. Muddy footpaths and tangled gardens lined overgrown country lanes that looked like green tunnels. A sign outside a school advertised a jumble sale, and I could have sworn I saw another warning of slow-moving horses and carts. To my surprise, I felt a physical ache at the sight of hills swelling on the horizon, with their promise of views and breathtaking descents. The train rocketed high over the Medway and then the Thames. And there, appearing quite suddenly on the horizon, was London: grey and grimy and nearly obscured from view by fog, electricity pylons and vast Tesco warehouses.

I disembarked at St Pancras station into a strangely multicultural zone, with announcements in French and Dutch, a train guard who wished me *'Bonjour'* and even a uniformed French policeman eating a croissant on the platform. Beyond the ticket barriers, however, was unmistakably Britain, with its endless infantilising announcements over the station loudspeakers: not just 'mind the gap' but also 'don't forget your bags', 'don't block the doors' and 'mind out for the floor, which might be slippery'. It wasn't yet lunchtime, but a drunk man walked past clutching an enormous bottle of shandy as if it were his first-born.

Britain felt at once both familiar and unfamiliar. I knew instinctively which direction I should walk in to find the station exit, and where the toilets would be. Yet when I paused to buy a coffee in a busy station café, I was confused by the new contactless credit card reader, and the waitress smirked at me for not knowing what a 'Flat White' was. My drink cost more than double what it would have in the Netherlands. When the waitress handed me the cup, I accidentally thanked her in Dutch.

I left the station and walked south towards Covent Garden. I'd been this way a hundred times before but found myself looking at London as if I were a tourist, fascinated by the new double-decker buses, the red phone boxes and post boxes, the black cabs and the unarmed policemen wearing helmets shaped like pen lids. After years of thinking the Netherlands was horribly overcrowded, I was surprised to find that London seemed even more so: noisy and chaotic and so packed with cars and buses and idling tourists that it was impossible to move quickly. Crossing the road in front of the British Museum, I looked the wrong way and was almost flattened by a cliché: a white builder's van hurtling recklessly through a pelican crossing. Winding down a grimy window, the fluorescent-jacketed driver hollered a perfect London welcome: 'Oi! Mate! Get yer eyes tested!'

Wandering south, I came to Seven Dials, a tall obelisk with blue sundials encircling the top. An inscription carved into the granite base read: 'Unveiled by Her Majesty Queen Beatrix of the Netherlands, 29th June 1989'. Across the street, a pair of young Dutchmen were talking loudly in their native language about the anatomical features of a woman bending over nearby, assuming that no one could understand them. I wished them a brief '*Fijne dag*' as I passed, and they blushed the same deep red as her underwear.

After forty minutes or so I arrived at the passport office, where an elaborate numbering system had been established to process customers as slowly as possible. Perhaps a hundred other people were already waiting in complete silence; in Britain, talking to a stranger was clearly still unheard of. When I asked a woman of about my age for the time, she seemed to assume I was hitting on her and quickly moved to another seat. Eventually, having paid an exorbitant 'Express' fee, I left my old passport with a friendly Jamaican woman and was told I could collect the new one later that afternoon. Passportless, I felt suddenly stateless. Having gone years barely setting foot on British soil, I was now unable to leave.

With several hours to kill, I resolved to do exactly what returning expats usually did: browsing for books, visiting pubs, shopping in Marks & Spencer and stocking up on Marmite. Like any good tourist, I also ended up spending a great deal of time eating and drinking: a bacon sandwich in Covent Garden, a slice of carrot cake at St Martin-in-the-Fields, a warm ale in a draughty pub near Charing Cross. Down by the river, near the London Eye, I bought a steaming meat pie and mash from a roadside vendor who spotted my largish backpack and asked where I was going on holiday. 'Not going,' I replied. 'Coming. I'm just visiting for the day, I live in the Netherlands.' 'Oooh, lovely,' she said, another great British cliché brought to life. 'What are the house prices like there?'

The last time I had spent any significant time in London was in the days after David Cameron's 2010 election victory – a victory I'd worked to help bring about. I was therefore curious to see what had changed during my time away, and whether any of the incoming government's promises to transform the country had been delivered. According to the media, they hadn't: the newspapers were still filled with talk of economic crisis, an overstretched health service and duplicitous bankers. Looking at a bank of wide-screen televisions in the window of an enormous electrical goods store, I saw politicians from the three main parties stroppily debating immigration policy. Did, the reporter asked, the 'tsunami of media coverage' and 'bitter partisan divide' politicians had to deal with make it harder for them to debate good policy? Was Britain moving towards a European-style system where coalition governments were the norm? All three ducked the questions.

Judging by London's skyline, though, the city was thriving. A host of new skyscrapers looked almost Dutch in their refusal to blend in with their surroundings. Areas I remembered as green were now crammed with flats and office blocks; buildings I recalled as dilapidated had been converted into gleaming open-plan apartments. Cycling seemed more popular than it had been before, although it evidently still involved running a fearsome gauntlet of buses and lorries, riders dressed in fluorescent clothes in the hope of avoiding certain death. Bars and cafés all seemed to have been refurbished in the same style, offering craft beers and expensive coffee in echoing faux-industrial spaces of reclaimed wood and unpainted concrete. Despite what the papers said, people didn't look like they were teetering on the brink of destitution. Celebrity magazines were filled with hysterical coverage of things I'd never heard of: *The Great British Bake Off* and something called *Gogglebox*. Everything was expensive – roughly the same price in pounds as it was in euros in the Netherlands. Seeking an answer to the pie-seller's question, I paused to look in an estate agent's window and saw that for the price of a large family home in Rotterdam, I could buy a shoebox in a rough part of London.

Most striking of all was the food, which was omnipresent. In contrast to the Netherlands, it was almost impossible to walk a hundred yards without being tempted by an artisan sandwich, gluten-free cake, sushi platter or stone-baked pizza.

Sugary snacks were on sale everywhere: flapjacks and cakes and chocolate bars and bags of sweets piled up next to every checkout. Perhaps as a result, people looked more unhealthy than they did in the Netherlands, sporting muffin tops to match the muffins they always seemed to be eating. In a busy Parliament Square, I found I could see easily over the crowd: at 6'2" I was taller than most people, rather than merely average. Waiting to cross the road, I did see one young woman who looked a little healthier and happier than everyone else, smiling to herself behind a curtain of long blonde hair. When she opened her handbag I saw a book inside, and realised she was Dutch.

It wasn't all bad, though. Compared to Dutch cities, London crackled with energy. People walked quickly, dressed smartly, had passionate debates about current affairs. The shops were filled with enormous selections of food and gadgetry, and the streets were lined with posters advertising new plays, new books, new museum exhibits and new fashions. I remembered the German poet's quote about everything happening fifty years later in the Netherlands, and thought he was probably right.

I was also reminded of many things I had missed about Britain, like the simple pleasure of walking down a sloping street with a view across the city. I loved how polite everyone was, queuing nicely and eating carefully and holding doors open for one another. I liked the way patches of green land and trees were allowed to run wild, rather than being pruned and levelled and tarmacked into submission. The way people sat quietly in the train without nosying into each other's business or talking loudly about embarrassing problems. The way even the smallest supermarkets sold a dozen types of breakfast cereal and a dozen types of cake. The way people said 'cheers' instead of thank-you, and called people they hardly knew 'mate' and 'love' and 'dear'. The way people were scrupulously polite to strangers, and hilariously rude about their friends. The way they seemed to love their dogs almost as much as they loved their children. The scurrilous newspapers with their punning headlines, ever ready to puncture the egos of the grandiose or corrupt. The way even mundane street furniture – hand rails and lampposts and letter boxes – was ornate and antique and not made from the same extruded grey steel. Black cabs and M&S lingerie models and round-abouts and real ale and bookshops. Twiglets.

Being back in Britain – albeit very briefly – also made me realise the extent to which I had 'gone Dutch'. In the course of nearly five years in the Netherlands I had, I thought, become rather more laid-back. I was less concerned about career and money, and more inclined to prioritise quality of life over status. If I met someone at a party, asking their occupation might be my tenth question rather than my first. I had developed a deep love of cheese sandwiches and good coffee, and a curious affection for the colour orange. I even nurtured a strange kind of love for the unappealing Dutch landscape, learning to see past the flat boggy polder to the wide pano-ramic skies and magnificent sunsets beyond. I was insepa-rable from my bicycles and motor scooter and didn't miss my old car at all. I had perhaps even become a little more cheerful, less inclined to the natural grumbling and cynicism of Brits, and more uncomplicatedly optimistic like the Dutch. I was more likely to speak openly and ask difficult questions directly, and had changed the way I spoke English – adopting the Americanised vernacular of people who had learned the language from subtitled MTV and *Sesame Street*. A pavement was a 'sidewalk', rubbish 'trash', a motorway a 'highway'. I had even come to sympathise with the prevailing Dutch view of British people: that they were funny and fashionable, but also a little too pale and unhealthy and stressed and obsessed with social status. Compared to the hale and hearty Dutch, every-one in London looked like Ron Weasley.

Politically, living in the most liberal country in Europe had in some ways made me more conservative. There were many things the Dutch had got right, but other areas – such as prostitution – where they had been slow to foresee the negative consequences of letting everyone do whatever they wanted. Legalising prostitution had helped ensure the success of many a stag party, but also caused untold misery to thousands of trafficked women. On the vexed issue of multiculturalism, avoiding the subject seemed merely to have caused the Dutch more trouble in the long run. As a governing philosophy, 'Anything Goes' clearly had its limits.

Overall, though, I was inclined to think that the Netherlands had avoided many of the mistakes other countries had made. In particular, being removed from the circus of British politics and the media had strengthened my view that parts of the governing elite were deeply nepotistic, unrepresentative and short-sighted, focused more on partisan bloodsports than on improving people's lives or protecting the vulnerable. While Dutch passivity and rule-making could be annoying, I suspected there was much that the British elite could learn from their competent, uncompetitive Dutch counterparts, forever working together to find a sensible solution. The Netherlands, for all its faults, was happier than Britain, more efficient than France, more tolerant than America, more worldly than Norway, more modern than Belgium and more fun than Germany.

As a people, the Dutch were healthy, creative, curious, friendly, worldly, always willing to chat with strangers or help out a friend. The mythical 'work–life balance' for which others strived in vain seemed to come naturally to them. Compared to citizens of almost every other country, they worked fewer hours, took longer holidays, spent more time with their children, but enjoyed a higher standard of living. In an era when much of the world was cynical and pessimistic, most Dutch remained tolerant, internationalist and open-minded. Challenges like immigration and economic stagnation meant that some freedoms were being trimmed, but I couldn't help thinking that if the Dutch could preserve even a fraction of their distinctive, happy-go-lucky outlook in the coming years, then the future of orange looked very bright indeed.

As London's streetlights flickered into life, I walked back to Victoria – a place whose very name conjured up fading imperial glories – and collected my shiny new passport. I was British again, and I could leave the country. After a quick stop to buy sausages and Twiglets, I took a crowded tube to Paddington and caught the first train to Heathrow. From there I could make the short flight to Rotterdam, where my new wife, the skinny girl, was waiting. It was getting late, and I wanted to go home.

Selected Bibliography

A Brief History of the Netherlands by Paul F. State (Facts on File, 2008)

A Short History of the Netherlands by P.J. Rietbergen (Bekking and Blitz, 1994)

A Time of Gifts by Patrick Leigh Fermor (HarperCollins, 1977)

Ajax, the Dutch and the War by Simon Kuper (Orion, 2011)

Amsterdam: A Brief Life of the City by Geert Mak (Harvill Press, 1999)

Arnhem: The Battle for Survival by John Nichol and Tony Rennell (Penguin, 2012)

Brilliant Orange: The Neurotic Genius of Dutch Football by David Winner (Bloomsbury, 2001)

Bury the Chains: The British Struggle to Abolish Slavery by Adam Hochschild (Pan, 2012)

Culture and Welfare State by Wim Van Oorschot, Michael Opielka and Birgit Pfau-Effinger (Edward Elgar, 2008)

Discovering the Dutch by Emmeline Besamusca and Jaap Verheul (Amsterdam University Press, 2014)

Edge of Empire: Rome's Frontier on the Lower Rhine by Jonah Lendering and Arjen Bosman (Karwansaray, 2013)

Eichmann in Jerusalem by Hannah Arendt (Penguin, 2006)

Going Dutch: How England Plundered Holland's Glory by Lisa Jardine (HarperPress, 2008)

Governance and Politics of the Netherlands by Rudy B. Andeweg and Galen A. Irwin (Palgrave Macmillan, 2009)

Holland by Adam Hopkins (Faber & Faber, 1988)

In Pursuit of Pepper and Tea by Els M. Jacobs (Walburg, 1991)

In the City of Bikes by Pete Jordan (Harper Perennial, 2013)

In the House of War: Dutch Islam Observed by Sam Cherribi (Oxford University Press, 2013)

Infidel by Aayan Hirsi Ali (Pocket Books, 2008)

Inverting the Pyramid: The History of Football Tactics by Jonathan Wilson (Orion, 2014)

Land below Sea Level: Holland in Its Age-Long Fight against the Waters by Johan van Veen (LJC Boucher, 1953)

Marked for Death by Geert Wilders (Regnery Publishing, 2012)

Murder in Amsterdam: The Death of Theo Van Gogh and the Limits of Tolerance by Ian Buruma (Penguin 2007)

Nathaniel's Nutmeg by Giles Milton (John Murray, 2000)

Nomad by Aayan Hirsi Ali (Simon and Schuster, 2011)

O Louis by Hugo Borst (Yellow Jersey, 2014)

Reflections on the Revolution in Europe by Christopher Caldwell (Penguin, 2010)

The Awful End of Prince William the Silent by Lisa Jardine (Harper Perennial, 2014)

The Book of Rotterdam by Arie van der Schoor (W Books, 2010)

The Development of the Dutch Welfare State by Robert Cox (University of Pittsburgh Press, 1993)

The Dutch and their Delta by Jacob Vossestein (Scriptum Books, 2011)

The Dutch Atlantic by Kwame Nimako and Glenn Willemsen (Pluto Press, 2011)

The Dutch Revolt 1559–1648 by Peter Limm (Routledge, 1989)

The Embarrassment of Riches: An Interpretation of Dutch Culture in the Golden Age by Simon Schama (Harper Perennial, 2004)

The Girl from Rotterdam by Elisabeth de Graaff (iUniverse, 2007)

The Hunger Winter by Henri van der Zee (University of Nebraska Press, 1998)

The Netherlands: Revolt and Independence 1550–1650 by Martyn Rady (Hodder Education, 1990)

The Savage Shore by Graham Seal (Allen & Unwin, 2015)

Tulipomania by Mike Dash (Weidenfeld and Nicolson, 2011)

Vermeer's Hat: The Seventeenth Century and the Dawn of the Global World by Timothy Brook (Profile Books, 2009)

Wanted Women: Faith, Lies and the War on Terror by Deborah Scroggins (Harper Perennial, 2013)

When Ways of Life Collide: Dutch Multiculturalism and its Discontents by Paul M. Sniderman and Louk Hagendoorn (Princeton University Press, 2009)

William of Orange by Daniel R. Horst (Rijksmuseum, 2014)

Year Zero: A History of 1945 by Ian Buruma (Atlantic, 2014)

Acknowledgements

It's common for authors to thank long lists of people for their help in bringing a book to life, but in this case I'd like to go even further, and thank an entire country. In the five years since I wandered out of Schiphol airport in the snow, the people of the Netherlands have never made me feel less than entirely welcome. I'm grateful to the countless people, most of them strangers, who have made living there such an enjoyable experience, and unknowingly contributed anecdotes and ideas recorded in these pages. I hope that Dutch readers can see beyond the criticisms of their country that I've made here, forgive my lack of enthusiasm for Zwarte Piet, and recognise this book for the love letter that it is.

More specifically, I'm deeply grateful to my in-laws – Ed, Ineke, Bob and Simon – for the warm welcome to their country and for providing an enjoyable crash course in Dutch family life. Thanks also to the many friends, Dutch and English, whose company on days and nights out from Bristol to Brabant taught me more about why the Dutch are different than any textbook or museum. Thanks to my friends at IAVI, particularly Arwa, for conversation over cocktails in Amsterdam, and over strong coffee the morning after. Thanks to Salma, for the encouragement. And thank you to Simon and Jessie, for insight and inspiration.

In London, I owe a huge debt to my publisher, Nicholas Brealey, for his skill in transforming a rough manuscript full of holes and oddities into something worth printing. Thanks also to the team – Sally Lansdell, Ben Slight and Louise Richardson – who did sterling work in editing, designing and promoting the book. Thanks also to Monica for providing speedy assistance with the Dutch translations, despite having a baby to look after.

Thank you to my parents, for encouraging me to write and for putting up with years of chaos while I ignored their advice. Without their support and encouragement, this book wouldn't exist. Thanks to my sister, Laura, for a Queen's Day to remember. And finally, thanks and love to Kim, the infamous skinny girl, for being the perfect guide and companion, in the Netherlands and everywhere else.

Apologies to those I have forgotten to thank. Any other errors are entirely my own.